W9-AQI-454

LIBRARY
UNIVERSITY OF NEW HAVEN

LIBRARY
UNIVERSITY OF NEW HAVEN

# Soweto's Children:

## The Development of Attitudes

This is a volume in
EUROPEAN MONOGRAPHS IN SOCIAL PSYCHOLOGY

Series Editor: Henri Tajfel

A complete list of titles in this series appears at the end of this volume.

EUROPEAN MONOGRAPHS IN SOCIAL PSYCHOLOGY 20
*Series Editor: HENRI TAJFEL*

# Soweto's Children:
## The Development of Attitudes

BERYL A. GEBER

*London School of Economics and Political Science,
University of London*

AND

STANTON P. NEWMAN

*Guy's Hospital Medical School, University of London*

1980

*Published in cooperation with*
EUROPEAN ASSOCIATION OF EXPERIMENTAL
SOCIAL PSYCHOLOGY
*by*
ACADEMIC PRESS
*A Subsidiary of Harcourt Brace Jovanovich, Publishers*
London  New York  Toronto  Sydney  San Francisco

ACADEMIC PRESS INC. (LONDON) LTD.
24/28 Oval Road
London NW1

*United States Edition published by*
ACADEMIC PRESS INC.
111 Fifth Avenue
New York, New York 10003

LA
1544
S6

Copyright © 1980 by
ACADEMIC PRESS INC. (LONDON) LTD.

*All Rights Reserved*

No part of this book may be reproduced in any form by photostat, microfilm, or any other means,
without written permission from the publishers

*British Library Cataloguing in Publication Data*

Geber, B A
  Soweto's children.—(European monographs in
  social psychology).
  1. High school students—South Africa—Soweto—
  Attitudes
  2. Students, Black—South Africa—Soweto—
  Attitudes
  I. Title    II. Newman, S P    III. Series
  373.1'8'1096822    LA1544.S/    80–40159

ISBN 0–12–278750–1

Filmset in Monophoto Baskerville
by Latimer Trend & Company Ltd, Plymouth
Printed by J. W. Arrowsmith, Bristol

# Acknowledgments

One of the pleasures of research is that it brings contact with a wide variety of people. This study has been spread over two continents and over many points in time; it has been particularly pleasurable, and owes its existence to the support, co-operation and help of a number of people. We would like to thank the headmasters, teachers and students at the four schools in Soweto who gave freely of their time, interest and advice over a number of years to make the research possible. At their request we do not specifically name them. Thanks are due to Dr Jack de Ridder for permission to use his African Thematic Apperception Test, and to Phil Sealy and Michael Katz for their help with statistical analysis. Sue Sharpe helped with the data analysis and we are particularly grateful to her. At various stages of the production the manuscript was typed by Margaret Oates and Lorna Norman. We would like to thank the Counter Information Service for allowing us access to their interviews and cuttings after the events of June 1976.

Our colleagues have been of particular assistance, and although the conclusions and interpretations are our own we are indebted to Henri Tajfel and in particular to Hilde Himmelweit without whose constant support and prodding this research would never have seen the light of day. Their vision of Social Psychology has been of critical importance in setting the context for the work. We may not have done them justice, but our debt is strong.

Anyone who has produced a book knows the tremendous burden it places on friends and family. We want to thank Marie Smith for the endless cups of tea and coffee made over many months. Our special thanks to Michael and Susan for keeping us going through all the expected and unexpected crises, and for all their support while we were busy.

This book is dedicated to Jan and Nick, in the hope that it will help them understand.

May, 1980

BERYL GEBER
STANTON NEWMAN

# Contents

# 1

# Introduction

In a paper written in 1975, Morton Deutsch argued that the task of social psychology was to answer the question: "what kinds of social structure, social organisations, social pressures will give rise to what kinds of social psychological consequences". This book attempts to find a partial answer to this question, by examining the social psychological consequences of being young, educated and Black in a social system which is clearly and firmly structured on the basis of race.

This detailed study of a particular situation affords social psychology another valuable insight to a society already placed under the microscope of politics and history, of economic and sociological analyses. Moreover, South Africa has been frequently written about in terms of approbrium, culminating in, and continuing to come under the moral censure of the world community since the first meeting of the United Nations in 1946.

> The question of the treatment of people of Indo-Pakistani origin in South Africa appeared on the agenda of every session of the General Assembly from the first in 1946 through the sixteenth in 1961–62, with the exception of the fourth in 1949. At the seventh session in 1951–52, the Assembly added to its agenda the "question of race conflict in South Africa resulting from the policies of *apartheid* of the government of South Africa". For the next ten years, the Assembly dealt annually with both items; but since 1962, the specific problems of the Indo-Pakistanis has been merged with the larger problem of non-White South Africans generally. (Leiss, 1965)

There are many studies, analyses and touching novels about South Africa that are a reflection of the imprint of the society on the researchers and writers. As social psychologists, we are relieved of the creative tasks facing the novelist because we allow our respondents to do the talking. Our primary task is to organize information so that it can be of more than private value, and give support to particular theories.

Understanding the thoughts and beliefs of young urban Black South Africans also affords the opportunity of examining the broader question of the interaction of the individual and society. This is a study of the social psychological reactions of Black high school students in Soweto, South Africa. By examining young people in high school in the process of preparing for and deciding their future, we find both an avenue for and a focus into the understanding of the individual in interaction with the wider society.

The social anthropologists in the main have chronicled and categorized the change taking place as industrialization and urbanization spreads to the more remote parts of the world. The anthropologist describes changing patterns and structures by examining changing rituals, social networks and economic systems, by examining cargo cults and millennial movements, by looking at shifting bases of social control. With his emphasis on structure, on small scale communities, on participant observation as a technique and sensitive description as the outcome, the anthropologist has drawn a detailed portrait of changing societies.

The social psychologist, frequently seduced by the certainty of the laboratory and without a theoretical system facilitating the simultaneous handling of large scale structures, has been less concerned with chronicling major social change. Until recently experimental laboratory work has been regarded as the appropriate province of the social psychologist, with field studies as a scientific poor relation. McGuire (1967) has written that, until recently, the term "experimental" has been misused by "followers of the establishment who interpret it as referring only to manipulative research, or still more erroneously, only to manipulative research in the laboratory." In its "etymologically correct meaning of 'to test, to try' " it could include "hypothesis testing in natural settings or even testing in natural settings without manipulation by the experimenter of the independent variables" (pp. 127–128).

However, the dominance given to the laboratory experimental investigations has slowed the growth of a social psychology able to do what Deutsch has claimed we ought to be doing. If one asks questions regarding the relation of the individual to the broad social system the answers will be less than satisfactory if sought in an encapsulated environment, divorced from a sense of time. In an experiment by Haney et al. (1973) students were assigned to play the roles of prisoner and prison warder in a simulated prison setting. The experiment was stopped after six days, during which time the students were found to be considerably influenced by the social structure. How much more potent might be the continuous influence of a socio-political structure which defines roles, rights and obligations with almost as rigid a clarity as is found in a total institution, a system which is not based however on the arbitrary assignment of roles, but on prescription. To discern clearly the implication of any such social situation is, of course, almost impossible. To define the impact of one social system in contrast to any other system, on the lives of the individuals who comprise it is an enterprise of terrifying ambition. In the South African context this task would seem to demand an ability to separate class from race, the effects of a migrant labour system from those of economic decline in rural areas, personal restrictions from political disenfranchisement.

We will therefore define our task more realistically. We are interested to chart the effect of the school on the assumptions and behaviours of its students. Tajfel has written:

> . . . in an infinite variety of situations throughout his life, the individual feels, thinks and behaves in terms of his social identity created by the various groups of which he is a member and in terms of relation to the social identity of others, as individuals or *en masse*.

At any point in his life cycle the individual is involved with and is influenced by a variety of forces. These arise from developments within him/herself, and from outside, in the social world. The relation between these is not arbitrary, nor is there only one direction of influence. The external world both offers and insists; the individual both constructs and demands. At various times one force may be stronger than another. For the young person the period of adolescence and early adulthood is one during which a multitude of choices are made. The nature of these choices varies in different societies and the number of choices and options may differ from one social system to another. In that there seem to be two major social systems that influence choice at this time of life—home and school—this work concentrates on establishing the relative importance of these in relation to the way the individual sees his future within the wider society.

Any event can be depicted with varying amounts of detail and against a variety of backgrounds. We have started from the assumption that it is not useful to study the elements of the whole in isolation. Rather, it is important to see how they derive meaning from each other and from the larger whole which they constitute. The family and the school operate in a wider socio-political context and therefore their influence and role will vary from society to society. It is only in looking at a range of societies and systems that general statements can be made about the nature of the relation between the individual and the environment.

This, however, is more than a case study of a particular group of young people in a specific social system. It is able to relate the perception of society evidenced by the group, to later social events.

In June 1976, trouble broke out in the African townships to the south-west of Johannesburg. The protestors were Black* school students, who live and study in the complex of housing estates known collectively as Soweto (South Western Townships) which houses the majority of the African (Black) workers who work in the factories, industries, shops and houses which have made Johannesburg, with its surrounding gold mines, one of the most productive and prosperous cities in Africa. The course of the rioting, the reactions of the authorities to the rebellious students, to their parents and teachers, and to the issues which apparently triggered the protest were reported in broad outline by the world's press. The coverage served to focus attention on the particular dilemma of the young, educated Black students in South African cities. What this book plans to do is to detail the social psychological forces which were implicated in the series of outbursts of protest and violence of the Soweto school students, to describe the insights which can be derived from charting the interaction of individual and social systems and its psychic and experiential reality, rather than focussing on purely socio-economic forces. We do not claim that one analysis is "right"—any social event can be described in a multiplicity of ways.

However, it is important to understand what the individual experiences and feels, to chart differences amongst individuals and to perhaps indicate further what personal and social influences converge to encourage the particular forms of response at particular historical

*This study is only concerned with the attitudes and beliefs of students of one of the racial groups that comprise South Africa. For reasons of historical context this group will be described in a variety of ways—Africans, Black, Bantu all refer to the same group. The terms Whites and Europeans are also used interchangeably, but where necessary we distinguish between those who speak English and those who speak Afrikaans. The two further groups the society distinguishes are Coloureds (of mixed blood) and Asians (mainly descendants of immigrants from the Indian sub-continent).

moments. In no way does such an analysis deny the validity of alternative disciplines' contributions to the understanding of social events—politico-economic perspectives, dramatic interpretation, social class and role analyses may all offer interpretations of the same event. Soweto has been and will be analysed in terms of political forces, economic factors, personal biographies. A social psychological perspective allows for the integration of at least aspects of all these in illuminating the experiences of the individual in his social world.

Most disciplines have found it difficult to reconcile the specificity of an individual process oriented approach with the generality of societally oriented analyses. Yet it is these that must be integrated if social change is to be described and if its effects are to be charted. One way to do this is by investigating the developing individual within the system through the channel of the individual student's aspirations and expectations, forged in the family and the school of a society in flux. It is a way of studying the role of particular socializing agents in fostering and shaping the individual. Furthermore, such a study (if related to the opportunity structure of the wider society, which may be hostile or lend support to his needs and wishes) can help in understanding the basis of the individual's evaluation of his society. When related to group membership, this evaluation can be seen as part of the shared assumptions which define social norms and ideas about the appropriateness of particular types of behaviour.

These norms and evaluations define the way individuals view their changing world. This in turn influences the way they perceive the systems of choices and decisions which confront them. Tajfel (1972) sees social change as a system of choices the individual has to make. He writes that "new choices can best be explained and predicted from an analysis of conditions under which conflicts between and within the systems of expectations and evaluations are resolved in one direction or another and may at the same time give rise to the creation of new styles". It will be argued that the process of education is one which encourages changes in the expectations and evaluations of those who are involved in it. To the extent that the society within which the educational system operates is able to satisfy these aspirations there will be a general endorsement of its values and aims. If, however, the relationship between the school and the outside world is one of poor fit, where the wider system neither recognizes nor rewards the values imbued by the school, nor offers the opportunity for the achievement of the aspirations that the educational system encourages, then there will be conflict. The nature of the resolution of this conflict, the choices that are made, will influence the creation of new systems, both intra-individual and inter-group. South Africa presents a society within which the chance of conflict from a mismatch of expectations is maximized, and this will be clearly demonstrated by an analysis of the social system, and the history of the education of its population. The conflict is exaggerated in the areas of high industrialization and urbanization, which demand specific sorts of skills from the population. Of all the urban areas in South Africa, Soweto is the largest, housing the largest urban Black population, involved in the complexities of a highly industrialized economy. The young person growing up and being educated in Soweto, exposed to the norms and values of big cities, with the demands of a sophisticated economy, and the varied perspectives presented by the media, may well be particularly sensitive to the relation between the world of school and the world beyond it.

A study of the aspirations, expectations, values and beliefs of 1000 high school students at four schools in Soweto was carried out in the 1960s. The study sought to examine the demographic and the educational variables which influenced the way the young Black viewed his or her world. A cross-sectional design was employed, comparing the responses of students in their second, third and fourth year of the five year high school programme. Such a large study of so large a sample has been rare in South Africa. The difficulties facing the researcher are different from those normally faced in such a research project, and chief amongst them was the considerable anxiety on the part of the respondents that they should not be identified. The reasons for this will be discussed later, together with the nature of the sample and the materials and methods of research. However, it is important that one of the bases for co-operation was the undertaking on the part of the investigator that no details of the study would be presented until the last of the students was out of the school system, and that the results would be available to a restricted audience. Parts of the study have been reported previously (Geber 1971; 1972; 1976; 1977), but the schools and the students have not been identified.

The events of June 1976 brought about a reconsideration, not of our obligation to the subjects of the study, but of our previous decision to restrict the publication of the study. The students involved in the protests, demonstrations, strikes and political actions in Soweto and elsewhere in South Africa are not the same individuals as those who participated in the study—but their aspirations, values and hopes are not different, and through a study of their predecessors we may better understand them. The conditions under which they live and learn are unchanged, the schools are still the same. What was learned on an earlier group of Soweto students is of considerable interest and pertinence.

There is a further reason for presenting this study. It is rare for a social scientist's predictions to be confirmed. In this instance they appear to have been. Written in a previous report appears the following:

> While it is perhaps true that in all societies those values taught at school are not necessarily directly relevant to the life that is led outside it, it is not all societies which present such firm, race dominated obstacles to the translation of these school values to adult working life. It is possible that the reaction to this frustration will be rejection and aggression, and the whole system of values will be discarded. (Geber, 1972)

The report then continued to suggest those constellations of aspirations and attitudes which might predispose to rebellion, and the societal structures which fostered them. Following closely the events of recent times it appears that the suggestions were correct.

# 2

# Past and Present: The South African Experience

Removing social psychological research from the laboratory to the field demands that the context in which the observed behaviours occur are described with great clarity. In this study, the context of behaviour is particularly important because we attempt to understand the way the developing individual accommodates his behaviour and his needs to the demands of his world, and how this process of accommodation shapes the perspectives and the assumptions he has about his world. The social system is a powerful determinant of action but it is, or can be differently viewed according to one's position in the network of relationships of which it consists. The demands that the world places on the individual depend on the particular nature of the social structure and on the more direct system of social organization and social networks in which the individual lives.

In South Africa the young African has not only to reconcile his desires with the opportunities the society offers but he has also to reconcile the demands of varying cultural commitments. These emanate from the dominant White minority, from the immediate neighbourhood of the Black urban township and from the vestiges of tribal organization. Each of these systems operates with varying degrees of strength on the individual and his responses to them will in part depend on his position in the intricate network linking the three.

The most dominant feature of the South African society is that it is based on race. Power is allocated on the basis of racial group membership, and as far as possible divisions between racial groups are maintained. Seventy per cent of the population is Black, living in towns, in villages, on the farms of White farmers and in tribal reserves. Approximately 21% of the population is White, speaking either Afrikaans or English, and the remainder of the people are of mixed blood (Coloureds) or of Asian origin. The largest percentage of Coloured people live in the Cape Province and of the Asians in Natal, and there are substantial communities of both in the Transvaal where this study was carried out.

Most Africans in the Transvaal and the Orange Free State are from the local Sotho-speaking tribes, and drawn from further afield to the mines and industries of the Witwatersrand.

There is no need here to give extensive details about the political and social structure of South Africa: it is a structure based fairly firmly on race, within which rights and obligations, privileges and power are allocated on the basis of racial membership, where to be born Black or White determines the civic status one will enjoy. The structure can be viewed as comprising two parts—a core of politico-economic institutions and a fringe of personal and social interactions. The ideological dressing which integrates and lends coherence to the system is the concept of separate development—Apartheid in Afrikaans. It is important to stress that although apartheid as a guiding ideology, has operated since 1948, its roots lie much earlier in the history of South Africa.

Whites first settled in the Cape of Good Hope in 1652, as agents of the Dutch East India Company, to establish a provision station on the route to India. The first settlers in the Cape found Hottentots and Bushmen, and in 1658 imported a shipload of slaves from Malaya to provide labour. These slaves, Whites, Hottentots—and those Bushmen not hunted down and killed—were the ancestors of the present Coloured population. The Dutch, joined later by French and German settlers, were the ancestors of the Afrikaners.

Control of the Cape was finally wrested from the Dutch in 1806 by the British, who in 1820 landed parties of new immigrants in the Eastern Cape to encourage the development of the colony. It was in this area where the expanding thinly populated colony first met the Bantu, and the first clashes occurred:

> The Borderlands filled and the pressure from behind mounted, and the unending clashes over cattle increased. Then there was a concerted heave or two, and the truth finally dawned. The Kaffirs (Bantu) were themselves the fringes of a tide. Even if they had been willing to recede . . . they could not move. The free land had run out, and Africa was no longer endless. (Morris, 1973)

The Cape Dutch did not easily bear the yoke of British rule, and from 1834, groups of Boers (the Dutch for farmer) trekked away from the Cape settlements and founded their own Republics inland, the Orange Free State and Transvaal. It was particularly during these treks, and around the land taken for farming and settlement by the Trekker

Boers, that a series of bloody wars between Bantu tribes and Boers occurred. The expanding Boers, seeking political independence, met the Bantu who comprised a number of different tribes and clans involved in changing allegiances as the Zulu nation and the Sotho nations expanded; at the same time the British settlers in Natal were involved in a series of battles with the growing Zulu nation.

One of the factors which fuelled the trek of the Boers away from the control of the British was the movement for the abolition of slavery. For the Boers since "slavery was a matter of semantics, they could (even) accept emancipation provided they were compensated for their losses. What they could not understand, and would never accept, was the concept that their servants were their legal equals . . ." (Morris, 1973). One of the leaders of the Trek issued a statement of the aims of his party which included the resolve to "preserve proper relations between master and servant". The constitution of the Republic founded by the Boers in what later became the Transvaal embodied the principle that "the people will suffer no equality of Whites and Blacks either in state or in Church" (van den Berghe, 1965).

In 1867 diamonds were discovered in Kimberley in the Cape, and the independence of the two Boer Republics was threatened by the discovery of gold in 1886 at Langlaagte on the Witwatersrand. This was only 36 miles from Pretoria, the capital of the Transvaal Republic, and the rural isolation and ethos of Boer southern Africa was shattered. As a result, new people moved in, new centres were established (Johannesburg owes its existence to the discovery of gold), labour was in demand, and in turn, demands made on all services. Many of those who pursued the adventure of gold* prospecting, the soldiers of fortune, the gamblers and the satraps of the new industry were British; adventurers who had also been drawn to the Kimberley diamond mines, to the opportunities in the British colonies of the Cape and Natal. Conflict between the Boer Republics and the British colonies increased and from 1899 to 1902 this escalated into the Anglo-Boer war. Despite odds favouring the British, the Boers fought valiantly and well and their defeat was attended with great resentment. In 1910 the two colonies and two former Republics joined to become the Union of South Africa, which in 1961 declared itself a Republic and ceased to be a member of the British Commonwealth.

*For a report of the early days of Johannesburg see "Out of the Crucible" by Hadley A. Chilvers (1929). Published by Cassell, London.

This brief history underlines two major points, firstly that the development of Southern Africa has occurred against constant conflicts between Boers, Britons and Bantu, and secondly that the growth of the Afrikaner nation has taken place at the same time as the growth of larger Bantu nations, so that the clash of nationalisms has been a constant part of South African history. The competing aspirations of these groups and the maintenance of power by the minority White group, has been reflected in the pattern of legislation which was passed by the South African Parliament. Increasingly it led to the protection of Whites against the competition from non-Whites, to the removal of the rights which existed for non-Whites in the common central political institutions, and to the emphasis on the separateness of the racial groups. At the same time a conflict over political and economic power between the Boers and the English-speaking South Africans increased. The early days of the Union of South Africa saw industrial power and control over the mining resources firmly in the hands of English-speaking South Africans; the civil service, the media, and even political power was associated with English. The Afrikaners' resentment at their defeat and treatment by the British smouldered, and found expression both in the Nationalist Party and in the secret society called "Die Broederbond", the Brotherhood, which strove to expand Afrikaner influence. It was also in part implicated in the support offered by some notable Afrikaners to the Nazis in the Second World War.

Although Smuts (1870–1950), the South African Prime Minister (1919–1924; 1939–1948) who was leader of the United Party, was an Afrikaner it was not felt that he embodied the aspirations of the growing nationalist movement and in 1948 the Parliamentary elections brought to power the Nationalist Party. This party not only embodied the hopes of the Afrikaner but it also propounded a particular political theory—the theory of apartheid.

In its most idealistic form the concept of separate development sought to harmonize White and Black rights by proposing that although both groups were entitled to rights it was against the interests of both groups to exercise these rights in a common society. This would sweep away the ethnic heritage of both groups. Thus, two parallel but equal societies were to be developed, one for Whites and one (or more, as notions of tribal affiliation gained strength) for Blacks. Each could enter the society of the other only temporarily for work as long as they were needed, but no social or political rights would be enjoyed outside their own territory. To this end, 13% of the land of South Africa was set aside for the Africans.

The Nationalist Party was able to campaign so profitably in 1948 on its *apartheid* policy because, among other factors, three processes converged at that time. The urbanisation of the Afrikaner which began after World War I and gathered momentum in the 30s, reached the point where by 1948 nearly two-thirds of the Afrikaners lived in the cities (in 1911 the figure was under 20 per cent, in 1936 it was 52 per cent). Urbanisation of the Africans also increased sharply in the 30s and the influx swelled considerably as a result of the demand for African labor created by the tremendous increase in industrialisation brought about by World War II. In fact, the number of non-Whites employed in secondary industry more than doubled between 1935 and 1946. In the cities resentful and fearful Afrikaners in the lower social and economic strata found themselves not only competing for jobs with Blacks, but often living cheek by jowl with them.

The third process was the escalation of non-White hopes, expectations and political activism consequent on the shattering defeat of fascism and tyranny by victors who had in a series of reverberating declarations from the Atlantic Charter to the United Nations Charter proclaimed their dedication to the ideals of freedom and human dignity. Fuelled by the same declarations and by the enlarged role of the Soviet Union as one of the principals among the victors, were endemic Afrikaner fears of the submergence of Afrikaner rule and hence "White civilisation" under an engulfing tide of racial egalitarianism.

The Nationalist Party offered the Afrikaners a remedy . . . the doctrine of *apartheid*. In a pamphlet issued in 1947, the Party said, in effect, that by preserving and safeguarding the White race, the Nationalist Party would promote the happiness and well being of all citizens, non-White as well as White. Apparently the happiness of the Blacks would be advanced by arresting the process of detribalisation and by treating them in the urban areas as migratory citizens not entitled to political or social rights equal to those of the Whites. *Apartheid* was also to be applied to the Coloreds, while the Indians, since the Nationalists regarded them as an unassimilable element in South Africa, were offered only the prospect of repatriation to India.

In this policy of *apartheid* the Nationalist Party found an election winner. (Melamet, 1977)

The legislation which gives formality to the structure of South African society can be seen in two categories. The first deals with the "core" of the politico-economic power system, and the second consists of those regulatory acts which organize social and personal life. It is almost as if a series of hurdles, or a mined area, were set up around the very essence of the system so that it itself does not suffer direct attack.

It is debatable how one should characterize "apartheid". One approach is to see its roots in the system of ownership of the means of production, particularly the mines and large, heavy industries, and the need to supply and control cheap labour for these. Another would be to see political power as the essence, and the maintenance of privilege as its result. In the economic and the political structure of the society, racial group membership is the basis for the allocation of rights and rewards. Africans have no representation in the South African Parliament and are not enfranchised except in their own tribelands. The State President is delegated as the protector of the Bantu and a Department of State controls the affairs of the African population, directly and through a system of White commissioners. The Africans living in cities and towns or on White farms, are really regarded as residents and citizens of existing or proposed independent homelands (Bantustans) and their tribal chiefs have representatives in town to liaise with the central government or to link the African to his tribal territory. Africans are not regarded as having any political rights in the White areas which constitute 87% of the country, and political influence or change from within the system is therefore impossible for the Black communities. The rights of the ballot box, the lobby, the processes of exerting influence on the policies of local or central government within the system which maintains a bi-cameral Parliament and provincial and local Councils, is the prerogative of Whites. The rights of the Blacks may be exercised only in tribal homelands; for Coloureds and Asians whose territorial rights are less defined, the situation is even more complicated. The White Parliament has the right to legislate for the total population, even those who are not directly represented in it.

There are a number of laws and controls that follow from the political core of apartheid. Firstly, the notion of tribal homelands implies that all Africans, if not to be seen as totally dispossessed, must belong to a tribe, and that the tribal authority system must be maintained. Since one of the effects of a long history both of industrial development and growth, and of conquest and loss of land, has been the dislocation if not disintegration of the traditional tribal system in all the industrial urban areas, this has not been achieved without difficulty. The tribal system, where it remains, is strongest in the rural areas, both on the White farms and in the land held in trust for the tribe. Frequently tribal land is scattered, with White farms splitting one area from another. The logic of homelands has led to the removal of large, mainly Black, populations from one location to another in order to consolidate the tribe, but without any guarantee of equity in the exchange.

A system which allocates political rights on the basis of race, which does not have universal franchise, must have some basis for ensuring the correct classification of each individual. This is performed by the Race Classification Act, which formally locates individuals in appropriate groups. Thus marriage between Whites and non-Whites is forbidden by law, and sexual relations are also proscribed. Children of those liaisons which escape the law are most likely to be classified as non-White.

The second important correlate of the system of political apartheid is that where the majority of the population is theoretically not resident or permanently settled where they are living and working, some method of ensuring that people know where they belong is imperative. The Black population is alien, and must be registered and controlled. This registration and control is effected through a series of Pass Laws, which determine who (if Black) shall be where, for what purpose and what length of time. Rights to be in and remain in the industrial, urban or White areas, is dependent on the economic function the individual can fulfil within that area. The political and economic faces of apartheid are related like the two halves of the classical reversing pictures of wife and mother-in-law. Each defines the other, and now one, now the other, seems to be the predominant. That the maintenance of economic power relies on the maintenance of political power and vice versa, especially where a minority is in control, is indisputable.

The pass laws are the direct personal experience for Blacks of both political and economic control. Africans need permits to live outside a tribal area, and also when they return "home" to the homeland. If regulations are not complied with, one may be "endorsed" out of an area. Visitors are allowed in for short stays, work-seekers have 72 hours' grace and people changing jobs may be permitted to stay on for a while. However, wives and children of workers have no right to live in the White areas without permission, and children may be sent back to the homeland area even if parents are in the cities. Because of this view of the African as only "guests" in the White areas, even if born and bred there, and their fathers before them, they have no property rights outside the homelands, no security of tenure, no real protection from the arbitrariness of bureaucratic decision.

In the House of Assembly, 18 March 1964, the Deputy Minister of Bantu Administration* explained the situation:

> An unmarried Bantu male qualifies to be in an urban area on the ground that he was born here or that he has been employed here for ten years by one employer or for fifteen years by different employers, and wants to marry a woman outside that urban area. The woman can only enter if she is given leave to do so. Housing is one of the factors which must be taken into account and it must be clearly understood that that means housing only in the Bantu residential areas and not housing in the backyard of the employer where that woman's husband is already employed and living in the premises. It applies only to housing in the urban Bantu residential areas and subject naturally to the regulations of that particular authority.

A second example was the following:

> A Bantu woman who qualifies to be in an urban area wishes to marry a man employed there but not yet qualified (he is not born there, has not been employed for ten years by one employer or for fifteen years by different employers). The couple may marry. If the man ceases to work in the area, he has no longer a right to remain there. If that Bantu male cannot obtain employment he will have to go, but that is something which the Bantu woman knew from the first day; the Bantu male himself knew it; they entered into this union with their eyes open. They both knew that if he lost his employment then the last vestige of justification for his presence here would disappear. If he has to leave therefore she will have to accompany him. But there is still the possibility that the bureau may find a new job here for him. If he goes to the bureau and proves bona fide that he lost his employment, there is the possibility that he may get a new job here and in that case they can remain here.

The control of labour has many further aspects, including both a basis in a migrant labour policy and the reservation of particular jobs for people according to race.

Anthropological literature has described the effects on traditional patterns of social structure of an economic system that depends on migrant labour—labour which serves the mines on fixed contracts for particular lengths of time as well as labour which is drawn into cities and towns to earn money to supplement the poverty of depleted farmlands. The system is not unique to South Africa and its effects can be documented for many communities: the continuing impoverishment of a community whose able-bodied men earn elsewhere, leaving the women, the young and the old to scratch a living from the soil; the disadvantages for the stability of family life of absent fathers and

*House of Assembly Debates (Hansard), 18 March, 1964, Col. 3192–3194.

husbands; the stress of separation on the migrant workers themselves. The mines and urban areas provide compounds and hostels for the thousands of migrants living away from home, and the system is implicit in the structure of the economy. The migrants usually do those jobs which are the least skilled and least attractive—working underground in the mines, working on roads and as cleaners, collecting garbage and stoking furnaces.

The principles of apartheid not only minimize the rights of the work force, they also determine the nature of the work performed by members of various racial groups. By a series of Acts of Parliament certain occupations are reserved for members of particular racial groups and others may not do the designated jobs. The particular jobs so reserved are altered according to changing economic demands, but the main purpose is to protect the White labourer from the competition of cheaper Black labour, and to ensure that the percentage of Africans in certain skilled trades is restricted. Employing a skilled African artisan will very often mean that a White overseer will have to be appointed to ensure that the status balance is maintained.

Whereas White doctors and lawyers may have as clients people of all races, professional and business Africans may only service Blacks, and if they work outside the homelands, may operate only from the segregated townships. Circular A12/1, 15 July, 1969, from the Secretary for Bantu Administration and Development, said:

> It has come to the notice of the Department that certain local authorities, in conflict with policy, grant consulting room and office facilities in urban Bantu residential areas to non-European medical practitioners and other non-European professional persons. It is, therefore, necessary to set out the policy of the Department in this regard.
>
> It should be borne in mind that urban Bantu residential areas, although set aside for the purpose of occupation by Bantu, are situated in White areas, and taking into consideration the application of the principles of the policy of separate development, it follows that each national unit should be served by its own people in its respective homeland. It is therefore imperative that non-European medical practitioners and other Bantu who pursue professions should practise amongst their own people.
>
> Local authorities are, therefore, requested to ensure that non-Europeans who render professional services are not granted consulting room and office accommodation in urban Bantu residential areas. The Bantu should be persuaded to offer their services in the Bantu homelands where an acute shortage exists in the field of professional services and where, as a result of

industrial and other development including the provision of hospitals and clinics, excellent opportunities for their establishment exist.

Professional services in urban Bantu residential areas should be rendered by Whites in terms of the provisions of section 42 (g) of Act No. 25 of 1945.

Bantu who are at present legally exercising such rights may be permitted to continue to do so but should, by way of persuasion, be activated to establish themselves amongst their own people in the homelands.

Your cooperation in this matter will be appreciated.

The principle of separate development with its logic of separate homeland areas for different tribes and for each racial group is reflected in the urban areas as well. Residential districts are segregated with the Blacks housed in areas frequently distant from the economic and industrial heart of the city. They form, not dormitory suburbs, but city complexes lacking the economic basis for their own existence: huge reservoirs of labour. Within these separate areas the repetitiousness of discrimination continues. Schools, churches, creches, hospitals and administrative complexes exist separately for each group.

We argued earlier that the legislative basis of South African society comprised a core of critical statutes which determine political and economic power and a supporting system of laws which regulates interpersonal segregation. These laws range from the trivial—separate park benches, entrances to public buildings—to more crucial discriminations. Blacks are given less pay for jobs than Whites, even in occupations of high status (doctors, teachers); transport, entertainment, sport, access to parks, beaches are segregated. In welfare and health facilities and in housing and public expenditure, per capita payments and capital investments are lowest for the Africans, highest for Whites. All these facilities and the institutions that administer them are separated for Blacks and Whites.

In addition to the provision of separate facilities by central and local government agencies, apartheid separates also on the informal level. Societies, political groups, pressure groups are discouraged, if not even forbidden, to cross the colour line. This is the structure of "petty apartheid". It is in this peripheral area of separation that concessions can be made when the tensions of the system threaten. Mixed sports matches, joint worship, alterations in the racial classification of lift-operators, or railway brakemen do not actually undermine the overwhelming structure of political control.

The vastness of the legislative structure which supports and gives form to apartheid has necessitated the construction of a large force to police and ensure its implementation. There are over 300 pieces of legislation relating to race, and over 60 relating to security, from the control of movement through the Pass Laws, which can entail spot checks of people in the streets, or dawn raids on sleeping houses, through the normal policing functions to the suppression of dissent through censorship, and the implementation of various internal security measures. The majority of the White community is Afrikaans-speaking: the bureaucracies and arms of social control are mainly Afrikaners.

> The effect of Apartheid has been to drive Whites and Blacks further apart so there is virtually no contact between them except at the level of master and servant, employer and employee.
> The end result has not been the flowering of mutual respect as the architects of apartheid envisaged, but of bitterness and resentment (Ashford, 1977).

This then is the structure of South Africa. Its elements are not unique. Other societies operate totalitarian systems controlling the lives and thoughts of their citizens. Other societies have uprooted large populations or encourage a system of labour migration. There are other cultures where class and colour converge, where poverty, hunger and morbidity are to be found. There are few, if any, societies where all these converge to influence the lives of their citizens, offering little chance for escape through changing beliefs, through accumulating wealth or skills. What one is, is defined at birth.

# 3

# Tribesman and Townsman

Who are my people? I am supposed to be a Pondo, but I don't even know the language of that tribe. I was brought up in a Zulu-speaking home, my mother being a Zulu. Yet I can no longer think in Zulu because that language cannot cope with the demands of our day. I could not, for instance, discuss negritude in Zulu . . . I have never owned an assegai or any of the magnificent tribal shields . . . I am more at home with an Afrikaner than with a West African. I am a South African . . . "My people" are South Africans. Mine is the history of the Great Trek, Gandhi's passive resistance in Johannesburg, the wars of Cetewayo and the dawn raids which gave us the treason trials in 1955. All these are South African things. They are a part of me . . .          (Nakasa, 1964)

Within the social structure defined by apartheid two systems, related but often polarized, are characterized which shape and define the young African. We focus on two groups, the tribal system associated with Bantustans and Reserves and the urban proletariate living in the Black townships. There is a third group—Blacks living and working on White farms—which we do not consider. As a force its influence is minimal on the young people who are the focus of this volume.

It must be stressed that in examining the two systems of tribe and town we are not dealing with unrelated entities, one reflecting a traditional past and the other a progressive present. The idea of a "traditional" society is not tenable, given, as Monica Wilson (1961) has shown, that the contact between White settlers and Bantu communities has changed both Whites and Blacks, and reports of tribal structures are based on observations made after these influences have had many decades, indeed centuries, within which to operate. Tribesmen are fundamentally people who have not been permanently separated from their rural roots. Townsmen are not necessarily a dispossessed peasantry (although they may be). Rather they represent the Black community which exists alongside and interdependent with the White, Coloured and Asian urban groups.

The theory of Apartheid is founded on the concept of separate homelands for racial and tribal groups. As we have seen this demands that all Blacks are identified in some way with a tribal group, within whose tribal area they will find recognition of their political aspirations. The blueprint for this policy was found in the Tomlinson Commission which reported in 1954.

The Commission examined the implementation of Separate Development and recommended the development of a fully diversified economy within each tribal area. These areas, 13% of the area of South Africa

> ... consists of fertile agricultural land, with an excellent rainfall. The territories have become denuded and eroded, as a result of bad and primitive agricultural methods employed by the inhabitants. In general they are underdeveloped and poor, mainly due to the fact that industrial and urban development has been confined to the European areas. (Olivier, 1954)

Despite the most optimistic acceptance of the feasibility of implementing the policies of apartheid, the Tomlinson Report did not predict that the homelands would be able to absorb the entire African population. More than twenty years later only seven million Africans reside in the homelands, eight million live in "White" areas, over five million of these in urban areas.

> Even then the true nature of the position is distorted because Africans living in large townships . . . which are situated within homeland boundaries but which adjoin "White" cities where the township residents spend their working hours, are included in the homelands for census purposes. (Randall, 1972)

Residing in the tribal areas, therefore, are less than half the African population, and even then many will live in the homeland but work in the nearby White town. In addition, the poverty of the soil in the homelands and the demands of efficient farming necessitate a change in the agricultural policies of the homelands. The soil cannot support its population, and they have to find alternative sources of income— either in the "White areas" or in specially created industries within the homelands. Thus, "tribesmen" are no longer what they were when the anthropologists described the vestiges of tribal society.

Traditional tribal society, even after its history of contact with other social systems, was a society based on agriculture. The kinship group was the basic unit of social organization, and its economic base was either cattle or cultivation. It was essentially a subsistence economy, although from the mid-nineteenth century young men and women were drawn for various lengths of time into the economy outside. The attempts to retard the process of "detribalization", by returning to an agriculturally based system of homelands, within which the tribal structure could flourish, have not succeeded. Essentially agricultural productivity is too low to enable the family unit to earn sufficient to maintain itself, and population growth too great to be sustained on insufficient land. Therefore, even those working the land within the tribal areas have to earn cash wages in centres of employment.

This migrancy has changed the essence of the tribal system of social organization, and although tribal identity, common heritage, language and rituals may give a sense of ethnic unity, the politico-economic basis of the tribe has long since been eroded.

> While the majority of residents of the Bantustans belong to what might be termed a "lumpen-peasantry", maintaining traditional ties with some aspects of the tribal religious, communal and authority systems, together with an identity based on language and ethnic grouping . . . all are deeply affected by the system of circulating labour which takes a larger proportion of the adult men into the common economy, gives them experience of the urban situation and returns them to the Bantustans to transmit much of what they have learned to their fellows. (Whisson, 1972)

Despite the demise of a stable, unchanged, traditional tribal system, the vestiges of values and assumptions which were associated with it remain in the myths about Africans believed by many Whites, and in the belief of many urban dwellers that the tribal system was and remains a better one for raising children.

Literature describes the tribal community as a small scale community, whose cohesiveness was historically emphasized and supported by the centrality of kinship to the economic and political life of its people. The kinship system was basic to the organization of the society. The nuclear family was the basic unit—a stable group as a result of a low divorce rate. Polygamy was approved. The father was the head of the household—marriage was patrilocal and inheritance and succession (except among the Ambo of South West Africa) patrilineal. Each household was subdivided into houses which consisted of a married woman and her children. As the sons of the household married, they would settle in the kraal with their wives and children. The people who shared a homestead descended from a common ancestor and were grouped into a lineage, which co-operated in common rituals, and consulted about property and matters arising from the provision and return of cattle. Lineages were grouped into clans which claimed descent from common ancestors.

This strong kinship system lent to the society cohesiveness and unity. The welfare, health and prosperity of the society were believed to be dependent on the unity of the kinship group. The kinship system and territorial organization overlapped—the homestead with a segment of a lineage, a sub-district with a lineage and a district, under a chieftain, with a clan. In some places kinship and territory were so closely related that it was impossible to hold land outside the kinship area. Members of a homestead co-operated economically, in ritual (where ancestor worship emphasized the common dependence on the goodwill of the shades), in defence (except among Swazi and Zulu), and were legally responsible for the behaviour of their members.

Traditional society was one which placed great emphasis on masculinity and seniority. Men held higher status than women, controlled property and had complete authority over children. Women were minors, and, unless the senior wife of a head of a homestead, their status was low and their actions strictly controlled. Not all men held equal status. The senior son of the senior wife commanded greater respect and had greater authority than either his younger brothers or the senior son of a junior wife. Birth too, determined social position. Age also brought increasing status to both men and women and it was thought that age brought wisdom.

The traditional tribal system, as described above, no longer exists even in the Homelands. However, its influence is still felt, first through the vestiges of the traditional structure that remain in the rural areas, and perhaps more important, in the influence of the mythology about the past and about the certainty and stability which that represents, both to the urban African and to the Whites. Each urban African is legally required to have a tribal identity and a tribal homeland as well as a chief to whom he owes allegiance. For many this is an artificial imposition of identity, for others it simply expresses their continued affiliation to a traditional way of life (Mayer, 1961; Hunter, 1936).

At the end of the last century when gold was discovered, the first major influx of Africans to the Witwatersrand area occurred. As the area flourished, developed and settled down into a large city, so the African population grew, developed and became more stable and organized. The Non-European Affairs Department estimated the

African population figures for Johannesburg in 1927 at 136 000. By 1946, following the labour influx to the war industries, the official number was up to 395 231, although the unofficial estimates placed it at over 400 000. By 1959 the number of Africans living in the urban area was over 500 000. By the 1970s the number reached over 1 000 000.

The one million Africans living in and around Johannesburg live in what de Ridder (1961) has called "a city within a city". Except for those who live as domestic servants or miners on the property of their employers, Africans live in segregated townships some distance from the heart of the city.

White Johannesburg lives well, in well laid out suburbs radiating from the industrial and financial centre of the city. The standard of living is high, and the climate delightful. Even the suburbs to the south and east where the White working classes live are pleasant to look at and the inhabitants enjoy a standard of living generally higher than their counterparts in Europe.

Surrounding this "island of privilege" are the townships where the Africans live. Until very recently the provision of social amenities and housing took place slowly and in random fashion. Shanty towns and squatter camps sprawled over the veld and provided their inhabitants with little more than a rather precarious roof over their heads. "In 1939 the City Council of Johannesburg had built one house for every estimated 28 Africans living in the city. The rest of the African population were living in shacks and squatter camps without water or sanitation. Housing progress was limited; all building was undertaken by European artisans; costs were high, small cottages were costing up to seven hundred pounds each" (de Ridder, 1961). In the early 1950s new legislation resulted in a great increase in the rate of building.

Most of the building has taken place in the areas to the South West of Johannesburg. These areas are separated from the White areas by a buffer of mining land and industries; they are about 15–20 miles from the industrial and commercial concerns where the inhabitants earn their living. The population housed in the South Western townships was drawn from the camps, the shacks and also from areas declared "White". Sophiatown was one of these areas; a place of large, squalid houses, surrounded by shacks and lean-tos, where life was "poor, nasty, brutish and short, a nightmare of overcrowding, poverty and violence". Yet when people were about to be moved to new townships there was a great deal of opposition.* In spite of its disadvantages Sophiatown had one advantage—the Africans could own not only the houses they lived in and let out to many families, but also the ground they stood on.† It was an area devoid of regimentation and control and as a result Sophiatown gave birth to and nurtured both the best and the worst of township life, in much the same way as Alexandra township to the North East, still does.

TABLE 1
Black workers in major occupational groups (1970)*

|  | Number in thousands | Economically active % | % of total Black population |
|---|---|---|---|
| Professional, technical and related workers | 93 | 1·6 | 0·6 |
| Administrative and managerial workers | 3 | 0·1 | — |
| Clerical workers | 96 | 1·7 | 0·6 |
| Sales workers | 111 | 2·0 | 0·7 |
| Service workers | 1012 | 18·1 | 6·7 |
| Farm, forestry and fishery workers | 2052 | 36·6 | 13·6 |
| Mining, production, transport workers and labourers | 1689 | 30·1 | 11·6 |
| Unspecified | 549 | 9·8 | 3·7 |
| Economically active | 5605 | 100·0 | 37·3 |
| Not economically active | 9431 |  | 62·7 |
| Total population | 15 036 |  |  |

*From Department of Statistics, reported in "South Africa: An appraisal". The Nedbank Group, Johannesburg, 1977.

The new townships are less dense than the old slums and the small plots of land on which they stand are not cluttered by lean-tos. But there is little to break the grey and brown monotony of rows upon rows of square houses; 96 000 for an estimated population of 1 000 000. The houses are small, almost all with outside toilets, and none with baths or kitchens provided, and none have electricity laid on. New houses are handed over without ceilings, floorboards, plastering, hot water and internal doors. All these must be provided by the tenant. Only the

*For the description of Sophiatown, see "Naught for your Comfort". (1956) by T. Huddleston. Published by Doubleday.
†In 1976 leasehold ownership was introduced on a highly restricted scale.

main streets of the township are tarred, and street lighting, where provided is inadequate.

The townships house all those Africans not housed on their employer's property (miners and domestics). Table 1 gives the occupational distribution of Africans across the country as a whole in 1970. This indicates clearly, that of the active work force, 94·5% are to be found in unskilled and semi-skilled occupations. A survey by Market Research Africa in September 1977 revealed that the unemployment rate for Blacks over the age of sixteen in Johannesburg was 19·5%, and in the Johannesburg, Pretoria and Reef areas it was 18·8%. Table 2 gives the distribution of this group by level of education and by age.

TABLE 2

Unemployment in Johannesburg, Pretoria and Reef area (1977)*

| By education | | By age | |
| --- | --- | --- | --- |
| No education | 14·9% | 16–24 | 22·5% |
| Primary | 22·1% | 25–34 | 20·1% |
| High school | 8·5% | 35–49 | 18·1% |
| | | 50+ | 10·4% |

*51% of the unemployed had been out of work for more than six months. Based on information in *Survey of Race Relations in South Africa.* 1977, Vol. 31. South African Institute of Race Relations, Johannesburg, 1978.

It is worth noting that the highest unemployment is in the youngest age group, and this is important to bear in mind when later we turn to consider the aspirations and attitudes of the high school students.

The monthly earnings of the African population is significantly lower than that of Whites employed in similar sectors of the economy. Figures based on information released by the Department of Statistics reveal that the ratio of White to African wages ranges from 3·1:1 (in banking) to 9·3:1 (in mining and quarrying) (Legum, 1977).

The estimated annual income of Black families in the Johannesburg area was R2272·72* for a multiple household in 1975. The average income per earner was put at R1394·19 resulting in an annual income per capita of R445·69 (South African Institute of Racial Relations, 1977). From a minimum monthly income for a family of four calculated in 1975 at R122·27, 51% was spent on food, 12·5% on clothing,

*Approximate exchange rate in 1975 R1·80 = £1.

8·6% on housing, transport took 6·2% and fuel and light 5·2%. The remaining 16·5% includes education, personal and domestic care, hire purchase repayments, medical and taxation.

The African population in Soweto is increasingly urban born as one goes down the age scale, and almost all the population are fully urbanized in the sense of being solely dependent on their city earnings, unsubsidized by earnings from the rural areas. There is evidence from studies by Pauw (1963) in East London that urban families are unstable and that almost one half have female heads. A large number are three generational, that is they include unmarried daughters and their offspring. Although there is no recent survey of the family structure in Soweto earlier evidence (Non-European Affairs Department, 1959) indicated a similar pattern for the Johannesburg townships, with almost one-third of the women having children born out of wedlock, and only one-half of the households surveyed being nuclear.

There is a growing middle class in the townships, but it remains disproportionately tiny. For its members life is economically easier, but their demands are greater than those of the working classes. They are paid less than equivalently qualified Whites, and are more circumscribed in the practice of their professions. Africans may serve, as lawyers, doctors, teachers, social workers, only their own race; the political and legal control exercised over them limits the way that their income may be spent. Inadequate numbers of segregated theatres, holiday resorts, restaurants, hotels,* poor transport and the restrictions on movement limit the opportunities available for the African middle classes and consumers. This affects both economic power and the ability to enjoy the fruits of higher status. The population on whom the African professional man or African shopkeeper, trader or entrepreneur is dependent is poor and this factor too is a limiting one. The major caste division of race acts as a damper on the expression of class differences within the African population. Writing of the African intellectual, Ezekiel Mphahlele (1958) said, "except that I have these interests and was to this extent allowed to pursue them (reading for a degree by correspondence) I, and the many like me, come from the same kind of home and live under the same uncertain conditions and in the same way as our fellow African townsmen".

This picture is of a poor community, with a high level of instability,

---

*A number of hotels are granted "international" status, which allows them to admit Blacks from outside South Africa, and also from within.

living in a geographically separated area, selling skills or labour in a market that it is not able to influence. It may be the frustration, the poverty or the instability—or all three—which is related to the high crime rate and the violence which are characteristic of township life and which add to the economic and political insecurities of the population. Reported figures for violent crime in Soweto for the year July 1975 to June 1976 totalled 10 442. Of this total 557 were murders and 1336 rapes, 8239 were assaults and the rest culpable homicides. Approximately 60% of these were brought to trial (Hansard, 1977).

It is necessary to emphasize that townsmen and tribesmen are not exclusive categories, and that the transition from the latter to the former, in South Africa, has been made by many individuals for many generations. And the transition is not only made by men. Although the obvious employer of migrant labour—the mines—does not employ women, women have been entering cities and towns to work in domestic and factory jobs for many decades. What one is perhaps dealing with is a matter of balance, whether the individual perceives himself as urban or rural, and whether the structure of the system allows this image to be happily realized.

There is no logical reason why one should ask the Black man in South Africa to make a clear affiliation to one group or the other. It is perhaps only in looking at a static, momentary representation of reality that a clear belonging to one system or the other is to be seen. Much of the literature written by psychologists about Africa emphasizes the process of acculturation and the way that the individual "becomes modern" (see Wober, 1976). Anthropological literature also deals either with the vestiges of the tribe or the *traumas* of rapid social change. It is worth noting that with very few exceptions (Hellman, 1948; Hunter, 1936), most anthropological studies and ethnographic reports of the peoples of Southern Africa describe the traditional rural social structure often as if it were only marginally influenced by both the Whites and the availability of urban values.

And yet we do not assume that the urban-rural dimension in other societies is discontinuous. We are unabashed by big city dwellers who tell us that they are really only "small town" at heart or whose ethos and ambition is to retire to the country and raise chickens in an attempt at self-sufficiency.

A second misconception that encourages the view that Africans should be either tribal or townsfolk is that which suggests that South

Africa is in a transitional stage of industrialization, similar to that of some other African states. It is worth emphasizing a point made earlier, namely that South Africa is an industrial nation, one rich in minerals and highly organized in its capital and manpower, as well as one with many natural blessings to support its agriculture. It cannot be compared with its neighbours, the old British protectorates, nor with Angola and Mozambique. South Africa cannot really be regarded as an undeveloped nation. What is equally important is the fact that unlike many countries whose development occurred under the auspices of a colonial power, which often saw the colony simply as a source of support for the metropolitan country, the two areas of the Transvaal and the Orange Free State were independent republics until defeated by the British during the Anglo-Boer war, and even the Cape and Natal were not regarded in the same way by the British as their other African colonies. And, as we have stressed before, the indigenous population was integrally involved in industrial and mining development from its inception. Given the prevalence of the system of migrant labour and the evidence for the concern that those who have worked in town may "contaminate" their rural brethren, it can be assumed that even if the individual under consideration has not previously been to town, in some measure he will have been influenced by urban culture. It is always difficult to put together the personal and the historical reality.

It is also important to emphasize that the country is large, and that regional differences will and do occur. In East London for instance, where a fairly comprehensive study of the Xhosa in town has been undertaken (Pauw, 1963; Mayer, 1961; Reader, 1959) only 14% of the population of Africans studied were urban born. One reason for this may well be the closeness of that city to homelands allowing the continuing force of family and tradition on urban sons and daughters.

In his analysis of labour migrancy and the process of urbanization Mayer suggests there are two types of rootedness—structural and cultural. Structural rootedness refers to:

> ... social ties formed and maintained; of incorporation within a town community; or of roles played in town and roles elsewhere abandoned or rejected. (Mayer, 1961, p. 6)

Cultural rootedness is assessed on the basis of a "way of life", of attitudes and values, of subjective intentions. Both of these modes find a home within the psychological reality when one assumes as Mayer does that they are independent of simple stabilization, that is of the actual length of time spent either in town or out of it. Although his 1955 figures suggest that only 15% of the population are urban by birth, Monica Hunter's study of the area reports that from 1828 "Kaffirs" desirous of entering the service of farmers were let into the colony, and by 1850 they were employed to work in the docks in East London.

Examining the development of the policy of segregation in South African towns and cities, Swanson (1970; 1976) argues that from the early 1900s South Africa's development was influenced by urban factors. Writing about Durban he says:

> Economic expansion inevitably concentrated African labourers in the urban centres . . . To stimulus of trade was added the thrust of military conflict, and by 1901 Durban was a war-swollen city of 55,000 of whom 15,000 were Black Africans, 14,000 Indians and 26,000 Whites. By 1904 the numbers rose to 68,000 with proportions of 19,000, 16,000 and 31,000 respectively.

Swanson's analysis, especially of the togt or day-labouring class of workers, leads one to suggest that this population, although consistently growing, was not necessarily composed of the same people at all times, so that these totals represent a far larger number of Africans who were for longer or shorter periods employed in and influenced by the urban environment.

The essence of the argument is this. It is possible to suggest that the African is part of three cultures—his rural society, the industrial work environment controlled by Whites, and the bonds and relationships that flourish in the African urban township. By doing this one may seem to imply a trichotomous system each static and separate from the other with the individual a member of one or other of these groups. It could also imply that the individual may move from one to another, i.e. be in transition. These implications often confound the description of an abstract social system with the real experiences of the individuals within it. The Africans in South Africa are not an "emerging people", newly in contact with the complexities of industrial society. Any single individual may be, but his experience is personal. They are a people who have for generations worked and lived in modernity, whose traditional system was shattered long ago. However, the present always bears the traces of the past and the values which characterized a different situation may be found in the present. The British have not shaken off some of the assumptions of their imperial past, nor the Americans their tradition of frontiership. The Afrikaner's history is freshly kindled on occasions of public ceremonial when victories against both Bantu and British are marked. In the same way the strands of these three systems reflect the history of the African in South Africa, and values of each, in varying combinations, characterize the psychological assumptions against which experience is evaluated.

Mayer has suggested that the traditional and the urban values suffuse different realms, that the traditional values are maintained in relation to personal domestic and familial experience, whereas the values which are correlated with urban life will be important in public life. The way in which the individual structures these values may be critical for understanding his view of himself, and his evaluation of the society as a whole.

Although it is clear that South African society is founded firmly on distinctions of race, it is not undifferentiated within the castes themselves. The power of race is great, but although it might be able to account for differences in political and economic power, which are to be found between groups, within each group there are to be found variations in roles and obligations according to age, to sex and to occupation and education. The clarity of the racial divide has frequently taken the attention of investigators from the less obvious and subtler variations which are associated with other lines of social organization.

There are few societies where sex or age, where skills and expertise, do not bring with them obligations, rights and expectations about behaviour. Societies which are stable, where development and change are consistent in pace and direction, are able to offer fairly clear norms which people can follow, even to providing ritual celebrations of changes in status and obligation as age or skills increase. Ceremonies of birth and marriage publicly mark changes of status; graduation or promotion mark alterations in skills. In gender even with modern scientific genius, the average individual does not alter. As with race it is given at birth and as with race the extent to which the society holds this distinction to be important will vary according to place and time. If it is deemed to be a critical social variable then the demands associated with it will be set out with clarity.

Where the rate of change in a society is rapid, either because of technological development, or conquest or revolution the clarity of expectations associated with social positions and roles blurs, and the expectations alter. Although one does not need to posit a reaction of the extreme encompassed by the idea of "future shock" it is possible that those whose rearing has geared them to a different set of expectations may find that they are bewildered by changes which are rapid, and that the continuity of the society which occurs as one generation prepares the next, on the basis of assumptions which are no longer appropriate, appears to be undermined.

There are difficulties to be found in relating the psychological experience of individuals to the complexities of more abstract social structures. This is not to suggest that it has not been done. Social class, generally assumed to be directly related to and reflected in the occupational status of the male of the household, in particular, has been correlated with a variety of psychological indices. Sex, and indeed age are likewise taken to be variables on which other behaviours are dependent. It does not need to be stressed that these studies cannot make causal links between one level of analysis (economic or social) and another (personal or interpersonal). All they can do is to suggest a set of relationships which might be directly linked or might be related via a third, often unspecified factor. Where the studies merely catalogue correlates they might add a dimension to the general range of phenomena encompassed by a sociological variable, but, as argued forcefully by Holmes (1970) to list as a catalogue does not change a fact into an explanation. Holmes argues that to be more than transient, more than a passing piece of information, a fact must be integrated into a coherent theoretical superstructure, it must be subsumed in something bigger than itself to have lasting meaning. The numbers listed in the telephone directory, or the information between the covers of "The Guiness Book of Records" are indisputably factual. They do not constitute science. Likewise listing the correlates of social structural dimensions does not explain, any more than specifying the merchandise of Harrods or the stock of Bloomingdales tells one how the retail trade functions. Piaget makes a distinction between figurative and operative knowledge—operative knowledge is the true field of mature cognitive functioning, and reflects the processes of scientific thinking, whereas figurative knowledge enables one to recognize a phenomenon:

> The operative aspect of knowledge, however, assumes that one knows the object by acting upon it in order to transform it, and one discovers its properties through these transformations. (Geber, 1977, p. 6)

We therefore need to be able to do more than list a set of relationships. We need to be able to go beyond the information given to understand the processes whereby the parts relate, by which the structures of society are reflected (if indeed they are) in the psychological processes and assumptions of the individuals.

# 4

# My World: The Subjective View
of the Townships

One can examine the social reality of the individual in a number of ways. There is his behaviour, the actions he performs and the reactions he receives, the regularities of relationships which he displays, the symbols of speech or other systems of social signalling he uses and from these we can abstract the position and function of the individual in the network of behaviours that constitute his social world. Or, we can examine his beliefs, his values, the way he construes and orders his social world, and from these make assumptions about behaviours which the individual is likely to display in particular contexts. Additionally we may look across the particulars of any one individual and abstract consistent patterns of beliefs or behaviours for many individuals and relate these to specific social structures and social experiences. This intersect of the societally defined and the individually experienced is a fruitful point for discovering the essence of social psychological experience. The sterility of the nature-nurture debate, of the argument as to the primacy of the individual or of the environment, has no part in such an examination. One is searching for the interaction within a dynamic context of the experiences and beliefs of the individual and the environment, both personal and impersonal, within which these are shaped. One is seeking an understanding of the "fit" between the individual and the social moment so that one can predict how the individual or group of individuals will behave under particular conditions. One is looking for the key to relating the individual's beliefs about himself and others to his actual behaviour.

For a number of reasons, in our role as social scientists we seem to be reluctant to ask directly a question that can be asked indirectly. We are also reluctant, for a variety of historical and methodological reasons, to get direct information from those in whose lives and experiences we are most interested about their lives and about their feelings. The problems of the status of the information given to us is the same whether we ask direct questions or try to glean our data in more roundabout ways. We are still dependent on the reports of others.

There are some studies that give support to the direct approach, to the technique which enables the subject to provide, with as little intrusion from the investigator as possible, the basic data for analysis. Danziger (1963) in his studies of South African youth has shown that it is possible to derive a great deal of insight from the way people perceive their future. Although one may quibble about the objective reality that the reports represent, one cannot deny that they reflect the psychological reality of the writer. It was possible for Ezekiel (1968), in his study of Peace Corps workers to use the "future autobiography" successfully as a predictive tool against later objective and independent assessment of the individual's performance in the field.

We used as sources of information, reports written by 14 final year Soweto high school students about life in the townships. These 14 were part of the original sample, and were selected from those who remained in the final year of the high school programme. They were chosen in order to represent some of the background variables that we thought might influence attitudes, but were not necessarily a representative sample. A number of subgroups were defined within the final year group: girls and boys; lower and upper ends of the age range; urban born or country born; unskilled, skilled, clerical and professional family background. Quite clearly these are not exclusive groups. From within the groups students were chosen randomly to take part in a series of interviews and discussion groups. They were asked to write essays to describe, as if to foreigners, what it was like to live in Soweto, and what the life of a child and a teenager in the townships was like. This technique produced insights which it was not possible to achieve as an outsider, nor by the reading of demographic facts and figures. We know too little about the basic building blocks of individual psychological and phenomenological experience to be able to move from an aesthetic appreciation of an environment to an understanding of the way that the individual construes it. While it might be feasible to rely on tested covariance to predict the influence of social environments on the generalities of experience and functioning, the particularities necessitate a level of abstraction at one less remove from the individual's interaction with his particular world.

In this study, where the investigators were not Soweto residents, we felt it was risky to base too many assumptions on one's own reactions to the townships. And even when one is not aware of the separation from the life of one's subjects it is possible to err in judging the effects of particular environments on the psychological functioning of individuals. Studies of high rise housing for example have shown that many young mothers and children living at the top of tower blocks are distressed by their conditions, at their isolation and by the physical difficulties of running a house and family so far from the ground; but it is possible to imagine that penthouse living, at the same height from the street could indeed be a delightful experience. The evaluation and effect of the built environment is filtered through a complex of needs, and reflects the personal and social networks of the individual, the family and the community. Without espousing a romantic view it is possible to have a full and rewarding life even in dense and unaesthetic surroundings, and there is no guarantee that fulfilment and contentment comes with edge-to-edge carpets and large gardens. What one needs to know is how the individual reacts to, copes with, and performs within the social world that is encompassed by the bricks and streets, the playgrounds and shops, that constitute the physical frame of his immediate world.

The world that emerges from the essays about Soweto is remarkable in the similarities of the issues selected as foci for comment and at the same time individual in the particular way that the common themes are reported. It is a world that is characterized by poverty and brutality, but is also warm, lively and intimate. It must be noted that where comparisons are drawn they are with the White suburbs of Johannesburg, and not with a tribal past. Nor is there evidence of the decaying inner cities of Liverpool and London, Detroit and New York being used as reference points. The young Black resident of Soweto looks out on White Johannesburg then back at his township, and draws his own conclusions. What are these conclusions?*

> Life in the township is summed up by the words, starvation, fear, evil, privation and dissatisfaction. (George)

*The essays have been excerpted for presentation here. However, except that spellings have been corrected the extracts have not been edited nor has the grammar been altered. It would have been impossible to present the essays in full because of constraints of space. Where it was thought necessary, more than one writer's work has been extracted to show how the theme is dealt with across respondents.

The poverty of the townships, their physical desolation and the violence which characterizes life within them are constant themes of the descriptions.

## The environment

Dirty, corrugated windowed semblances of streets, dirty urchins half naked running about the streets every hour of the day and several of the night. Bedraggled old men and women along the streets, some selling dry shrunken fruits. Small nearly collapsing houses, others with planks for window panes, doors that creak as if their hinges never knew oil in their lifetime. Evenings that are darker than an Ethiopian because of the smoke issuing from innumerable braziers. Buses full of cramped, tired, uncomfortable labourers one after the other deliver the breadwinners of hundreds of families to find wives red eyed because of smoke, bending over braziers preparing a scanty supper. This is the general outline of the physical and social structure of South African townships. (Isaac)

Putting this as something that has to be read, I take it my readers are aware of this, that I am granted freedom of speech. The conditions and pressure of township life has led me and others who are experiencing the same fate to think not less than once of quitting ourselves from existing. The "loud-sounding-nothing" that is termed "government" has turned us into instruments to further its own ends—the ends that are unknown to those who live in the townships but only known to those who are considered and recognised as human beings.

My aim is not to criticise anybody, but to state, in actual fact the type of life that Africans lead in townships. I regard the township as an "open jail for free prisoners" . . . The things that we live in are not houses but segmented cocoons with four small rooms in which I cannot move freely. Nevertheless we are expected to appreciate that. An artist, a man who sees beauty in almost every object, has surely nothing to appreciate in the way our "modern" houses are built. I wonder whether the Conquerers of Nature are of this saying that everything is good as it comes from the hands of the Creator, but becomes bad when it gets into the hands of man. We were free when we were called barbarians but we are now chained by civilisation. We move within limited bounds within our own yards. Let us forget the house and consider what is outside it. The daily setting of the sun has nothing save bringing sorrow into the hearts of those who live in the townships. The streets are very badly illuminated; the roads are badly constructed. These things result in nothing else but an increase in death rate. These conditions do not demote but promote delinquency.

Every street in a European town is paved, and most of the streets have special paths for pedestrians. Township roads are narrow and dusty and pedestrians have to decide whether to walk in the middle of the street or to crouch themselves against the fence. The only tarred roads are those that are used by the official vehicles of municipality and the government. Roads that lead to the railway stations for the collection of money, to the Superintendent's office; to the hospitals and to the beerhalls.

The badly illuminated streets bring doubts to everybody. Children doubt whether their parents will reach home safely from work because every dark corner has been made a hive for the thugs. Instead of improving the conditions the landowners put big boards on each available space, written in capital letters thus:

BE SAFE IN THE STREETS TONIGHT, CARRY A TORCH

I wonder whether we are advised or expected to carry torches even inside our supposed houses, because even there the lights that are used are no good. We cannot use electricity—it is not up to our standard. We deserve candle lights; and we are however satisfied. After all beggars can't be choosers. (Aubrey)

To a stranger the township appears to be a military camp . . . The plan of the township resembles that of military camps. The houses are small (in fact not fit to be called houses); the yards are overwhelmingly small; the roads are not well constructed. Most streets are not macadamised. They have rocks jutting out of the ground, broken bottles hidden beneath the sand. Life in such conditions is surely a curse. If man was not capable of adapting himself or herself to the environment then the hospitals would be full and specialise in treating fractures due to the rocks found all over the streets.

The size of the houses affects the social life of the African community. The houses are dreadfully small, the families are big, and thus overcrowding prevails . . . In a two roomed house one finds eleven people living there. There is evidently disorder in such a house. The children are noisy, the air is stuffy, and no one can do anything properly. (Thomas)

The essays focussed essentially on three themes. The first was the poverty of the people and the associated deprivations, the second was the violence and lawlessness of the township and the third was the eventfulness of life. Additionally special events or groups were singled out for description—the religious sects, politicians, New Year celebrations and marriages.

## The daily round

On ordinary days the township boys will be found either playing football in the dusty street with tennis balls, sometimes playing marbles or flying kites. Girls sometimes play games such as skipping or marabaraba (a sort of draughts game, played with stones and on arrangement of holes in the ground). These help in forgetting their miserable lives at their homes, and will help them to grow healthy and intelligent. (John)

If you want to experience the saddest part of township life take a short walk just immediately after lunch hours. What you will see is what will remind you of the peasants that were once mentioned in France, you will see a ragged, almost naked, hungry and lonely child with a big tummy filled with 'mealie-pap' and tears streaming down his grey cheeks, standing and admiring others who are eating what his parents cannot afford to buy.

The facial expressions of that child will reveal a sad story. "How am I going to get what that child is eating, and who is going to give me the money to buy it?" These are the problems that the little chap is trying to solve. (Agnes)

On week days lucky men and women go to work; their children run merrily to school. After eight o'clock the townships are cleared of all the better off people. Those who remain are the cursed lot, they roam around the township with no definite destination. Their eyes under drooping lids are always scanning the streets for policemen. The sight of a policeman sends these poor outcasts of fate scuttling for cover for fear of being arrested for not paying polltax when they cannot raise enough to clothe themselves decently. In the afternoons these people flock to the bars, waiting for their more fortunate friends to come back from work and buy them some beer. The children of the unfortunate hover around the shops and eating houses waiting to grab a piece of bread if the chance offers. They usually wait at the eating house until a customer has eaten his fill and if he leaves some in the plate they rush in and grab it and run.

The mothers are the ones that do something for the unfortunate families. They go to town or the suburbs to wash European's clothes, for a scanty salary. Some work for about four Europeans simultaneously. They collect the large bundles of clothes and wash them at their houses. From morning till sunset they wash and rinse until their backs are sore and their hands bruised. Then they have to prepare food for the hungry members of the family. The next day they have to iron the clothes and by the time they are through their bodies are just a symphony of pain and hunger only a single instrument in the symphony. (Isaac)

At evening time when everyone comes from work, township life reaches its climax. Taxis, overloaded to the extent that some passengers are packed into the boot and some even sitting on the bonnet, hurtle along at breakneck speed as they carry their passengers from the station to their homes. Extremely over-crowded trains one after another come to pour out their heavy burdens at the stations. As the passengers alight they rush like frenzied bulls to the station exit. When they get to narrow exits they push each other this way and the other, as each one tries to carve his way out of the station. Then as they one by one gain exit some rush to the beerhalls, some to the taxi rank to board taxis home, and some who may be fortunate enough to be staying near the station walk in small groups to their homes conversing on the news that may be in the headlines. (Nathan)

Such is the general atmosphere of the townships as seen by the young educated Soweto students. Their descriptions in general can be summed by the phrase used by one:

> In the township life is characterised by poverty, misery and untold suffering for the African people. (Shadrack)

The poverty of the population intrudes even into the liveliest and happiest scenes, and is a constant theme of the descriptions.

## Violence

Another recurrent theme is that of violence. No report omitted descriptions of gangs, or of robbery, or of murder. At times this was attributed to the prevalence of beerhalls, sometimes with the explicit suggestion that the beerhalls are part of general policy designed to keep the African people in a state of subjugated compliance.

> Groups of boys who usually have nothing to do turn themselves into gangsters and start displaying their excess energy mischievously. They will buy knives to fight against each other and even against innocent people. Such things are in fact indirectly encouraged by the Government who think it an honour to the people to have in any newly built township a bar or what is usually referred to as a "BEER GARDEN". . .
> These beer-halls have in them the seeds of destruction to the African. Their youth is easily corrupted because they are allowed to enter and have as many scales of beer as they possibly can afford; dreadful diseases are passed from one person to another because many share one scale of beer; they are the mother of irresponsibility in both men and women. (James)

Or this extract:

> It seems it has become a compulsory labour for the municipality to build beerhalls in every township, and what is questioning is that these beerhalls are built near railway stations. There is definitely a motive behind this. When a worker gets off the train especially on Fridays he is logically expected to get to the beerhall first, use his wages and then get home with empty pockets. Why do they not build secondary schools instead of beerhalls? The beerhalls do more harm to our fathers than any good. (Agnes)

This excerpt has a similar assumption:

> Every evening all beerhalls are packed to capacity—not to make mention of the multitudes who spend most of Saturday and Sunday at the beerhalls . . . Some intoxicated people get themselves hurt or make a disgrace of themselves, lying hopeless on the ground, sometimes badly hurt, talking endless jargon, and perhaps retching or even vomiting. Indeed this makes every decent African feel ashamed and gives the African's enemies ground for maintaining that the African is a very wild and uncultured people. (Simon)

The violence of Soweto is seen in contrast with the joys of nature:

> It is early in the morning. A cold westerly breeze is lazily blowing. The sky is clear and bright. The sun is not yet up, only the brightness of the east heralds its coming. The smoke from chimney tops seems to be drifting in the direction of the westerly breeze. One can hear the yelping of a dog or two here and there whilst the little birds twitter on the trees scattered in the South Western Townships. There is the occasional click-clacking of the heavy laden trains as they speed the Africans to the city where they work and are usually referred to by their employers as "natives", "kaffirs", "boy", "girl", "Jim", or "Jane". One listens to the birds happily twittering and the doves cooing in the trees, then one wonders if most of the people in the trains heading for work are happy or sad . . . One actually wonders why should people wear grim faces while nature was bright and alert.
>
> Yes, around the corner of Letsasti Street near the D.O.C.C. lies a cold lifeless body besmeared with blood and having quite a number of stab wounds. A short robust policeman is guarding the lifeless form on the ground. Passers-by just pass a remark or two and hurry on to be in time for their trains. The clear air is rent by a sudden scream of untold deep rooted grief and sadness. Turning round I saw a woman holding the lifeless form to her breast. I knew that it must be her husband for soon the children came running towards the body. The short robust policeman tried in vain to keep them away. The tears trickled down the cold grief-stricken faces. (Stanley)

Other descriptions of violence are less specific:

> People live under perpetual fear in the townships. In the first place a policeman infuses so much fear that the very sight of a police car attracts the attention of all the people. The reference book is the chief source of fear. Fear is further increased by the presence of hordes of hoodlums in the location . . . Butcheries are perpetuated in the townships in a degree unprecedented in the world, of course, excluding wars. The child who has left school because of incapability of the parents financially, who has followed an undesirable profession because of reference book difficulties becomes a danger to society. As we all must live, their means of livelihood becomes the butchery and robbery of others. (George)

They (the youth) hang around the street corners and the shops. There they way-lay smaller children sent to the shops to buy. They rob them of their money. And some go to the extent of exploiting young girls . . . The young robbers do not end at street corners, but they go to the station and the bus-stops. There they mingle with the workers and start their pick-pocketing campaign. The braver ones do not just pick-pocket but actually relieve the poor defenceless old man of his whole wages by force. But since this is always accompanied by some struggle these miscreants carry danger-ous weapons which when drawn would scare the victim into giving up his wages without any struggle. But some of these delinquents are so desperate that they kill the victim after taking his money. (Aubrey)

One fact about the townships is universally known, and condemned; the proficiency of juvenile delinquents. Every pay day the street corners are alive with dark shadows that flit from shelter to shelter, scanning the crowds for a likely victim. If a victim comes along a brick is deposited quickly and painfully over his head and his pockets emptied the minute his cadaver touches the ground. Every Monday morning numerous workers are missing from their jobs and the casualty wards of the hospital over-flowing; evidence of vigorous action on the part of young delinquents over the week-end. (Isaac)

The drunks are preys of robbers and the screams of the preys go un-heeded. (Thomas)

## Colourful events

Thus far therefore the world of the Soweto youth is bleak, poor, violent, desolate. However, the grimness is not unrelieved.

In general, the township is a life of joy in misery. On Mondays to Fridays most people go to work and children go to school. On Saturdays and Sundays there is sport, dancing, and church going. The most thrilling day is Sunday. This is when we see the different sects in religion worshipping in diverse ways . . . The most interesting are the diverse little sects that have cropped up. There is the "Watch Tower" or Rutherford Church . . . there are those churches which as a result of one man being poor and hence making a means of obtaining money from easier sources are born. The man decides to ask some neighbours to assemble in his house, and he being the unordained priest starts worshipping and collecting the money intended for alms giving. The most vast and widespread, but the most unconstitutional sect is that of the Zionists Churches. These people wear blue, white and green clothing. Some wear white research workers' coats and garbs made of green and blue cloth, and a large white cross sewn to the back of the garb. The queerest thing with these people is the way they worship. Tom-tom drums are used to keep the rhythm constant. And then they start jumping about in a circular motion with the priest or bishop running in front with his goat-beard (which is indispensable). The hymns they sing cannot be written down as they have no specific words at all. (John)

The most universal movement among the females in the township is the Christian Mother's Union. In all the churches in the township there must be a mother's union. Every Thursday the women assemble in their respective churches to pray for the whole of humanity. Every church has a special uniform. On this day the diverse colours of the diverse uniforms presents a lively and lovely picture. (John)

Not all reports of the Zionists are as tolerant, nor is Christianity generally favoured:

These Zionists beat drums every blessed Friday night until Saturday morning and we students are supposed to concentrate on our studies under these conditions . . . When there are no Zionists the Sangoma (Medicine man) and his numerous deputies make another nerve racking noise and strange odours of different herbs fill the night air. (Stanley)

Sunday, which is according to the Christian doctrine a holy day . . . on this day the Africans show clearly their flouting of what they call the White man's religion. (Nathan)

The White man under the pretext of civilising the African turned them into tools through Christianity. Luckily most Africans are beginning to realise the futility of praying to a White God as is evident from the fact that more and more All-African churches are being formed and that more and more Africans stay away from Churches on Sunday. (Simon)

Township living is not all misery and suffering, and the more light-hearted aspects of urban life do get mentioned though rarely in such detail as the more dismal. Each of the students described the hardships of township existence, whereas only half wrote of the gayer aspects, and each one of these interspersed their descriptions with asides to show that the miseries of township life are never far away.

However, the Africans being a gay and carefree nation by nature have or are trying to make the best out of the worst. The town-ships are buzzing with life at all times, weekday or weekend. People are always moving to and fro and conversing about the day's experiences or some other thing. There is never a dull moment in the townships. (Nathan)

Weekends are the most lively days in the townships. Invariably there are three or four wedding celebrations within a radius of eight hundred yards. Invitation cards fly from place to place among the elite. The down-at-heel out-at-elbows is always on the look out for a white flag on a gatepost that announces louder than news headlines the close proximity of the day of festivities. Before the wedding day there are choirs practising wedding songs every evening at the place where the wedding will take place. In the choir one finds many kinds of people, in fact a deputation representing every class of people in the township. The wedding day provides great excitement for all concerned. Cars, decorated with multicoloured paper ribbons, take the bride, groom, bridesmaids, best man and close relatives to the church. From church they go to the groom's house and there is dancing, singing and general entertainment. The patrons of the wedding are not limited to the invited. Ninety-five percent of the people present invite themselves. (Isaac)

One final extract perhaps sums up the impressions given by the others. It is autobiographical, describing the student's first introduction to the world of the Townships:

On New Year's Eve some years ago a boy arrived in Johannesburg from the rural areas of the Northern Transvaal. It was his first visit to the big city. His brother stayed in one of Johannesburg's townships. This boy, named Shama, had lost both of his parents during a revolt in his home in the Northern Transvaal. After their death Shama had no home, and his sole relative was his brother, and thus he was forced to come to stay with him.

Shama was met by his brother and wife and after they had shown him some new scenes in his life they took him to their home in Moroka township. When the taxi carrying Shama and his brother and his wife entered the location after the twelve mile ride from Johannesburg he was baffled at the sight of so many people and so many houses. He saw that everybody looked clever and active, whilst he felt like a lost sheep. After a few yards drive the taxi stopped at a shanty that was to be his future home. He was warmly greeted by his brother's neighbours, and by his brother's in-laws and his nephews and nieces. Within the end of the day Shama's sheepishness had declined tremendously because everybody welcomed him. That night he was told that everybody was going to sleep early, because at twelve midnight everyone would wake up to welcome the new year. At five minutes to twelve everybody woke up. Whilst he was puzzled by what was going on he heard the noise made by tins sounding from afar. At the same time the neighbourhood was filled with ear deafening noises from tins, drums, firecrackers and happy voices shouting or howling HAPPY! HAPPY NEW YEAR! Old people, middle-aged people, young people, teen-agers and even small infants all shouted and welcomed the New Year. Fires lighted the whole township. The one tarred road of the location was barricaded with dustbins full of ashes and rubbish or even buckets from the unseweraged latrines. At this instant no cars used the tarred road. Anybody who owned a car had to remove the tyres on New Year's Eve because they would be stolen or burned five minutes before the New Year. Sometimes car owners had to sleep in their cars to guard them from being "kidnapped" by the celebrators. Shama was puzzled by all these events which occurred too fast for him. To his amazement he saw a group of teen-age boys and girls who entered the dark passages where they indulged in acts of indecency. The "celebrations" went on until about three hours after the first minute of the New Year when most people felt tired and drowsy and the noise declined tremendously . . . When Shama awoke he found the main street strewn with ashes and full of dustbins and latrine buckets, their contents mostly being spilled. The whole place looked untidy and stinking. A boy of Shama's age, who lived opposite, saw him and befriended him. The other boy, who was called Bushu told Shama about life in that township. Whilst they were still conversing a group of teenagers who knew Bushu joined them singing and shouting "Happy New Year". Shama thought he saw amongst the group some boys who looked like girls and some girls who looked like boys. Bushu told Shama that during New Year's day boys wear girls attire and vice versa, and they go from house to house shouting HAPPY! and after that they would be given beer in gallons and drink until their stomachs protruded. This was a shock to Shama who considered drinking beer when still young a sin. During that day Bushu showed Shama all of the township with people drunk nearly everywhere. Some of the drunk people would vomit whenever they felt like doing so and in some instances others would sleep in the middle of the road. Bushu told Shama that murders were at their highest peak during this time. Ten lives would be lost during that day because when people are drunk they usually forget everything concerning their safety and walk about aimlessly during the night. This gives a chance to thugs, thieves and robbers who do their jobs well at this time. Late in the afternoon the two new friends returned to their homes. On arriving at Bushu's home they heard that Bushu's elder sister who had drunk beer for the first time that day had been kidnapped by thugs. Fortunately she was returned that same night after midnight having been assaulted. This to Shama's surprise was life in the township between New Year's Eve and New Year's Day. (Samson)

## Attributing responsibility

Even the extracts given here indicate that the young students of Soweto look at their world and question it. The poverty, the drunkenness, the violence, the ignorance and the neglect that they describe are seen in the light of experience. There is no attempt to find purpose in poverty, or destiny in the dreary desolation of the townships. In all but one essay, the political system which governs the life of the country is held responsible for the misery and suffering that are described.

Thus the African is what he is today due to the extenuating circumstances under which he strives. Thus life in the township could be developed along good and proper lines. The whole blame rests with the Government, that demands more than what it offers to the Africans. (Henry)

They (the Blacks) are termed uncouth and backward but those who decide their destinies do nothing towards their uplifting. Instead they isolate them and give them no chance to voice their opinion in politics. (Aubrey)

The status quo causes much concern in the townships. People are now aware of the injuries inflicted on them and are aware of the national bonds that hold them together. This is the fountain of revolts in the townships. People who have the initiative and drive lead and are thus termed inciters. This leads to the arrests of the so-called inciters thus inflicting misery and hardships on the dependents. (George)

Apartheid is the mother of the townships. To elaborate this statement I would say that the incurable policy of the government has been put into practice and it has stopped us from being given what we deserve, viz: the privileges that are enjoyed by the light complexioned nation, the so termed "Whites". We deserve unity and not racial discrimination that makes us feel inferior to be classified as people. Human beings live in cities, they use electricity and they are described by civilisations and courtesy as "ladies and gentlemen". We live in townships where the principles of apartheid and agents of the government call us Amadoda* and Abafazi*. The offices for European affairs are written Ladies and Gentlemen but our toilet houses have written males and females. Offices are written "dogs and natives not allowed". (Agnes)

Africans! Have hopes and the day will come when we shall also live under pleasant conditions. (Stanley)

Oh! What a curse to be an African in a township, to be a tool, an instrument, a possession without right. (Agnes)

This theme is expanded in one of the essays, the only one to deal in any depth with the question of leadership:

There is, however, a section that is apart from all that has been mentioned above. They are the township politicians. They are greatly concerned with the lot of the people, they are disgusted by the conditions prevailing in their country. They compare the White child, with his pleasant comfortable house illimitable means of advancement and all that money can buy, to the poor ill-fed handicapped African child. These people convene meetings and deliver fiery emotional touching speeches, that inflame them and the audience that happens to be there, to a raging hatred of the White man. They enumerate the grievances, perpetrated by the White man and quote grandiloquent passages from speeches made by prominent politicians in the world. These people have been so influential that the African regards the White man as no more than a usurper, coming

*Males and females.

to exploit them and their country for his own good. The Africans are now biding their time waiting for the day when open rebellion shall flare out and sweep through the country like a raging inferno, putting to end forever to the abominable White domination. (Isaac)

This dissatisfaction stems from the unpleasant thought that in their mother country, their birthright and heritage, they are congested in their millions into an area of a few square miles and made to stay in houses no better than pigstys whilst the foreigners in their land live in posh air-conditioned mansions. (Nathan)

This then is the student's construction of Soweto, their world and their reality. Poor, brutal, uncertain, but lively. All the time their world is informed by and anchored to the political system which fashioned it. This is the world in which Soweto's children grow up—it is where they are educated and socialized.

# 5

# Township Socialization

A great deal of research in Africa has been concerned with processes of social change, and much has focussed on the idea that there is a dichotomy between the traditional, rural tribal system, and the modern, Western or urban one (see Chapter 3). The alternative proposed is that there must be a continuum, whose "extremes are 'traditional' and 'western', but that the various constituent elements of such a continuum will cluster together" (Jahoda, 1970). Jahoda continues: "This view is in conflict with my observations". Change is not a process of moving from fixed point to fixed point, but a dynamic, in which the elements of the old and the new are intermingled in the production of a unique system which may well share some things in common with other places and times, but whose mix is particular.

This view is important for understanding the process of socialization, the experiences that shape and mould the behaviours and beliefs of the individual and lead to, and are part of, the way he is integrated into the social world. One could be forgiven when reading some of the relevant literature, for believing that the purposes and techniques of socialization were based on formalized, intentional programmes, whose means-end relations were clearly understood not only by the observing psychologist, but also by those directly involved in caring for the growing child. Alas, reality is not as clear as that, and very often the processes involved in the socialization of the child are the unsought consequences of external factors and demands. It is an imaginative idea that social and personal history have psychogenic sources—that economic change is the consequence of altered practices regarding the swaddling of infants (see Mause (1974) for a discussion)—it seems to these investigators at least, that within the primary socializing group, the family, how the children are reared and guided is more often a fortuitous confluence of circumstances than the outcome of deliberation. Reports about growing up in Soweto lend support to this belief.

The pattern of development in the African townships differs considerably from that reported for tribal societies. In tribal communities change was slow; social roles constant, accepted and understood. Men, women and children had well-defined positions in the social scheme. Marriage was stable and the extended kinship system was vital to the functioning of the society. Economic functions were clear, and children were important, both as an additional source of help and as a status determinant. Parents knew the personality characteristics approved by the community and could encourage these in their children. Rules of conduct were agreed upon, understood and enforced. The knowledge necessary for successful adjustment to the world and to society was not formalized, but was the consequence of experience, which allowed the older generation status and deference.

In the cities these circumstances no longer exist. Change is rapid and social roles fluctuate. Men and women no longer have separate functions, as the poverty of the community demands the direct involvement of women in the economic life of the society. The kinship system is no longer essential for the structure of the society and the extended family obligations strain meagre financial resources. Marriage is unstable, children are no longer easily integrated at an early age into the economic activities of the family, often proving additional burdens in the stresses of the cities. Knowledge is specialized and vast, and the older generation, far from being repositories of relevant experience are frequently less well prepared for the demands of urban life than their children.

In these circumstances children growing up in the townships do not automatically have before them the example of the older generation to follow. Instead, they are subjected to the influence of a variety of more or less successfully adjusted adults and age mates. They are no longer sure of what is required of them and all too often those parents who have firm ideas of the role of children find that these are unsuited to the demands of the township. Their authority is both questioned and flouted.

Monica Hunter (1946), writing about the urban African family:

> Always when I asked a middle aged or oldish person what were the changes in Bantu life they saw as a result of contact with Europeans, the decrease in parental control was mentioned.
>
> The economic conditions produced by the coming of Europeans have been a primary factor in disrupting social relationships. The old system of economic interdependence of father and son was adjusted to a culture in which no money was earned, but each performed certain reciprocal

services which on the whole were fairly balanced. When sons went forth to earn money the system was upset and has never since been satisfactorily adjusted . . . Further, the fact that both men and girls are actually self-supporting and not economically dependent upon their father as under tribal conditions, gives them the power and possible revolution or emancipation.

In addition, she writes:

. . . the fact that young people have learned more of European ways than their parents . . . makes them feel superior, they understand things which their fathers do not understand, therefore they are the wiser.

Philip and Iona Mayer (1961) studying the same area some 25 years after the Hunter study, found that many parents, both those oriented to the city and educated and those attached to the tribe and illiterate, preferred their children to be brought up outside the city, in country areas. The moral danger facing the children in the city was as important a factor as the economic benefit of children in the country.

Rearing children there (in the town) was supposed to mean loss of parental control with disastrous consequences for the child's morality.

Additional causes for the decline of the older generation are often mentioned. The need for both parents to go out to work and the absence of an older relative at home to take over the care of the children means that many are left all day without adult supervision. The presence of a large number of adolescents in the townships, without work and unable to continue at school does not help in maintaining control and order. The facilities for child-care and for pre-school education are poor and even when the youngster starts school pressure on the resources means that there are double sessions and that for much of the day the child is left unattended.

The life of the child and the young person in Soweto was detailed by the 14 final-year high school students. As in their descriptions of the township, all of them stressed the effect of poverty on the early life of the child, directly in terms of the effects of malnutrition and hunger, indirectly through parents having to go out to work.

An African child experiences hindreds (hindrances) even before he is born. The parents wonder whether the superintendent will accept the still-to-be-born child into their permit or not, and the child, after being born is neglected because the parents are anxious to get to work so as to earn money and feed the child. (Agnes)

The parent being unable to afford proper food for the child only manages to get food substitutes for it. For an instance, if the parent buys a bag of mealie-meal the child might have to thrive on liquid porridge—or even the very hard variety suitable for adults. Of course, the parent should not be blamed for unwillingness to sacrifice for the proper maintenance of his children, as most of them are quite ignorant as to what type of food is best for the child—to them anything that the child can shove down the throat to set the belly at ease is good enough; furthermore it might be a matter of "want not, waste not" if the child is as brave as to complain about the type of food. Then it is always carbohydrates, carbohydrates, year in and year out. This accounts for the fact that malnutrition is shockingly rife in the townships. (Simon)

The majority of the population of the townships is composed of poor people and people who just manage to check starvation . . . In average homes the parents do in a way manage to create favourable conditions for the growth and good health of their small babies. They buy warm clothes, warm nightgowns, nourishing infant foodstuffs, bathe it every day and allow it enough time for sleep. In poorer families especially with illegitimate children, which are not un-common, the mother fails to provide her child or baby with things that would promote good health and growth. She (the mother) starves herself, and as the baby lives by sucking from her, when she is hungry the baby is underfed. The baby is usually exposed to cold because the mother fails to buy enough coal for making a fire everyday. The mother stops bathing the child regularly for fear of promoting the cold. Sometimes the mother becomes so financially stranded that she starts looking for work in the town before she is actually fit and strong enough for it. She either carries her baby on her back and boards the heavily loaded trains with it or leaves it under the care of her older children. These children tend to ignore the child when the mother is away. They feed it soft porridge and send it to bed and they themselves dash out of the room to play with their mates in the street . . . They leave the child not properly covered, they force it to sleep before it is even satisfied with eating the soft porridge that they feed to it . . . It is only in the late afternoon when its mother is about to come home that they leave their playmates and attend to it, to give the mother the impression that they look after it well. (Shadrack)

An alternative source of care is described in another essay:

More often than not these young people find it necessary for both of them to go and work; and at a very puny age the poor creature (baby) is left to the care of an old woman who is only there to earn a living (rather) than to impart to the child the love he deserves. The child will grow up in that way with very little idea of what love is, but a more vivid and acute idea of what hatred is . . . The relationship between the parents and the child is usually not as it should be, because the parents come back home late and wake up early in the morning to catch their trains, and the child is usually tired in the evenings and has very little time to spare and enjoy the company of his parents. (James)

The students reach a number of conclusions about the lack of constant parental care and supervision:

The child begins to feel the importance of independence. He is left the whole day to do whatever he wishes and in this way the hatred of parental control crops in. He begins to hate control of anybody. When he comes to schooling age he cannot be told to do anything which he does not want. (Thomas)

Because the child is neglected from the moment he is born there is no one to preach integrity and honesty, and no one to see that he attends school regularly. (Agnes)

What happens to the child during the day and what it does is as dark to the parents as is daylight to a blind man. When the school goes out the child may be compelled by hunger to go home; if he is not hungry he is likely to go with his friends to play-grounds and he will leave when he realises that it is time to go home and do his daily routine. This he will do haphazardly so as to avoid punishment from his parents. It is more fear than a sense of duty that compels him to do his work. This becomes second nature to him and that is how irresponsibility comes about. (James)

The problems of parenting and of control are not alleviated when school age arrives:

Schooling is much of a problem. Sending a child to school means spending more money. Parents getting little salaries almost cannot afford it. This, and the fact that some of the parents regard education as a meaningless waste of time, contributes to the parent's reluctance to educate his children. Of course, to keep the child out of the streets the parent sends it to school, but, unfortunately, does not provide it with books, clothing, and all paraphanalia needed by a school child. The child feels very unlike those children whose parents can afford to give them all they need, and hence begins in him a loathing for going to school, and perhaps a detrimental inferiority complex. This might lead the child to play truant regularly during which periods he comes into contact with the very dregs of society. (Simon)

The issue of control and discipline is one that features in all reports. The violence that is portrayed in the township essays, is reflected in descriptions of the temptations to which the children are exposed when parents are at work, not only all day, but for extremely long hours. It was frequently mentioned that the parents have to get up before dawn to start the journey to work, and return after nightfall, that the children are left to the control and care of other children or to an "old woman". Grandparents are not mentioned at all—and the absence of creches and nurseries in sufficient number was stressed.

> Besides the already mentioned obstacles (poverty, neglect) African parents, especially in the townships have no mode of shaping the characters of their youth. In rural areas a child is taught to be loyal, honest and respectful, to know what is good and bad for him. That leads to the formation of what we call society—a community where a child, a man, are aware of the next man's existence. Unlike in the townships where every man is for himself. The primary education of every child should in fact be the education that a child gets from home from the parents. Such things as these should be taught: respect for elders, distinction between honesty and dishonesty, integrity, responsibility, love and understanding; and in addition to love the child should be taught and shown the appreciation and happiness of life. (Agnes)

It is clear from the essays that the absence of parental control is attributed to two sources. The first, the economic, we have already mentioned. The second is the use of strict discipline without discussion.

> In the average home, strict discipline has to be observed. The parent even goes to the extent of flogging the child for petty wrongs as he firmly believes in the expression "a burnt child dreads fire". The child can thus not object to anything that the parent says lest he gets himself into trouble. This turns the child's life into a nightmare; he develops a great fear for the parent, which sometimes turns to hatred. One might even be led to think that he grows up with these ideas of parent despotism firmly embedded in his mind and later on embarks on a vindictive policy against his own children. (Simon)

> Our parents should be exemplary: they should teach children manners so that the children in turn will know how to treat their children. (Agnes)

Problems are also seen to some extent in those families who are financially secure:

> A child whose parents are well-to-do, finds himself a misfit in society. A wealthy man is out of place in a poor community. He looks upon the poor with scorn and hatred and is considered to be haughty by the poor. In this way he then falls into the lot of the poor for nobody can live alone in a community. In a similar way a child who is born of rich parents, just has to fall into the lot of the poor and deteriorate into a worthless street jack. (Thomas)

With the parents out all day the young child has early to take on domestic responsibilities. Not only do the older children have to look after the younger through the day, but they also have to fend for themselves.

> At this age (when he starts school) the child is big enough to make tea for himself before going to school and he is therefore able to make breakfast for himself; his parents have very little to worry about him. All they do is to leave money for the child to buy meat for supper. Now the child has some responsibility, he has to see to it that he is early for home so that he can have enough time to make a fire and clean the house which was left uncleaned by his parents in the morning. The age at which the child can start making fire, cleaning the house etc. has no limitation because it all depends on the child's intelligence. (James)

Frequent mention is made of the attraction of playmates and street activity:

> Usually the favourite games are pushing and running behind old bicycle wheels or car imitations made of wire and empty shoe polish containers as wheels. Another favourite sport is the imitation of gangsters at "war". They divide themselves into two equal groups, the one group calling itself by the name of one "cunningly brave" gang and the other with the name of an equally notorious gang. They then throw stones at each other or use pieces of wood as knives for "stabbing", just as they see the gangsters do when fighting. Their parents scold and punish them when they see them playing this kind of a game, but when the parents are not in sight they play them. They love to call themselves with the names of notorious gangsters who say they do not "long for being trusted by anybody". (Shadrack)

The issues which are discussed in relation to the life of the young Soweto child are still relevant when teenagers and young persons are described. The conflict between becoming a responsible and reliable adult or finding one's life in the sub-world of the out-of-work and the delinquent is drawn constantly and clearly. The relationship between parents and children does not seem to be very different either—there is little evidence that the students see an improvement in mutual trust and understanding as the child passes into adulthood. The fathers seem to rule by decree, and discussion of problems is rare. Only one of the students had ever discussed any of his problems with his parents—and that was to do with religion—and all the others complained that they were unable to get guidance from their parents on the social, moral and intellectual problems that confront them.

Many parents establish a form of dictatorial government over their children . . . The child is a human being, she has some understanding . . . and it is tragic when parents cannot welcome such an exuberant young person who is filled with life and enthusiasm and talk with her at the time when she wishes to blurt out all the joy or heart-ache that is in her mind. The African parent cannot suffer him/herself the indignity of discussing teenage problems with the child. The child is left alone to wander in the darkness, and be taught only by experience. (John)

The dictatorial attitudes of parents and the absence of discussion and advice is seen by the informants as one of the reasons for the high rate of illegitimacy in the townships, and indeed illegitimacy or pregnancy is one of the main reasons given in a study of Durban youth for girls dropping out of school (Perry, 1974). Most of the essays about adolescence dealt with the problems of growing sexuality and indicated absence of guidance. They are characterized by coercion, meetings in dark alleys; in only one was the boy-girl relationship portrayed in terms of growing respect and understanding, rather than exploitation and force.

One day, before they were three months in the high school Rory asked Pearl to escort her home. She agreed. That day after school, they talked about their last two years in the Primary School, that is from the first year they knew each other. The following day, they escorted each other home after school. This went on for more than a week, a month, and now they are both in Matric. Fortunately, it does not end at escorting each other after school. They are now very great friends who are going steady. They usually date for the movies, spending a day at the Zoo together or sometimes go on a picnic on New Year's day with Pearl's elder twin sisters and Rory's elder brother.
Next year, they are going to miss each other if they pass their Matric. Rory is going for a Bachelor of Science degree; she wants to be a midwife. (Samson)

There are two distinct pictures drawn about adolescence in the townships. The first would be recognized by any other child growing up in a city, except perhaps for the lack of mention of coffee shops, or hamburger or ice-cream parlours and the absence of cars and motor bikes from the culture (see Coleman (1961) for a description of American adolescent life and Andersson (1969) for a comparison with Sweden).

The township teenagers are, like any others, normally very active. For instance most boys are affiliated to some of the local clubs—football, youth clubs,—where they participate in such games as soccer, softball, volley ball.

There are indoor games too . . . In organisations such as youth clubs girls also take part. The football associations have special competitions arranged according to age. There are competitions for a trophy set specially for the under sixteen group and those from sixteen to twenty.

Those who are not keen on soccer play softball, baseball and tennis. The latter is very popular and on every Saturday and Sunday scores of white-clad youths can be seen crowding most of the tennis courts in the townships. There are basketball teams which cater for those girls who could not get any other game . . . Not all teenagers take part in sport. Some like going to the shows and bioscopes.* Of course most of these are coming from well-off families who can afford every Saturday's transport fares and bioscope fees.

There is a group of teenagers who have record players. These during week-ends come together at one of their friend's home. Each brings his record collection and they have a sort of picnic. Those groups of teenagers are school-going most of them to high school.

Since these childrens' lives are not only games and pleasure-seeking it is only meet to take a glance into their homes. Some of them wake up very early in the morning to do the usual morning chores—such as making a cup of tea for the parents before they go to work, cleaning the home. Boys too are not exempted because not all homes have girls to do this kind of work. After cleaning and preparing breakfast for the little ones who may be going to a baby-school or a primary school, the house is locked. By this time both parents have long gone to work and off they go to school. After school the young ones are fetched from baby-school, fires are kindled to make ready for the mother who would come home carrying a piece of meat to cook for the evening meals. Then the teenager is relieved to attend to his or her homework or studies. In most cases the child cannot study because the houses are small, most of them being two roomed. Saturday morning is washing time. The teenager washes his own clothes and if a girl, washes all the clothes to be washed. In the evening the clothes are ironed and put ready for use on Sunday and Monday when going to school. (Aubrey)

The second picture drawn focusses not on the routine of a life lived happily within the community, the family and school but rather on street corners, idleness, lack of direction and rejection of control.

Coming back to the youth who have turned themselves against their own people, we find they are entirely beyond the control of their parents. They are self-supporting and independent. They hang around the street corners and shops, where they waylay smaller children sent to the shops to buy. School girls are the victims of these boys who are not given the opportunity to improve themselves. School boys also fall victim to these wayward sons of our continent. They pay protection fees which are used by the recipients

*Bioscopes are cinemas.

for purchasing dagga.* The boys who do not pay are slapped and kicked around every day until they make up their minds. The parents of these errant boys have absolutely no control over them for in failing to provide them with education and food they failed in the most important of their duties and have therefore no right to keep the other minor rights. (Jonas)

There is however, another group of teenagers, who are idle. These are the boys and girls—especially the boys—who have been turn out to be gangsters. They can be seen walking up and down the streets right through the day. They do not work and most of them have no reference book, and they are never at ease when they see a policeman passing by. These teenagers are most dangerous to the people living with them in the townships. They have indulged in the smoking of cigarettes and dagga . . .

They begin to haunt the shebeen† houses—they are usually heavy drinkers until they are again penniless. They never care to buy proper clothes. They are always in jeans and khaki trousers or overalls. In short, these are our "tsotsis" who have turned out to be jail-birds. (Aubrey)

The views expressed by informants to Hunter, and later to the Mayers are echoed in the reports of Soweto. Rearing children in the towns presents the parents with a number of problems, some to do with their own assumptions about appropriate behaviour between parents and children, and some beyond their own control, produced as a result of the peculiar socio-economic circumstances which prevail. The main source of complaint about parents is not that they neglect their children. Neglect is found and stressed but seen to be beyond the control of the parents. Their absence from the house for much of the day is regarded as a necessary response to unfortunate circumstances entirely beyond the control of the parents. The main complaints were to do with the relationship between parents and children during the time they spend together—the dictatorial attitudes of the father, the lack of acceptance of the young person as someone with opinions and feelings, the absence of discussion and consultation. Parents were blamed for not teaching by example, for not giving the child clear guidelines about behaviour and feelings. The cycle of deprivation, with babies born to young unmarried mothers, straining already meagre resources, being left in inadequate care and falling prey to the dangers of the township, was a picture constantly portrayed.

Care is inadequate, not because of wilfulness but because poverty does not allow for choice. The available help seems to be the young—

*Dagga is marijuana.
†A shebeen is a speak-easy, selling home-brewed liquor.

brothers and sisters—or the unspecific "old woman". The family group as an extended support system is seldom mentioned. The various regulations which determine urban residence is a further factor which restricts the range of relatives and retired grandparents on whom the working parents could rely for help.

For the adolescent there is conflict between the difficulties of delayed independence which is represented by school and the immediacy and power that various illegal activities present. The problems of the reference book which is the key to staying in town and finding work are frequently raised, and the distraction of unemployed youths no longer at school for those who are still students is a frequent theme. In fact it was a problem raised also by the schools themselves. Those who are no longer at school were often to be seen hanging around the school gates, taunting the students, occasionally threatening them. One of the informants was rushed to hospital after being stabbed by a gang of boys as he left the school grounds.

For the girls the problems are no less. They bear a heavy burden of domestic chores, and the sexual ignorance of which there was constant mention has its most serious consequences for them. There was frequent mention of the fact that women within the teenage groups were regarded as "property", "slaves" by the young men, and that they were in constant risk of attack.

The rejection of authority and the lack of respect for adults, both parents and teachers, was seen as a consequence of absent and insensitive parenting. It affects the child's adjustment to school, his willingness to take on the responsibilities appropriate for his work, to follow instruction and to respond to guidance. It also makes the peer group a very powerful controlling and socializing force.

# 6

# The Educational System

It is abundantly clear that unplanned education creates many problems,
disrupts the communal life of the Bantu and endangers the communal life
of the European.                                        (H. F. Verwoerd, 1954)

Western education had relatively early beginnings in South Africa. In
1658, six years after Jan van Riebeeck's three ships sailed into Table
Bay harbour, a formal school was opened. In the centuries which
followed the structure and organization of African education has reflected the economic and political relations between the racial groups
and through formal schooling the wider society has presented its values
to the young. In the first school young Black slaves, captured from the
Portuguese, were taught Dutch, elements of Christianity and how to be
good servants. A second school was opened for the children of Dutch
settlers, but since there were only 12 of these they were joined by four
slave children and one Hottentot (Khoikhoi). In the years that followed
additional schools were established, but slowly, so that there were
eight in 1779 catering for 111 White and 25 slave children. All these
schools were controlled by a commission—the *Schorlach*—which was
under the control of the Governor, while in the outlying districts
education was in the hands of itinerant teachers employed by farmers
to teach their children (Horrell, 1970).

On the Eastern frontier, trade provided the impetus for the association of Xhosa and Whites but it was the missionaries who were the
dominant force in education. In their driving desire to teach the
Gospel, the missionaries learned the Xhosa language, translated and
printed the Bible and taught their Black converts to read. At the beginning of the nineteenth century a Hollander from the London
Missionary Society spent over one year with the Xhosa chief and
following that an increasing number of missions were built, with their
attendant educational facilities. In 1841–1842 the first Teacher's
Training Seminary was opened at Lovedale.

The arrival of Sir George Grey as Governor of the Cape Colony in the 1850s was important for African education. He encouraged the civilizing of the tribes rather than their military conquest and gave grants of land and money for the erection of mission schools. He thereby established the principle and precedent for the central authority to pay for and vote monies for the establishment of new schools and the payment of teachers' salaries. Grey initiated the system of selective education for the sons of chiefs, and by 1858 they were being trained at a racially mixed school at Zonnelbloom (Welsh, 1969).

From the time the British took control of the Cape they attempted to anglicize the White settlers. The first of these attempts was the introduction of English as the public language. Included in this was an attempt to counteract the influence of Dutch fee-paying schools in rural areas by promoting free public schools, most of which taught in English. The Education Act of 1865 enforced English as the medium of instruction in first and second class schools and required this in the largely rural third class schools within a year. The Dutch resisted this introduction in the rural third class schools, and in 1875 a society was formed to fight for the rights of "Afrikaans" speakers, and in 1879 the Afrikaner Bond was formed to ensure the role of the Afrikaners and their language within the Cape. When the Act of Union was agreed, following the Anglo-Boer war, in 1910, the two Boer republics insisted that Afrikaans be placed on an equal footing with English in the Constitution, and that education for White children should be in the home language up to Standard IV.* The issue of language, though resolved constitutionally, remained prominent in the relations between the communities in South Africa, and symbolized the Afrikaners search for identity and power. It became critical too in the education in the African areas, and was a major factor in the Soweto uprising in 1976.

The question of how the younger generation should be educated, whether in segregated or in multiracial schools, was a prominent theme in the history of education. The earliest reported attempt to segregate schooling was in 1676 when the Church Council expressed the desire for separate schools. After the British took over the Cape the pro-segregationist lobby influence increased and the government had to

*The grading system within South African schools works as follows: there are two early classes, sub-standards A and B (also known as Sub-A and Sub-B, and less frequently as Grade 1 and 2). These are followed by five years of elementary schooling labelled as Standards 1 to 5. In African schools there was a sixth year in the Elementary or Primary system. High School classes are known either as Forms (1 through 5) or the Standard system is continued counting from 6 to 10.

resist pressure to exclude slave children from government schools. The arguments in favour of maintaining and extending an integrated system apart from being philanthropic were based on the need for the races, which would have to work together, to learn to understand each other. The forces for segregation, arguing often for superior education for Whites, were strengthened when gradual industrialization drew Blacks and Whites into competition for jobs where the extent of education could be a factor in obtaining employment. Some Whites even questioned whether Blacks should get any education lest it limit the availability of cheap labour (Horrell, 1970). Although mission schools continued to accept students of all colours, the number of White children at these schools shrank with the growth of free public schools, and in these the segregationists won the day. In 1911 the Appellate Division of the Supreme Court of the Union of South Africa ruled that part of the policy of the Cape School Board Act of 1905 was to establish separate schools for all racial groups.

In the other British colony of Natal the development of African education was broadly similar to the Cape, but aid to the mission schools was both slower in coming and more limited, being based on a percentage of all the monies raised by the taxation of Africans. In the early years the provision of education for Africans was seen very much in terms of the labour they would provide. In a speech in the Legislative Council of Natal in 1873, the Chairman of a select committee on labour said:

> I will not detain this house by making a long clap-trap speech about the mission of the white man in civilising our native population. In this resolution I propose to use civilisation, and morality and Christianity as a means to get labour. If these causes are at the same time advanced, so much the better for them . . . (Welsh, 1971)

Objections to African education were voiced by pagans amongst the Africans who were concerned that education would destroy traditional life, and by Whites who argued that educated Africans would be less obedient, reliable and honest, and would pose a threat to other Whites on the job market. Grants were restricted to those schools which produced goods that were not in competition with White controlled trade and no grant was given to those schools associated with the printing of African newspapers, which were considered potentially seditious. The most important difference between the provision of education in the

Cape and Natal was the introduction of a separate syllabus in Natal African elementary schools in 1886 which stressed manual labour, to the extent that one-fifth of the total time was to be spent on this, in line with the view that labour was to be produced for the Whites.

African education in the two Boer Republics was slower to develop than in the British colonies. Part of the reason was that the Boers remained essentially farmers, employing Africans as farm workers. The societies themselves were frontier states, with no schools and no banks; in the case of the South African Republic (later the Transvaal) no books were kept by government until 1867. What education there was for Africans was provided by the missions offering a fairly limited schooling in the basics of reading and writing. In 1904 the mission schools began to receive government funds, and a special curriculum was set up for Africans.

After Union in 1910 the control of African education was placed under the four provincial authorities who took over the inspection of the mission schools and established some of their own. Each province adopted its own system of taxation, which resulted in the uneven development of African education. In 1922 the Central Government stopped any increase in direct provincial taxation on Africans for education, and required the provincial authorities to maintain expenditure levels at the 1921/1922 level, given in the form of a grant from the central purse. Additional amounts were made available from general taxes paid by Africans and distributed to the provincial governments by the Minister of Native Affairs. At a later date a per capita grant was introduced to bring the financing of education of all races in line. The sum set for Africans was £3 12 9 in comparison with £5+ for Coloureds and over £20 for Whites. In 1945 it was decided that all funds for African education were to be drawn directly from the Central Government and that expansion was no longer to be dependent on taxes deriving from Africans. Monies allocated rose considerably until 1954, when the basis of financing was again changed.

When the National Party came to power in 1948, a Commission was established to report on African Education and it is in this Commission's report submitted in 1952, that the present system of African Education had its roots.

One of the original terms of reference given to the Commission clearly outlined its general political approach—one of separate development (apartheid):

The formulation of the principles and aims of education for Natives as an independent race, in which their past and present, their inherent racial qualities, their distinctive characteristics and aptitude, and their needs under ever changing social conditions are taken into consideration.

The general conclusion of the Commission was to centralize African education and to link it more closely to overall government policy.

The policies of this Commission were enshrined in law as the Bantu Education Act of 1954. This clearly separated the education of Africans from that of the other three ethnic groups, not only administratively, but also in terms of content. The intention underlying this Act was clearly illustrated in a statement by the then Minister for Native Affairs:

It is the policy of my department that (Bantu) education should have its roots entirely in the Native areas and in the Native environment and Native community. There Bantu education must be able to give itself complete expression and there it will have to perform its real service. The Bantu must be guided to serve his own community in all respects. There is no place for him in the European community above the level of certain forms of labour. Within his own community, however, all doors are open. For that reason it is of no avail for him to receive a training which has as its aim absorption in the European community while he cannot and will not be absorbed there. Up till now he has been subjected to a school system which drew him away from his own community and practically misled him by showing him the green pastures of the European but still did not allow him to graze there. This attitude is not only uneconomic because money is spent on education which has no specific aim, but it is even dishonest to continue with it. The effect on the Bantu community we find in the much-discussed frustration of educated Natives who can find no employment which is acceptable to them. It is abundantly clear that unplanned education creates many problems, disrupts the communal life of the Bantu and endangers the communal life of the European. (H. F. Verwoerd, Senate, 1954)

The logic of the Act demanded the separation of the races even at the university level. This was formally achieved by the University Extension Act of 1959. The Act gave to the Central Government ultimate control over appointments, entry, courses offered and followed and the content of the curricula at African universities.

The financial arrangements for African education arising out of the Commission's report were laid out in the Exchequer and Audit Amendment Act of 1955. The effect was to return to the system of 1922 whereby a fixed sum was passed to a special account for Bantu Education (now R13 million) added to which was a proportion of taxes paid by Africans (4/5 increasing to 100% in 1963). Included in this were recoverable advances made by the Central Government and monies derived from other sources.

In an attempt to keep the costs of African education relatively low, various measures were coupled to the new financial arrangements. Included in these were:

(a) The provision that part of the cost of erecting new primary schools in urban areas would be recovered by levying a special tax on Africans living in government homes in the area.

(b) All new post-primary schools erected were to be half funded by the African School Boards.*

(c) The daily work of cleaning schools was to be the responsibility of pupils under the supervision of teachers.

(d) To bolster the numbers at school, the "hot seat" or "platoon system" was introduced for pre-primary standards, where the number of hours teaching per day was reduced to three, and two groups of pupils were taught successively in the same classrooms.

A few years later, to cope with the monies required by African education, Central Government increased taxation from a basic level of R2 to R3·50 a year, increasing by 50 cents for every R120 up to R960.

The Bantu Education Act made explicit the relation between ideologically based policy and practice. The relative position of the racial groups in education can also be seen in comparing the Governments per capita expenditure on school students by race. The figures are given in Fig. 1. In Soweto many facilities were built and maintained by the Johannesburg Municipality which decided in 1968 to add 19 cents to the rents of all new houses to provide funds for the building of new Lower Primary schools. The African school boards and committees as well as the Soweto Urban Bantu Council suggested collecting additional funds for post-primary schools. Finally, in 1972, the Department of Bantu Education (a Central Government department) decided to levy the head of each family in Soweto 38 cents per month, 20 cents of which would be used for this. Additional monies are collected for

---

*Established by the Bantu Education Act of 1953. School Boards were placed in authority over a number of schools in a prescribed area. Each school had its own school committee established by the same Act.

African education from various voluntary bodies, commercial organizations and religious organizations. Secondary school students are required to pay towards their education, and Lower and Higher Primary schools may ask for donations.

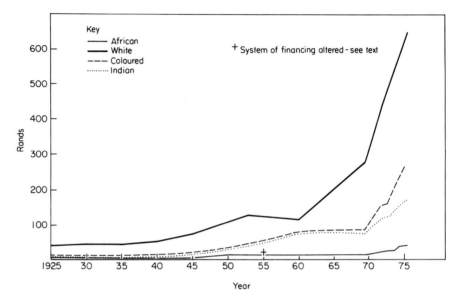

Fig. 1. Per capita expenditure according to group.

In addition to fees, taxes and voluntary contributions, parents are required to pay for the books and writing materials needed for school. These costs vary according to geographic area and for Soweto are estimated to range from R12·50 for the primary classes to R34 for the secondary schools. There was an agreement that by 1980 free text books would be available for African school children as for Whites, but although this undertaking was given in 1974, by February 1976 no free books had yet been issued (Hansard, 1976). School uniforms constitute another expense. Although not compulsory there is considerable social pressure to acquire the uniform, and the cost for this was assumed to be around R12 in the lower classes and R15 in the upper forms in 1971. At the same time the monthly wage for a Soweto blue collar worker was about R50 per month, of which at least 50% was estimated to be spent on food (S.A.I.R.R., 1972).

The organization of education for Africans is slightly different from that for the other three racial groups. Besides curriculum differences there are four types of school rather than a simple elementary-secondary school split. The elementary years are divided into Lower Primary (years one to four) and Higher Primary (standards 3 to 6).* The five year high school programme is divided into two courses. Junior Secondary consists of Forms one to three, and Senior Secondary Forms four and five. Junior High Schools offer only the first three years, Senior offer the full five year programme.

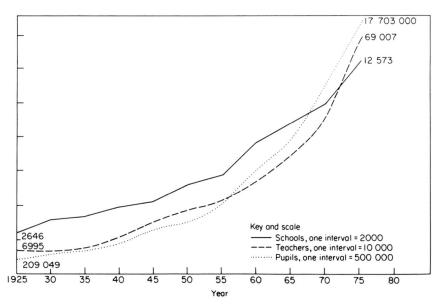

Fig. 2. Number of schools, pupils and teachers in African education. (Government and homeland controlled schools only.) From the Annual Report of Department of Bantu Education, 1975.

There is a shortage of school accommodation, especially in areas like Soweto, and at the start of the school year large numbers of children are turned away from schools, for lack of space. This, despite the considerable increase in the provision of schools and of teachers that has taken place since 1925 (see Fig. 2). The increase in Soweto over

*Standard 6, the extra year in primary school for Africans, was partially abolished in 1975 and 1976. The consequences of this are discussed later.

the period 1972 to 1976 is illustrated in Fig. 3. One of the causes of the upturn in the rate of increase of students at school from 1955 was the introduction of the platoon system. This doubled the number of pupils in the first classes by introducing two sessions daily, in the same class-room, with the same teacher. When introduced, the platoon system was seen as a temporary measure due to the shortage of teachers, but twenty years after its introduction almost a million pupils were being schooled this way.

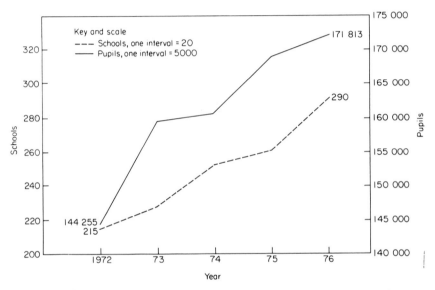

Fig. 3. Number of schools and pupils in Soweto, 1972–1976. From Hansard* (South Africa), 20 April 1976 and 31 January 1977, Minister of Bantu Education.

While the percentage of school-going Whites, Coloureds and Indians, relative to the total population of each group has remained static for a number of years, the percentage of Africans has grown steadily. In the twenty year period 1935–1955 the percentage of Africans in school relative to the total population almost doubled from 5·18% to 9·76%. In the following twenty years it reached 21·1%. Part of the rapid expansion is accountable for by the platoon system; there has also been a rapid growth in the African population, which has swelled the relative number of school-age persons in relation to the rest of the African population.

*All references to the Hansard are to the South African Hansard.

TABLE 3

Percentage of each group below 18 years and per cent, and number attending school*

|  | % Under 18 | % At school | % Not at school | Number at school, 1975 |
|---|---|---|---|---|
| White | 35·3 | 21·0 | 14·3 | 891 776 |
| African | 48·3 | 21·1 | 27·2 | 3 731 445 |
| Indian | 45·3 | 25·0 | 20·3 | 182 187 |
| Coloured | 50·2 | 25·0 | 25·2 | 594 339 |

*Hansard, 1 February 1977. Minister of Statistics figures are for 1976.

Hansard, 30 April 1976. Minister of Statistics Annual Report, Department of Bantu Education, 1975, p. 4.

Hansard, 11 Col. 795/6 March 1975. Minister of Indian Affairs. As corrected in *Survey of Race Relations in South Africa*. 1975, p. 237.

Hansard, 14 Col. 931/2 1975. Minister of Coloured Affairs.

One feature of African education is the small number of pupils in the higher standards. The proportion of Black students in high school has always been lower than that of the other groups. There are a number of reasons for this. The availability of places is less, the age profile of African students is higher—they start school later, and are therefore more likely to leave earlier to take up adult responsibilities. In addition

TABLE 4

Percentage of pupils in secondary school*

|  | 1945 | 1969 | 1975 |
|---|---|---|---|
| African | 2% | 4·2% | 8·62% |
| Whites | 26·9% | 33% | 37% |
| Indians | 5·5% | 23% | 28% |
| Coloureds | 7·5% | 10·8% | 13·3% |

*Hansard, Col. 783, 30 April 1976. Minister of State Department of Statistics.

Report 21-02-04 "Education Whites". 1969, p. 53.

"Education Beyond Apartheid". *Sprocas* Johannesburg. 1971, p. 23.

*Bantu Education Journal*. June 1976, pp. 20–21.

*Bantu Education Journal*. August 1976, p. 15.

"Stepping into the Future". Distributed by Department of Information of Republic of South Africa, pp. 26, 30.

Hansard, Col. 264, 18 February 1976, Minister of Indian Affairs.

Hansard, Col. 931/2, 1975, Minister of Coloured Affairs.

the extra year at primary school would also depress the number at high school, since in the other racial groups the eighth year of schooling (Standard 6) takes place at high school. Tables 4 and 5 compare the percentage of pupils of each racial group at secondary school and, in

TABLE 5

Percentage of South African scholars in each class according to group*

| Primary | Africans 1975 | | Whites 1975 | Indians 1975 | Coloureds 1976 |
|---|---|---|---|---|---|
| Sub standard 1 | 21·86 | | 10·03 | 12·05 | 17·00 |
| Sub standard 2 | 16·18 | | 9·27 | 12·65 | 15·07 |
| Standard 1 | 14·61 | | 9·10 | 5·99 | 13·91 |
| Standard 2 | 11·34 | | 8·71 | 11·13 | 11·99 |
| Standard 3 | 9·90 | | 8·82 | 11·21 | 10·58 |
| Standard 4 | 7·58 | | 8·77 | 10·28 | 9·29 |
| Standard 5 | 5·98 | | 8·40 | 8·74 | 7·52 |
| Standard 6 | 3·94 | | No Standard 6 in primary school | | |
| Secondary | | | | | |
| Form 1 | 4·04 | Standard 6 | 8·84 | 7·21 | 5·69 |
| Form 2 | 2·47 | Standard 7 | 8·40 | 6·82 | 4·25 |
| Form 3 | 1·37 | Standard 8 | 8·47 | 7·78 | 2·69 |
| Form 4 | 0·49 | Standard 9 | 6·29 | 3·55 | 1·40 |
| Form 5 | 0·24 | Standard 10 | 4·91 | 2·60 | 0·60 |

*Bantu Education Journal. June 1976, pp. 20–21.
Bantu Education Journal. August 1976, p. 15.
Hansard, Col. 783, 30 April 1976. Minister of Statistics.
Hansard, Col. 264, 18 February 1976. Minister of Indian Affairs.
A Survey of Race Relations in South Africa. 1976, p. 341.

more detail, in each year at school. The rate at which African pupils drop out of the school system is excessive. Despite some progress in recent years the final class in 1975 constituted a mere 2% of those who had entered school in 1963 and therefore could have graduated in 1975. This is illustrated in Table 6.

A particularly large number of African pupils leave school after Standard 6, the final year of the primary school. At this stage (until the form was abolished in 1976) there was a set examination which was moderated by the Department of Bantu Education. Pupils who pass with a third class pass are not entitled to go on to high school, and in 1971, of the total who sat the examination 84% passed, but only 47%

## TABLE 6

Rate of drop out in African schools (figures are given as a percentage of enrolment in first class Sub A)

| Year of entry | Entry Sub A | 1 year later Sub B | 4 years after entry Standard 3 | 7 years after entry Standard 6 | 8 years after entry Form 1 | Secondary school 10 years after entry Form 3 | 12 years after entry Form 5 |
|---|---|---|---|---|---|---|---|
| 1963 | 100·0 | 75·5 | 44·7 | 30·5 | 12·1 | 8·4 | 2·0 |
| 1964 | 100·0 | 79·3 | 47·8 | 33·2 | 14·2 | 9·5 | |
| 1965 | 100·0 | 74·3 | 45·5 | 31·3 | 13·7 | 9·9 | |
| 1966 | 100·0 | 74·0 | 46·6 | 32·4 | 14·7 | | |
| 1967 | 100·0 | 75·2 | 48·9 | 34·6 | 25·9* | | |
| 1968 | 100·0 | 75·8 | 49·6 | 24·0† | | | |
| 1969 | 100·0 | 77·7 | 51·3 | | | | |
| 1970 | 100·0 | 79·2 | 53·2 | | | | |
| 1971 | 100·0 | 79·4 | 54·1 | | | | |
| 1972 | 100·0 | 80·1 | | | | | |
| 1973 | 100·0 | 79·2 | | | | | |
| 1974 | 100·0 | 84·6 | | | | | |

*All students passing Standard 6 were eligible for Form 1 as well as many passing Standard 5.
†Standard 6 done away with in part, in 1975.

achieved a mark above third class. In 1974 the third class pass was abolished, and then the entire extra class was removed from the system in 1976.

Although the pupil-teacher ratio for African students is poor in comparison to the other ethnic groups, their examination performance, despite some variability year to year is not different from that of the Coloured group, although from 1972 the Indian school students have improved their performance relative to the other two groups. No comparable figures are available for Whites. The pupil-teacher ratio for Africans in 1970 was 60:1, improved to 54:1 in 1975; for Whites in 1975 it was 20:1, for Indians and Coloured at the Primary level it was 30:1 and 27:1 and for these two groups at secondary school it was 21:1 and 31:1. The actual figures do not necessarily give an accurate picture of what happens within particular classrooms, especially in urban schools where the population growth is often fastest. Cases were reported in 1976 of some primary schools in the Johannesburg African areas having 113 students in a class (*Rand Daily Mail*, 1976).

The effect of the variations in educational provisions for the four racial groups has been to lead to differences in the amount of formal schooling between them. One estimate of the percentage of Africans over the age of 15 with no schooling at all was 62·5% in 1960, declining to 51·8% in 1970 (*The Star*, 1974). The estimated percentage of each group over the age of 18 which had successfully completed four years of schooling by May 1970 indicates group differences as well: 98·64% of Whites, 77·42% of Indians, 68·3% of Coloureds and 40·13% of Africans (Hansard, 1974). The numbers actually completing all twelve years of schooling can therefore be expected to show similar dramatic differences across the racial groups. For instance, in 1975 5400 Africans were successful in their final matriculation, an impressive increase from 332 in 1953, but there were 43 776 Whites in their final year at school in 1975, and the Whites comprise 17% of the total population, as opposed to the 71% of the population that is African.

It is against these historical facts and figures that the role of the school in the process of socialization must be considered. To the young person living in South Africa socialization takes place against a background of differential provision of facilities according to race. The absolute level of provision may be better than in some other parts of Africa, and the percentage, even of Africans, completing their schooling may be larger. But Africa as a whole is not the standard against which the individual assesses his world. The essays indicated quite clearly that young Blacks compare what they have to that which young Whites are given, that the reference points are within the country, not outside it. The media and cultural tradition that education fosters, even when complemented by emphasis on home-language and ethnic distinctiveness, is based on a Western tradition, and the political and institutional structures of the society owe their form, if not their content, to the strong technological and Western traditions of the society.

# 7

# The School as Socializer

It is within the family that the earliest learning occurs. It is the first agent of socialization and its importance has rightly been stressed in psychological research. Much of the research in this field has examined the family within developed societies: its role in a situation of acculturation and change is more difficult to assess. To varying degrees the family represents the traditional past while providing the base for the individual's move into the changing world outside. In this movement the family, through the achievements, values and behaviour of its members may be a help or a hindrance.

A typical, but particularly thorough, study by Rosen (1961) of 8–14-year-old boys in the North-East United States related social class background, family size and ordinal position to achievement motivation. He found that the boys from middle class families produced the highest n-ach scores, with higher scores associated with smaller middle class families. In the upper classes the medium sized families had boys with higher scores. Family size is apparently an important factor since, in both middle class and working class families, the need achievement scores of youngest boys declines as family size increases.

Structural variables however merely represent interaction patterns within the family which are themselves the actual precursors of achievement motivation. While not denying these structural features some role, it is as well to guard against too simplistic assumptions. In a follow-up study by Sewell and Shaw (1968) of 9000 senior high school children it was found that the education of the father had a strong effect on boys' college behaviour whereas for girls both parents were equally important. Rehlberg and Westby (1967) showed that parents' occupation and education and parental encouragement are independent predictors of adolescent educational expectations, while Bennet and Gist (1964) looking at the occupational and educational aspirations of 800 urban high school students and their actual career plans found that aspirations and educational plans showed a significant variation. Their study also showed that the influence of the mother was stronger in lower class families than that of the father.

A further family variable that has been studied is ordinal position. There have been many attempts, not all successful, to link birth order and achievement. The study of Rosen mentioned earlier showed an interaction between social class, family size, and birth order; Elliott and Elliott (1970) reviewed studies where birth order and the age gap between siblings jointly determine aspiration level.

The stress on parents and on the static description of ordinal position blurs the importance to the growing individual of his siblings particularly insofar as they provide him with alternate models of behaviour and with a source of psychological and social support. Research has given the small family and primogeniture important roles in the achievement of the child. However, it could be suggested that the greater the number of people the individual has to call on for both social and financial support, the more likely he is to believe in his possible success. The youngest child of a large family is just such an example. Not only has he parents to support him, but older working brothers and sisters to call on for both money and advice. Rather than older siblings serving as positive examples of achievement for the younger to emulate, their very non-attainment in both school and jobs may lead them to encourage the younger children, to focus on them as sources of vicarious achievement. To anticipate that only middle class families would provide support for children is to ignore the social context within which such support is given. This does not deny that progress may be easier with the example of successful adjustment by parents and siblings to the social system. It simply suggests that there may be compensations for the child within the unskilled family.

In an analysis of the literature on ordinal position Zajonc (1975) has shown that the results of the research are best explained by a model more complex than that implied by a uni-causal system. His model relates the order of birth to the number of adults in the household and the differences in age of the children. His argument is based on the assumption that intelligence measures reflect the cognitive stimulation a child receives, which will be greater the larger the number of adults talking to and relating to the child. This can be assessed as the number of adults divided by the number of children in the household. Children are not simply the offspring of the adults—adolescent offspring can be counted as adult equivalents. Thus, the first-born child will have more adults available than the second born and so on. However, if the age differences between the children are large then the later born children will have the possibility of even greater numbers of adults as stimulators than the first born. Once again one is reminded that structural variables are only the framework within which the dynamics of socialization occur.

The emphasis on the family as an agent of socialization led to a tendency to stress its role in acculturation studies to the neglect of school and other formal socializing agents. Marris (1967) discussing the research on family and achievement in Nigeria, Kenya and Britain, states that conceptions of family relationships adapt readily enough to economic circumstances and change. Whether the adaptation will encourage individual achievement depends as much on how people perceive the opportunity structure of the society as on the family traditions of the society themselves.

What Marris's study illuminates is that family variables cannot be studied away from the structure and opportunities of the society. The fact that parents have not achieved either occupational or academic success may be due entirely to the absence of acceptable opportunities in their youth. Where the opportunities for advance within a society are of long standing, it seems proper to assess the family in terms of their success in utilizing these (as occurs in measures of social class). This may be inappropriate in rapidly changing and developing societies. Certainly the family in its patterns of support and help and in the quality of its relationships may be important: the family variables however are not a sufficient, nor perhaps a necessary condition for determining the variations in the individual's perceived present and future roles in a fluctuating and developing system.

A conceptualization which looks at the fit between traditional social and family variables and the dominant system, is probably more appropriate.

The work of Douglas (1966) has shown that family structure and social class relate to the child's performance at school, mediated perhaps by the teacher's expectations and evaluations of the child. In addition, research would suggest that middle class families, defined either by parents' occupation or education, make available to the child behaviours appropriate to the school situation, whereas the child of uneducated, unskilled parents, living in poverty and often with minimal parental care, learn behaviours and skills appropriate to their own cultural group, but not integration into the dominant system.

The educational system in all societies is the means by which the knowledge and values of the wider society are presented to the individual: in many industrialized and developed societies it has yet a further function, namely that of providing a means for social advance. Where formal education is scarce it serves as a pathway to potential membership of a variety of élites, both of power and of knowledge. The family system therefore becomes of importance to the extent that it permits involvement in and the utilization of the formal socialization system.

This formulation implies some sort of congruence between the goals of the family as primary socializer and the goals of the formal socializing agents. It suggests too that there is little conflict between the goals ascribed to the formal agents by the wider society and their actual operation. In Britain, for example, the educational system has traditionally offered an acceptable pathway to achievement and to influence, although the power of the system to do this has often been limited by the match between the values and norms of the home and of the school. Jackson and Marsden (1962) for example in their study of working class children at grammar schools, suggest that these pupils very often come from a "depressed middle class". Their parents were themselves often not able to take the opportunities for educational advance of which they were capable or which were offered, but yet espoused the attitudes and values, of education and of middle class aspirations that eased the transition of their children. Where the home and the school were in conflict the children often did not make full use of the opportunities that were available within the educational system. This is supported by Douglas's (1968) longitudinal study of 5000 girls and boys:

> By definition all the parents of (these) lower manual working class boys and girls had left school themselves before reaching the age of 15, but the pupils whose parents had attempted to obtain some further education after entering employment are nearly twice as likely to stay on as the rest. This applies equally to the fathers' and the mothers' education . . .
>
> A high level of parental interest, high employment ambitions for the child and a good record of visits to the school on the part of the father are all associated with longer school life.

The Independent and Public School systems have also provided pathways for the socially mobile who aspire to admission to particular social and political elites. Here perhaps the match between family, school and the wider society are most clear. Either through especial talent which wins scholarships or through the willingness of parents to pay for their children's private education, offspring of families whose birth does not immediately provide rights to positions of power and influence attempt to achieve them through the educational system. The close association between the Public Schools and success within the wider social system has been shown amongst others by Anthony Sampson ("Anatomy of Britain") and by Jonathan Gathorne-Hardy, who documents vividly the role of these schools since A.D. 625. It is perhaps an extreme example of the power of the educational system, but one which it is helpful to bear in mind to illustrate a variety of points.

The idea of fit is an important one to examine, because it is more complex than first it seems. That the family and the school can either reinforce each other or offer the child different codes and mores is fairly clear, as is the proposition that the integration of the child into the school and his acceptance of its values is easier if there is a good fit between home and school (but it must not be thought that the school cannot impress itself on a divergent child). The situation becomes more complicated when one looks to the match between the school and the wider social system within which it operates.

Again, bearing in mind the example of the English Public School, it is clear from the analysis offered by Gathorne-Hardy that the Public Schools have survived because they have constantly adapted to changing demands from the outside world. From the close link with Church, where they served to teach choristers to sing, taught Latin for use in services, and provided recruits for the Church itself, the schools moved to providing an appropriate education for the nascent clerical class to transact the nation's business in the Middle Ages. As times changed so did the schools, both in terms of the purposes they were supposed to fulfil, the boys they intended to educate and the nature of the matter that was considered to be the crucial elements in the process. By this constant adjustment and readjustment the Public Schools survived and maintained a close interaction with the wider society. Time and history fed into it, and the products of the schools influenced the world outside in their turn.

More recent history provides further instances of the close ties between the educational system and the context within which it exists.

Schools are not static. Issues within society reflect on to the schools—
questions about the type of skills that are to be fostered, the nature of
the social environment within which the process is to occur, the use of
the school systems to manipulate and alter the social order itself. At
different times it is possible to conceive of different types of homes
being more or less congruent with the school.

The history of education in Britain has been such that it has frequently encouraged and given support to the view that the individual
through his own effort (and perhaps the patronage of power) either by
developing his intellect, or through hard work, or creative ability in the
arts or technology could improve his status and alter his power or
influence in the wider world. The idea that the individual could move
as an individual was supported by many examples of mobility and
success. The schools and the society reinforced each other. In time,
education held out hope of advance for all, even though for many it
never really could succeed. One could talk of the myth of advance
through individual effort, which in its most extreme form is embodied
in the American Dream of log cabin to White House. No matter who
one is, how humble one's forebears, how wretched one's past, power is
possible through one's own making. Not through birth, not through
class or caste but through each person's will.

In their analysis of the motivational dynamics of Negro youth
Gurin *et al.* (1969) offer important insights into the relation between the
individual's own characteristics, the educational system and achievements in the world outside education. Using the concept of Internal-
External control of reinforcement, and focusing specifically on the
concepts of powerlessness and of blame, Gurin *et al.* examine three
groups of Negroes—one attending predominantly Negro colleges in
the southern USA, another a group of high school drop-outs attending
a retraining programme in a northern city and the third part of a
national sample of both White and Negro youth attending retraining
programmes. Their results are relevant in the context of the notion of
"fit" (see pp. 94–95 for their results).

Although the literature to date indicates that people who believe in external control are less effectively motivated and perform less well in achievement situations, these same effects may not follow for low income persons,
particularly Negroes, who believe that economic or discriminatory factors
are more important than individual skill and personal qualities in explaining why they succeed or fail. Instead of depressing motivation, focusing on

external sources may be motivationally healthy if it results from assessing one's chances for success against systematic and real external obstacles rather than the exigencies of an overwhelming, unpredictable fate. (p. 33)

Essential to their findings is the point in the system where the individual locates the blame for his condition. It could be seen as dependent on the individual Negro's personal inadequacies, or it could be located within the system. Their results were interesting.

> Students who were more sensitive to discrimination, who tended to blame the social system rather than individual qualities of Negroes for the problems that negroes face more often aspired to jobs that were non-traditional for Negroes (for instance, engineering or business).

When the blame system was related to readiness to engage in collective action, similarly interesting results appeared. Students were asked whether individual mobility and effort or group action represented the best way to overcome discrimination. Individuals who blamed the system were more in favour of group rather than individual action to deal with discrimination. They had engaged in more civil rights activities—picketing, boycotting and demonstrations, than those who saw the individual as responsible for his disadvantages. Those who accepted the self-blame point of view endorsed the traditional view that the best approach to dealing with problems is that of self-betterment, through effort and hard work. They supported the traditional Protestant ethic of the wider society.

In South Africa the young African is influenced to a varying degree by his tribal and traditional past as manifested in its modified form, the highly industrialized Western technology of the dominant Whites and the African urban proletarian communities fostered by the enforced segregation of the races. It is likely that the influence of the school and of other agents of socialization will vary according to the position of the individual in the interaction of these. The fit between family and school, stressed in the studies of Douglas (1967) and Himmelweit *et al.* (1969) needs to take account of other factors too, in a context of social change. One of these may well be acculturation. It is not easy to get indices of acculturation. One that is frequently cited is the degree of urbanization of the individual. Mayer (1961) has shown that psychological commitment to town life rather than the country is important in assessing the adjustment of the Xhosa in town. A study by du Preez (1968) of rural Xhosa showed that travel outside rural areas relates to the degree of field independence on the rod and frame test; others (Allport and Pettigrew, 1957; Hudson, 1962) have shown that perceptual responses differ according to degree of urbanization. Studies on American high school pupils have shown urban Negroes to have higher occupational aspirations than rural Negroes (Kuvlevsky and Ohlendorf, 1968), and urban Whites have higher aspirations than those from rural areas (Bureminal, 1961).

The rural-urban dimension in South Africa is an interesting one, and not only because of the differences in industrialization and complexity of social organization which it represents. The strength of tradition is greater in rural areas, allegiances to chiefs and to the tribe more powerful, change slower, the extended family more vital and parents more sure of the values and behaviours they wish to develop in their children. Within the urban context some traditional ceremonies may remain, but tribal links and strength of the kinship system are less, and intergenerational differences greater. There is also value confusion so that parents do not always know what values to teach. On the other hand, city-born children, familiar with the technological and organizational aspects of Western industrial society, are more likely than their parents to have developed the behaviours that town-living demands.

Growing up in either town or country therefore has both advantages and disadvantages. Theoretically, it is not clear how these should interact with the school system. It is possible that the stability and sense of identity fostered in a smaller, traditional and kinship-based rural society would provide the individual with inner resources to help in his adjustment to the wider society. This may outweigh the disadvantages of unfamiliarity and the extent of the adaptation demanded of the individual. Equally, the benefits of cultural familiarity to the urban child may well be outweighed by the disadvantages of social disruption, uncertainty and alienation which have often been the result of rapid social change. A study by the Ainsworths (1962) supports the advantage of cultural familiarity, while a study by Lystad (1970) gives strength to the benefits of rural stability.

Lystad performed a content analysis on stories produced by Black adolescents of both sexes in South Africa and Swaziland. Whereas the South Africans grow up in a modern industrial system, the early experience of the Swazis is of a more rural, less modern and less complex material and social system. Despite possible problems of acculturation for the latter group the nature of the actors and their relationships in the stories they wrote, suggest that it is the industrialized South Africans for whom the world is not rational, and for whom it produces few psychological satisfactions and many threats to the individual's welfare. This is supported further by a study by Gregor and McPherson (1966) which lends force to the view that rural living gives greater ego strength. They used the Clarke Doll Test on rural and urban Venda children and White children and found differences in ethnocentric and xenocentric choices for White and Black children with White children selecting dolls like themselves and Blacks not doing so. But they also found that the degree of identity confusion of the Venda children positively correlated with the degree of intensity of inter-racial conflict, with the rural Venda showing less confusion than the urban.

Within the towns and cities tribal traditions change and weaken; they do not always die. Tribal identity is maintained by government policy. Each African in town, even if second or third generation urban born, is regarded as being only a temporary urban dweller and as belonging to a tribal homeland. Tribal identity may further be bolstered by family ties, by language, by variations in cultural traditions. The extent of affiliation to the tribe provides another measure of the individual's acculturation, and a way of examining the fit between two systems: the educational and the traditional.

Where the traditional system and its accepted pathways to success are under stress and blurred by change, power is gained by a system offering the individual clear vision and possible prestige. It is an interesting reflection of this that the number of African pupils in schools increases while those participating in the tribal educational process of initiation, diminishes (Pauw, 1963); also that the careers of tribal chief and chief's wife have low appeal (Sherwood, 1957). In a situation of social change where status and economic benefits accrue from rapid acculturation the traditions which the family often represents lose out to the formal educational system. This is particularly so during the period of high school education, when the individual has not yet committed himself to a future role, but is mature enough to contemplate his future identity. It is not a matter of denying value to the family: it is a question of assessing the strength of family and school in interaction as influencing the individual. The school may well be a stronger influence than the family solely because it is a stronger system. Himmelweit and Swift (1969) define the strength of the school system in terms of its "coercive power over its pupils deriving from the nature of the objectives assigned to the school and their salience for the individual within the system". In South Africa race is the strongest system for the prescription of status: within the African community however, education rather than the family is the more powerful. The rewards the school offers appear to outweigh those offered by the family. This would suggest that variations in family background would be less effective than type of school in determining the values and aspirations of the child, and would diminish further in importance, the longer the child stays at school. The strength of the school system will be indicated by the extent to which what happens *in* school becomes more important than variations among the pupils on entry.

In the Johannesburg African townships there are two types of high schools—junior high schools offering a limited high school course of three years, culminating in the Junior Certificate examination, and full five year high schools providing education up to matriculation level, equipping the individual for a possible university career. In one case the high school pupil is presented with limited opportunities in his immediate environment (although with the theoretical possibility of shifting to another school after three years), in the other with extended opportunities both immediately and the more distant future. This difference between the two types of school provides the opportunity to test how far the structural differences in the formal system by which the society trains the child and presents itself to him, will influence the child's assumptions about his future role in the society.

The differences between the two types of school are not directly comparable to the secondary-modern/grammar school variations in Britain which have been so well documented by Himmelweit. Entry to the particular types of school is not determined by measured intelligence: firstly all high school entrants are a relatively small proportion of the total numbers who started school and are technically qualified for further education beyond the primary level, and secondly education for Africans is not compulsory.

In addition the four high schools which were studied are situated in different parts of the townships, and allocation to a school is mainly by neighbourhood. Whether a full course or junior high school is attended will depend on where the pupil lives. Unlike the English system there is little relationship between neighbourhood and social class. The African urban population is very poor, largely unskilled, and not free to select where to live. The close coincidence of type of school and social class which the English literature portrays is not found. If there are differences between the two types of school then these will be school effects, indicating the strength of the school system as a socializing agent.

However, it need not be anticipated that the school should make an immediate impact. The new entrant is still tied to his previous socializing agents, both his primary school and his family, whereas the high school graduate leaves his secondary school aware of the opportunities opened to him and of his potential utilization of them. Hence the length of time spent at school is an important condition for the strength of the system to make its influence felt on the subject.

The expected differences between the schools of each type due to variations in their structure does not deny the possibility of differences within each school with each increase in form. Each additional year within the school system should increase the influence of the system and decrease within group variations due to earlier socialization experiences. It would be expected that the range of responses produced would decrease and similarities increase as the individual spends more time at the school. Each year the potential rewards of the educational system increases and so does the need to justify the time and effort committed to education. Remaining on at school is expensive, not only in terms of educational costs but also in lost income. For a poor community the financial burden of voluntary further education needs justification. Perhaps, as the studies of severity of initiation (Aronson and Mills, 1959) would lead one to predict, the greater the cost, the greater the consequent commitment.

In addition, the potential rewards of higher education are highly prized. Education is valued by the African community and the educated middle class is very small. Mayer (1961) and Pauw (1963) stress that within the town "comparative status is measured 'in terms of education, occupation and living standards—the more civilized the better' " (Pauw, p. 176). Of these, educational achievement seems to be the single most important criterion for ascribing status to people in town.

Without doubt the highest status is generally ascribed to people like doctors, teachers, trained ministers and nurses, as well as prosperous business men who are less well educated. On certain occasions they are clearly set apart as a class, for instance being ushered to the front seats at a concert or beauty queen contest, or by being called to the first sitting at a wedding-feast (Pauw, p. 179). Although segregation de-presses and diminishes social class variations within the African community the doctor, the lawyer, the school teacher are still all better off, and more visible as community leaders, than the road-worker or factory hand.

What we suggest is that for the individual in the process of accultura-tion, a strong system, such as the school, is of major importance. Its influence will vary according to the opportunity structure the school represents and the length of time the individual is involved with it. The strength of the school system is thought to be such that individual differences in the goodness of "fit" of past experience (level of ac-culturation, community of origin, traditional bonds and family struc-ture) to present circumstances will be outweighed by the influence of the school and will diminish in importance the longer the individual remains within the system.

There are factors which may operate to weaken the influence of the school. One of these is age. Within most social systems the age limits between which critical events occur are relatively narrow. What is interesting about African high school pupils in South Africa is that the age at which they start school varies and therefore each classroom contains a number of pupils some years older than the median age. In part this is due to rural parents sending their children to the city for education when younger children can take over herding duties. In part it is due to the fact that schooling is not compulsory and therefore children start when it is financially and socially feasible.

Another variable which is important is sex. A major portion of the acculturation literature deals exclusively with the responses of boys, although some of the studies of West Africa have examined the de-velopment of economic power amongst the women traders. There is however a great deal of evidence summarized by Maccoby (1966) on sex differences in interests, and abilities and achievement. The study by Veness (1952) of English school leavers has shown not only the greater importance of work for boys than girls, but also that girls aspire to different sorts of occupations and for different reasons than do boys.

Traditional tribal society viewed women as minors with limited rights (although there were a few exceptions such as the mother of the Swazi king, and the Rain Queen of Lovedu). Sex-role differentiation was clear (Simons, 1958). Today occupational opportunities for African women in industrial South Africa are, apart from domestic work and primary school teaching, clearly different from those available to the boys. Thus, both traditional and present day role models available for girls leads one to predict clear sex differences in the subjects' responses. It is also likely that since the number of opportunities made available to the girls by the school system are less than those presented to boys the effect of the school will be weaker for girls than for boys. Both within each type of school and between the different schools less variation is expected to be found for the girls than for the boys.

If the school is a strong system variations in the structure of the school should be reflected in the aspirations and evaluations of the pupils. The strength of the school lies in its relation to the opportunity structure of the wider society: if this is differentially reflected in the school's organization it should exert differential influences on the pupil's expectations and aspirations.

One of the sources of the strength of the school system is to be found in its preparatory role for occupational achievement. Highly specialized social systems demand highly specialized training: high school education is a first stage in this process. Himmelweit and Swift (1969) in a longitudinal study have shown that the type of high school (grammar or secondary modern) attended by a boy bears a significant relationship to his occupational status at age 25. Of 138 working class boys who went to grammar school 84% were in middle class occupations, whereas of 156 who went to secondary modern school only 30% achieved higher status occupations. Their study shows too that 49% of middle class boys who went to secondary modern schools ended up at age 25 in working class occupations. The school provides a means whereby cultural expectations are made explicit and become personal wishes and, given the importance of occupation in defining one's status and role in society, the strength of the school becomes clear.

A recent study by Rahlberg et al. (1970) gives added strength to this view. Using a sample of 1455 high school males they tested two models suggesting a temporal sequence of adolescent achievement variables. The first model links adolescent educational aspirations with parental socio-economic status through achievement values and measured intelligence. The second reverses this by linking achievement values and measured intelligence with parental socio-economic status via educational expectations. The evidence from their study lends support to this second model rather than to the first.

A study of Swedish high school pupils by Andersson (1969) reports systematic differences between types of school on almost every measure of attitude motivation and peer group behaviour used, indicating a clear distinction in the impact of theoretical and practical schools. Coleman (1961) in his thorough study of adolescent society found that despite similarities between schools it was possible to classify them according to variations in the value climate of each school. Boyle (1966) too was able to demonstrate the differential impact of school structure on students' aspirations.

These studies support the proposition that schools vary in the strength of the influence they exert and in the content and nature of this impact on the aspirations, attitudes and self-evaluation of the pupils. Those schools which bring greater rewards—in opening opportunities and in leading to entry higher in the social status hierarchy— have the greater impact and strength.

Most models of the school as a socializing agent assume a fairly consistent relation between the school and the society within which it operates. Schools encourage particular attitudes, values and ideologies which are congruent with those of the dominant culture. They offer curricula which are geared to assumptions about present and future demands from the economy, as well as to providing the basic skills which are considered necessary for useful integration into the productive systems. Although Danziger (1971) argues that the school is not an agency of socialization he nevertheless writes:

> The school system presents the child with a simulated model of the bureaucratic society in which he will have to take his place as an adult and it does this not only as a form of training or preparation, but in order to gauge the child's ability to adopt the demands of such a social system. (p. 121)

That the school system changes with changes in the society of which it is part has already been illustrated. That any structural or holistic view of society cannot but assume interaction between the educational and other systems is not necessary to belabour. What is interesting is that the educational system itself can feed into the general body politic and create new roles and new influences. An increasingly literate population may demand new types of leisure activities, may force politicians to reassess their policies, may create new economic demands. There is an impressive literature on the effects of education within the independent African states which suggest that schools have increased the levels of demand and aspiration of the population faster than economic growth has been able to expand to satisfy them. Where the association between education and social advance has traditionally been a strong one, it is difficult for the present educated generation to accept jobs which were previously performed by the unskilled or the illiterate.

This situation pertains no doubt in Southern Africa as well. There has been an expansion of education and not an associated increase in the range and number of openings available for the newly educated. The longer the child is at school, the more he and the family invest both in time and money, the higher are likely to be the expected returns both in terms of personal progress and economic or occupational advance. But the relation between the educational system and the wider society for the Africans in South Africa is not clear-cut. The school system supports and encourages the concept of advance by means of hard work and individual effort, it ascribes value and worth to the individual on the basis of his own achievements. But the outside world reacts to the person not as an individual but as a member of a particular racial group. What the school may encourage, the outside world may deny. Where the school simply accommodates to the exigencies of a society where access to influence and privilege, to status and power is prescribed by race then the impact of the school may well be limited. Where the individual comes from a family which has adjusted and accommodated to the status quo, which has been mobile within the limits permitted the individual, he may well accept more easily the mores of both the school and the outside political system. However, were the school to take seriously the values implicit in its education then there may well occur a disjunction between the school and the world outside.

Education itself, that is, the process of becoming literate, may produce alterations in the thinking of the individual regardless of the structure of the system. Goody (1977) has argued that writing has encouraged the kind of scrutiny that makes possible the development of rationality and scepticism. By separating information and knowledge from a dependence on a person, by rendering it impersonal and external, it is possible to examine assumptions and evidence in a more detached manner, and bring to bear critical evaluations upon it. This process may encourage reflection that is independent of family, school structure and even the content of the curriculum. However, it may make more salient the cognitive capacities of the individual and his ability to deal with abstract representations. This means that we have to be cognizant of the psychological processes by which the individual comes to know, understand and represent his world. Structural variables are only a part of the story.

# 8

# Aspirations and Evaluations

This study is concerned with the interface of social structure and psychological functioning. It is formed by the premise that the individual's actions are neither the result of societal primacy, nor of biological determinism. This assertion raises the issue of how to characterize the intersection of the "undeniably individual character of human action and the undeniably systemic character of most of its manifestations" (Moore, 1969, p. 290). It is possible to see social behaviour simply as a reflection of societally determined rules and norms. It is clear that society is antecedent to the individual and that it is possible to see actors and their actions simply as elements in the system of relationships between components. Indeed, much work in the field of ethnography would argue that the responses of the individuals are simply manifestations of social order.

Without doubt the social system operates to set ranges of acceptable behaviour for the individual, and offers or denies choices and opportunities. No individual has to create for himself from birth the complex interactions of the elements of which society consists. But this view of the relation of the individual and the abstract collective demands stability and stasis, it is tenable only if there is no discrepancy between the real and the ideal. However the failure to achieve the ideal, to maintain absolute congruence between the expected and the actual is as clear a fact as the existence of the ideals themselves.

Nevertheless, we cannot see the interface of society and the individual simply as an area where the major activity consists of various ways of inducting the individual into a more perfect representation of the ideal. It does not consist simply of processes of social control, of the "society" imposing itself on an undifferentiated element. It is not possible to explain human psychology, or the actions of specific individuals at specific historical times and in a particular social system, by reducing the problem to role and norm demands. Social reductionism is no more adequate than psychological reductionism.

The fallacy of psychological reductionism lies in the belief that, since all social behaviour and structures are ultimately expressed through the behaviour of individuals, one can explain social norms, ideals and systems solely by reference to the behaviours of individuals. Even more fallacious are assumptions that attempt to find cause for the nature of social systems in the need-states of individuals. The individual is not isolated and unchanging. He is related intimately and ultimately to the other individuals and elements which comprise the social system, and it is in the relationships and interactions of the component parts of the totality that we can begin to understand the system itself.

However, rejecting the extremes of social determinism and biological reductionism leaves one with the problem of determining in what form the component parts interact, and how to represent the nature of that interaction. Psychology, like other disciplines, is not able to encompass "wholes". We cannot describe the totality of the individual's psychological world but needs must decide what phenomena are likely to be the most critical to our understanding, or given the specific circumstances of the individual's world, most likely to be influenced by his experiences. We have to ask precise questions in order to make possible even the simplest answers. The complexity of the problem is described, in another context, by Popper (1976). We are attempting to describe an objective theory of subjective experience, seeing that experience to be shaped by the interaction of the individual and his social environment.

Phrasing it this way, it becomes clear that the problem has been too broadly stated. To aver that all human experience is shaped by the social environment is to say nothing, while stating everything. It is likely that at different points in the individual's life certain parts of the social whole become more immediately pertinent and acquire greater salience in an understanding of his activities and his psychological functioning. For example, the family is perhaps at all times of importance; if however one is concerned with the individual's performance on a series of skilled tasks, the immediate salience of the familial constellation is reduced. It would therefore be feasible to specify those institutions of the society, or those experiences of the social reality, which are of particular relevance at particular times of the individual's life cycle or in relation to specified psychological developments.

It is this second that raises the major problem. What are the particular psychological developments that we should focus on at particular times of the developmental continuum? Various theories emphasize different factors according to their prime interest. For cognitive developmental theories it is the construction of cognitive systems that is critical, for it is these that relate to the way the individual functions in his understanding of the world, particularly the physical world, although many contend that the same processes may be involved in understanding the social world. Less important therefore would be the resolution of the psychodynamic conflicts, which some personality theorists would emphasize. These conflicts are different at distinct points in the individual's psychological growth, but can range from the questions of orality in Freudian theory to those of identity stressed by Erikson. For these theories and for the cognitive theories the development of brain systems, although accepted as important, is not of critical relevance in explanations and descriptions of the phenomena under scrutiny. When one looks at social psychological theories the range of relevant processes increases. Both cognitive developments and personality factors may have to be considered, but so too do other elements—questions of values, attitudes, relations to others and to the social system. While considering these it is possible to ignore the physiological substratum but it is not possible to do so for the social context.

During the period of high school education the individual is faced with a number of pertinent and pressing decisions about himself and his role in society. From varying vantage points this has been emphasized by socialization theorists, as well as by Erikson and by Piaget. For Erikson (1965) the adolescent period, which frequently coincides with high school education is a time of resolving a number of identity questions: who one is, what one will be, what the important principles are that should guide one and so on. In Piaget's formulation (1958) cognitive developments during adolescence, by allowing the individual to think about and operate on his cognitive schema, free him from the concrete, and permit the consideration of the non-existent. In other words the young person is able to think about worlds and organizations other than those which exist, and this allows the growth of ideals and idealism. In addition, since this is also the period when the young take their place in society, it is also the age of the formation of personality.

> Thus, to say that adolescence is the age at which adolescents take their place in adult society is by definition to maintain that it is the age of formation of the personality, for the adoption of adult roles is from another and necessarily complementary standpoint the construction of a personality. Furthermore, the construction of a life program and the plans for change

which . . . (are) . . . one of the essential features of the adolescent's behaviour are at the same time the changing emotional force in the formation of the personality. (Inhelder and Piaget, 1958)

Therefore, for Piaget the development of the capacity for formal thought is important as an element in the formation of personality. However, this is a concept slightly different from that used by Erikson, and linked rather more with social psychological considerations:

> A life plan is above all a scale of values which puts some ideals above others and subordinates the middle-range values to goals thought of as permanent. This . . . (corresponds to) the cognitive organisation of his work which the new member in the social body says he will undertake. (Inhelder and Piaget, 1958)

In addition, and of great importance is the fact that this life plan affirms the autonomy of the individual, in particular the moral autonomy which asserts that he is the equal of adults.

Like many of the theoretical concepts that Piaget has formulated, the ideas about adolescence provide a structure on to which the particular experiences and circumstances of the individual write the content. The nature of the ideals that the individual develops and the social roles he adopts, or hopes to adopt, are influenced by the particularities of the society. To the extent that choice exists and that the individual must or can make decisions, the nature of the choices open to him become important. To the extent that society prescribes some roles or proscribes certain choices, the freedom of the individual's "life-plan" is clearly limited. Adolescence and young adulthood are times of choice—educational, occupational, ideological. These choices are closely related to the individual's views of himself and of his society.

## Aspirations and expectations

There are a number of ways that the individual's future plans have been investigated. Danziger (1963) and Ezekiel (1968) and others have used a method of future autobiography, where the individual is asked to write about his psychological future. In this way the temporal schema and the life-goals and values integral to the individual are made explicit. McClelland's (1953) concept of need for achievement has proved a most popular way of discovering the individual's motivation to succeed. The level of achievement motivation within the individual is seen as the function of two factors—the situation and the strength of the motive within the individual's personality. McClelland and his colleagues examined two major antecedent variables, those located in the early familial experiences of the child, as in the Rosen study we have described in an earlier chapter, and those located in the ideological and economic systems of the society.

The measure used by McClelland and his co-workers is based on the content analysis of specific Thematic Apperception Test (TAT) cards, evolved from the original Murray set, and it is assumed to be a global and universal way of examining the individual's motivation to succeed. Both the concept and the test have been much used, and much criticized. A popular measure in cross-cultural research (Ausubel, 1960; Gough, 1970) and in investigations of ethnic group differences (Rosen, 1962; Lazarus et al., 1969) the measure has nevertheless been found to be of variable reliability (Feld and Smith, 1958). This has however not discouraged the measure's use, but it does make the results difficult to interpret. In addition, although the wide focus of the concept has many advantages, they do not necessarily make it applicable to a clear examination of the individual's view of himself in the society. The measure is not easily used to distinguish differing pathways which might be chosen as avenues of success, and for those interested in examining change it is not easy to differentiate those wanting to achieve in conventional or traditional ways or within the bounds of their present circumstances from those whose aspirations demand them moving away from them. In the Danziger method, for instance, it is possible to separate conservative from revolutionary concepts of change. This is not easy to do in the traditional McClelland investigation, and yet this may be an important variable if one is examining the relation of the need for achievement to life plans and to behaviour.

A more direct technique is simply to ask people what job they would like to do: to enquire directly into future aspirations. This has been done by Caro and Philbard (1965), by Garza (1969), by Hodgkins and Parr (1965) and Bennet and Gist (1964) amongst others. Although this approach is not necessarily free of interpretative problems at least these are focussed. However, even with the direct question it is necessary to do more than simply examine the responses; it is necessary to evaluate the tempering of aspirations by reality and so achieve a balance between fantasy and the expectation of success. This relation between aspirations and expectation is important, and applies not only to the general need-state of the individual but more particularly to his social and personal ambitions in work, in education, in friendship. For example, in their study Bennett and Gist (1964) found that whereas *aspirations* varied little by social class—the *actual* occupational plans showed differences. Wiener and Murray (1963) found no class differences between parents in their desire to have their children follow a college career, but there were clear class differences in their actual *expectations* that this would occur.

The benefit of examining expectations goes beyond their value in interpreting aspirations. By examining both aspirations and expectations directly, and by referring both to the realities of the social structure, it becomes possible to establish whether the impediment to achievement is internally located, as within the individual's own abilities, or is due to external factors, as would occur for example in a caste society. And the congruence or divergence between the individual's aspirations and expectations will give insights into his view of his place in the status system of his society. It may also indicate the amount of influence he feels he can exert over his own development.

## Locus of control

It is likely that members of groups, varying in the amount of direct control and power they legally and traditionally exercise, will perceive differently the amount of control over their lives that they exert. The results which have emerged from work on Rotter's (1966) concept of internal versus external control of reinforcement support this. Rotter's theory suggests that people learn, as a result of their experiences in society, to locate the source of reward for their behaviour either within their own control, or within the control of forces external to themselves —fate, chance, society.

> The fault, dear Brutus, is not in our stars, but in ourselves that we are underlings. (*Julius Caesar*, Act I, Scene II)

as opposed to:

> What can be avoided whose end is purposed by the mighty gods? (*Julius Caesar*, Act II, Scene II)

The concept of locus of control of reinforcement is similar to the idea of causal attribution which attempts to discover the assumed source of responsibility for an action or an outcome. The literature supports the view that the perceived locus of control varies with the position held within the larger society. The sense of personal control as measured by Rotter's I–E scale has been found in the U.S.A. to be greater in White children and adults than Black, in members of the middle class than in the working class (Battle and Rotter, 1963; Crandal *et al.*, 1965; Coleman *et al.*, 1966). Coleman, in his major study of public schools in the U.S.A., showed that at all grade levels Negro attainment was less than that of Whites, and that internality—the belief that the individual can exercise personal control over the environment—was related to academic achievement. An unusual result, one that does not follow the simple rule high status = internality, is that of Lazarus *et al.* (1969). In a study comparing middle class and working class White and Coloured (mixed race) school children in South Africa they found differences between the racial groups in need achievement scores (though not between social class groups in the White sample) but no differences in externality. In other words, where the social organization is rigid and control strictly enforced, all groups, regardless of their position in the dominance hierarchy, tend to see the source of control of rewards as similarly controlled.

These relationships, between achievement, expectation of success, a sense of personal control and social position, are complex and must not be oversimplified. People may assume different loci for success as opposed to failure, they may make assumptions for others that they do not make for themselves. And individual as opposed to group achievement may relate to different loci of control. Gurin *et al.* (1969) in a study of achievement of Negro college students writes: "When internal-external control refers to Negroes' conceptions of the cause of their condition as Negroes . . . it is the external rather than the internal control that is associated with more effective behaviours". What the Gurin studies showed was that people could have different assumptions about the locus of control of reinforcement for achievement related to their personal life—family and finance, for instance—from that related to socio-political achievement. For members of many groups achievement is closely tied to their condition as one of a minority or subordinate group and recognition of this fact may be essential for the development of appropriate behaviour. Perceiving externality may be achieving an accurate picture of the world. The control of reinforcement within one's family and informal world may, in reality, be found in a different locus from control in the formal occupational and political realm.

The locus of control is of relevance to more than just immediate aspirations. It may be implicated in the individual's choice of particular pathways to success. Those who believe hard work and individual effort sufficient to gain access to rewards are likely to endorse behaviours which reflect this when selecting the means to a particular end. Alternatively, if the individual is believed to be controlled by fate or chance, or by the external social system, then he is less likely to select personal effort actions in a context of choice. It is more likely that there would be attempts to appease the fates, accept passively what happens, or to seek support beyond one's self in the group, for satisfaction of one's desires. It is this latter approach that the Gurin study illustrates in those students who thought that the reason for their condition was located not in themselves but in their condition as Negroes.

The benefits of relating need for achievement to the perception of the wider social system are stressed in a study by LeVine in Nigeria (1966). He investigated secondary school students, boys only, and related attitudes and achievement imagery to tribal membership. Tribal differences were found in imagery, in attitudes to authority and in the value systems, and these tribal differences were cross-validated on a sample of men. LeVine offers three possible explanations for the differences he found. The first rests on the hypothesis of population pressure. This suggests that the relationship, high-achievement low authorization submission, which he found for the Ibos results from the move from agriculture to industry as a result of high population density. The second explanation is one proposed by Harper (1962, quoted by LeVine) based on the withdrawal of status and respect from a group by others whom they respect and esteem. The group so affected is first demoralized, and then attempts to regain status by assuming a role as innovator. There is some similarity between this idea and that which suggests that before a social group moves upward in the status hierarchy it needs to assert a positive reference point in opposition to negative judgements, which have previously forced them into an out-group role. This means that the very characteristic which has negatively defined a group in relation to others—race, ethnicity, religion—now becomes a positively valenced rallying point. Although this hypothesis can account for the results which LeVine found in respect of the Ibos, he prefers a third explanation which makes reference to current, rather than to historical, events. This is the contemporary status mobility thesis.

In his description of the thesis LeVine emphasizes both the need-states of the individual and the opportunity structure of the society, and also the nature of the information that the developing individual receives about this structure from the agents of socialization: the frequency of n-ach within a group would be determined by the perception that the growing child has as to the chances of him rising socially and the sorts of behaviour that lead to success within the society. Information that he receives about this comes from family, school, outsiders and media amongst others.

It is therefore clear that in order to understand the way the developing individual relates to his world one needs to know what he would ideally like out of life, particularly in relation to occupation, the extent to which he feels that the realization of his aspirations is within his own control and the way that the wider world relates to his aspirations.

The notions of control and of the opportunity system can be related both to factors within the individual (such as his abilities) and to those external to him. The locus of the perceived impediments to potential achievement derives importance as a source of possible discontent. If the individual perceives his progress hindered by forces external to himself the behaviour which will ensue is necessarily different from that which would follow an internally located impediment. Not only the locus of control but also the perceived location of the barriers are important in understanding aspirations and expectations. The way the individual evaluates his society, his traditions, his education, the political attitudes he adopts and the people he admires—indeed the whole value system that he employs—may be determined by the way that he sees society facilitating or preventing the satisfaction of his ambition and achievement.

## Relative deprivation

The relationship between aspirations and expectations can be either congruent or incongruent. Most of the literature is concerned with a description of incongruity because it is in incongruity that conditions of stress and tension are presumed to lie. However, congruent relationships should not be assumed to be free of tension. Since we take measures at one point in time the relationships which we observe may reflect previously felt tensions which have been accommodated with greater or lesser cost to the individual. The tension may not be apparent, but the cost of the resolution may yet leave scars. To the extent that the adjustment made is seen as satisfactory and the cost is seen as acceptable, so the relation will be devoid of tension.

Because incongruity is a potential source of action—either behavioural attempts to alter some parts of the system or cognitive reactions adjusting attitudes and values—it needs a detailed analysis to see how, and in what direction it exerts its influence. Gurr (1970) has utilized the concept of relative deprivation to describe conditions of incongruity and to indicate its behavioural consequences. Relative deprivation refers to the experience of a discrepancy between aspirations and expectations. Gurr quotes Hoselitz and Willner "Expectations are a manifestation of the prevailing norms set by the immediate social and cultural environment . . . Aspirations represent that which he would like to have but has not necessarily had or considered his due". Rather than aspirations and expectations Gurr refers to "value expectations" and "value capabilities": the first are those goods and conditions of life to which people think they are entitled, the second those that they think they are capable of getting and keeping. Rather like cognitive dissonance (Festinger, 1957) relative deprivation as an imbalanced state is psychologically uncomfortable, it leads men "over the long run to adjust their value expectations to their value capabilities" (Gurr, p. 46, 1970). In our terms, to make aspirations congruent with expectations.

Gurr defines three conditions of disequilibrium. Decremental deprivation occurs when a group's value expectations remain relatively constant, but their value capabilities are seen to decline; that is those goods, rights or services to which they have been accustomed are no longer available. The second source of disequilibrium is almost the obverse of decremental deprivation. Aspirational deprivation occurs where value capabilities remain constant but value expectations increase. This increase may take the form of a demand for new rights or goods, for more of an existing held value, or it may be an intensification of an existing but not previously salient value. The third condition is progressive deprivation, where both an increase in expectations and a decrease in capabilities occur simultaneously. This condition is less common than either decremental or aspirational deprivation, but occurs, for example, where there is a discontinuity in a previously smooth cycle of development and progress.

The South African social structure presents examples of all three of these conditions and all can give rise to the experience of relative deprivation by sections of the African population. Although aspirational deprivation is most common, with value capabilities remaining constant as value expectations increase, decremental deprivation is to be found in the loss of power and control by traditional tribal authorities. Progressive deprivation arises from the restrictions placed on the African's education and the work opportunities of the African middle class as segregation is more firmly imposed, and previously integrated institutions are closed to them. The intensity with which the deprivation is experienced will in part determine the behaviours which arise from it. This intensity will be influenced by the salience of the value thwarted, greater intensity arising with greater salience; by the size of the discrepancy between capabilities and expectations, and by the number of alternative satisfactions available to the individual. In addition, time is an important although not always a predictable factor. It is likely that in a short time-span the intensity of the relative deprivation experience may be increased. Over a long time period, even if aspirations do not shift, the discomfort caused by the discrepancy may be accepted. This tolerance of deprivation is also likely to be encouraged where the deterrents to forcing a change in opportunities are overwhelming.

Whereas the system discussed above leads one to expect tensions when aspirations and expectations are not balanced, it does not predict what attempts will be made to resolve them. The characteristics of the society in which the individual has to make his adjustments will determine the contents and objects of his attitudes and the nature of the values he expresses. The position occupied by the individual in his society will affect his view of the source of his discontent. It will determine his assessment of whether he can remedy the situation and how this can best be achieved. Gurr finds in the concept of relative deprivation the potential to political violence, by extending Dollard's (1939) frustration-aggression hypothesis to social events. It is equally possible that in the discrepancy between aspiration and expectation we may locate not only actions but also evaluations.

Where expectations are cut according to a racial cloth it is difficult for the individual alone to alter the pattern. If he wishes to effect change he will have to look beyond himself to do so. This would lead one to expect a number of interesting correlations with a high relative deprivation score. The society which presents barriers to achieving a state of balance between aspirations and expectations should be negatively evaluated; groups or individuals who exemplify various successful resolutions of the incongruence should be positively evaluated and serve a reference function. In addition those actions which are believed to produce community coherence should be favoured. The advance of the whole community will carry the individual with it. What follows from this is that one needs to assess the range of values, the reference groups admired, attitudes to society and to community traditions and to relate them to the aspirations and expectations of the individual.

## Value systems and motives: South African studies

Many of the studies carried out in Africa have been concerned with three main themes. The first has been related to the assessment of individual abilities, both in relation to general measures of intelligence (see for example the work of Vernon and of Biesheuwel) and in respect to specific abilities. In part these studies have their justification in attempts to derive "pure" measures, and they also stem from demands made by industry for assessment procedures that can both select and be used in training. The second main field of research is process oriented and involves cross-cultural comparisons of various aspects of cognitive functioning: studies of perception, of concept formation and particularly studies examining assumptions derived from Piaget's stage theory of cognitive development.

The third set of studies is more social psychological in that these attempt to assess the attitudes and value systems of the individual. Most of the studies in this group are concerned with acculturation, with measures which attempt to either order or divide the sample into traditional or Western, tribal or modern, conservative or scientific. In other words, the studies examine the position of the individual on a dimension scaled to reach a cluster of attitudes or a system of values which is similar to those that would be obtained from a European or North American sample. This could be in relation to economic and political values, in relation to scientific beliefs, in relation to health practices or child rearing procedures. There has not been a very consistent attempt to sample a wide range of behaviours or a variety of attitudes and beliefs.

The major value difference which the South African research has uncovered has to do with the focus of concern to which people admit. It has been argued that where one's condition is dependent on group membership, and not on individual actions and abilities, it is likely that the individual will turn his attention from himself to the community or group as a whole, since his progress is ultimately dependent on the progress of the group. Given this, it should be found that Whites in South Africa whose personal progress is not hindered by adverse legislation will seek purpose and pleasure in private activities; the non-White groups which consist of individual's whose personal merit will not be sufficient to guarantee maximum advance might see purpose and progress in the activities of the community. The research supports this—African and Indian samples are more concerned with political and social issues, Whites with private (Danziger, 1958). Bloom (1960) comparing White and non-White university students found that the latter were concerned with social change and with problems arising from the political system as well as with community problems and injustice, while the Whites lacked political and social concerns. The future views of the groups were also different with the Whites being relatively conventional and complacent in their orientations while the others' portrayal of the future was despairing and pessimistic. In general these results showing variations in values and concerns have been supported (Mann, 1962; Gillespie and Allport, 1955). Mann (1962) comparing White and non-White students on a social dilemma technique, again found consistent value differences. Non-White students inclined more to community service than private needs, and put public welfare above religious scruples. A later study by Danziger (1963) using the future autobiography technique suggests that the value system is responsive to politico-legal changes in that "the tightening of social and political restrictions has produced a relative de-differentiation of the psychological future and a decline in interest in both community service and individual economic success". He suggests that the observed changes indicate a "value oriented counter movement for which social reality is defined essentially in political terms".

Botha (1964) in a Uses Test, which assesses the purpose ascribed to people, objects and events in terms of seven value categories, found that African and White adults differed on six of the seven categories scored. The African sample were higher on sustentative values (those that refer to things that sustain life) and on benevolence (which refers to helping, receiving help, goodwill and friendship) while the Afrikaners were higher on the hierarchical category and on the religious, while all Whites were higher on hedonism and on aestheticism. Malevolence scores were low throughout the group. Comparing the observed differences within a range of age groups it was clear that the two groups which showed the greatest differences (African and Afrikaner) increased these differences with age. Value differences have been found by Danziger (1958) in relation to Western civilization, with Black students attributing negative and White students positive characteristics to it. Danziger (1958) found also that White students were more concerned with private issues, non-Whites with political and social. Bloom (1960) testing White and African students again found consistent differences between the groups in attitudes and values. The African students were concerned with problems which arise from the struggle for political and social freedom whereas the White students were little concerned with these issues. He found that the Whites' future view was complacent, that of the African student pessimistic and despairing. Some measure of expectation of favourable outcome may need to be taken into account in determining the behavioural correlates of values.

Not only values but also the needs which motivate the individual's behaviour may be influenced by context. The literature on the motives of Africans in South Africa has produced two views as to the nature of motivation. De Ridder (1961) found that the main expressed motivating factor in a large sample of African employees and prospective employees of a bus company was personal. He disputes the role of community service in determining job choice and assessing the value of education. Sherwood (1957) in her study of African clerks found that her subjects were positively motivated by group-oriented values and only secondarily by those that are self-oriented. There are no apparent differences in the educational attainments of the samples in the two studies which can explain the variation in findings. However an unpublished study by Lake reported by Reader (1963) may hold the clue to the answer. Lake studied job ranking in urban African high school boys and found that clerical jobs are not seen as ends in themselves, but as stepping stones to higher status jobs. Indeed Sherwood found that 40% of the clerks she studied were still studying through correspondence colleges.

It may well be in the process of achieving that the experience of deprivation is strongest. Brett (1963), examining attitudes of a sample of African middle class males, used a very broadly based questionnaire to assess the need states of his subjects. He found a preponderance of personal or self-oriented needs and a smaller number of what could be called altruistic-idealistic motives. What is interesting is that these occurred most frequently amongst those in the process of training, either at school or university.

A study by Ainsworth and Ainsworth (1962) gives evidence which indirectly supports this. They found that the level of acculturation in the schools which they studied in pre-independent Uganda related to to the level of occupational aspiration. Those schools which were most acculturated were most politically aware and more actively discontented with the political status quo than the pupils at other schools. What is particularly relevant is that these also responded most effectively to frustrations and were more likely to overcome barriers. While the more acculturated felt more frustrated by authority and by their own shortcomings they were less fearful of aggression and more likely to legitimize rebellion; they were more frequently intrapunitive and need-persistent and less frequently obstacle dominated and impunitive.

Given the particular structure of South Africa and the salience of racial and ethnic group divisions, it is not surprising that many of the researchers are concerned to discover the nature of the intergroup attitudes that are held by particular subgroups within the society. The first major social psychological research in the country was one conducted by MacCrone (1937)* into the race attitudes of Whites and he followed this by attempts to relate attitudes to the wider contextual background of personality traits and structures. He later studied the attitudes of the dominated groups, using a life history technique, and concluded that the reaction to domination was one of "counter-domination" through which, in aggression, suspicion, and dislike, the individuals expressed their resistance, focussing the greatest part of their dislike on the Afrikaans-speaking group. The aggressiveness cannot be overtly expressed and therefore was either turned inwards or found expression in acceptable techniques—ridicule, non-co-operation, rejection of the White man and of those things associated with him. The

*MacCrone's influence is to be found in the large number of studies which measure White's attitudes to Africans, Indians and Coloureds as well as to ethnic communities within the White group. These are not reported here since they are not relevant to the immediate concerns of this study.

engendered hostility MacCrone believes to be an aggravating cause of the problems of social adjustment. It also serves to minimize tribal differences by encouraging the development of a "racial" or national identity. Since the sample that was studied consisted of a group of social workers, most of whom had been teachers, he found that there was a conflict between the status to which they have claim by virtue of training and that to which they are assigned by the attitudes and behaviour of members of the dominant colour group. However, the African is not without resources in this situation. His group serves as a ground on which he can stand to confront the other groups; he develops a strong in-group identity strengthened by awareness of group heritage and tradition.

Edelstein (1972) found that the distinction between White South Africans according to language which MacCrone reported was strong within a group of final year African high school students. Using a social distance measure, the pupils were found to have more favourable stereotypes of English than of other White groups, and than of Coloureds and Indians. He also supports in some way MacCrone's findings about the reactions to domination—the students rejected the concept of Tribal Homelands, and would prefer Soweto to be undivided into tribal areas. They showed preference for English, nationalism and for multiracial government. In addition they were proud to be Black. The characteristic that is the basis for the condition of subordination begins to be positively rather than negatively valenced. In fact, the idea that self-esteem would be automatically lowered by being the underling in an hierarchical relation is further thrown into doubt by a research by Momberg and Page (1977). They found that the measured self-esteem of White and Coloured scholars in South Africa was not different. They comment on the similar rise in esteem amongst American Blacks, and Lobban (1975) found in a study of self attitudes of urban Africans that they have the highest positive regard for three groups—American Blacks, Independent Africans and their own group of urban Africans. (In common with other studies the least preferred group was the Afrikaans-speaking South African.) The groups they admired seemed to exemplify the characteristics they felt best described how they would most like to be, namely free, civilized and Black.

Lobban argues that the reason for high self-esteem is to be found in the fact that the social system easily allows the individual to attribute his failure to the external world. This was indeed found, as was the fact that the sample of high school pupils she examined displayed high agreement on the need for social change, rejecting accommodation in favour of militancy. This rejection is found too by van den Berghe (1962) in a comparative study of attitudes in Durban, Natal. He interpreted the association found between acceptance of out-groups and high levels of religiosity to imply that the African radical rejects Christianity, seeing it as an instrument of White domination. He also confirmed the original finding of MacCrone that Africans did not simply classify all Whites together, but tended to single out for the highest rejection those who speak Afrikaans.

It becomes clear that the social structure operates at the psychological level differentially according to position within the system, and that the socio-political reality is represented at the level of psychological reality. Biesheuwel (1957) demonstrated this neatly. In a study which showed that overall there was an acceptance by an African sample of Western ethical and social values he found that legal and administrative discrimination deprives both laws and social conventions of their moral base, and that therefore it is not necessary to observe the duties that are vested in one—not to pay tax, imprisonment is not a disgrace and so on. In other words the evaluations that are formed are congruent with the broader system.

If this is so then it should be that the actual position occupied by particular people should produce some differentiation within this broader context. It has already been suggested that aspirations raised by education should increase the amount of frustration that might be felt. However, very few of the researchers have detailed any developmental trends or shown clear within group variations. Botha's (1964) study suggested that the differences between her racial samples increased with age and education and Biesheuwel (1955) showed that the attitudes to law, justice and morality showed significant changes with age and education. However, neither of these reports enable one to unravel some of the dynamics of change and development. Danziger (1963) has in some ways attempted to resolve the question of change by using his future autobiography technique on different samples of high school students at three points in time—1950, 1956 and 1962. In this way he was able to document changes, and to show that the changes in the strength of the political system and the increase in the controls exerted over the African population were reflected in the protocols he collected. Both in the pre-occupation with socio-political problems and the limited amount of realistic personal future planning there were significant changes—more concern with political control, less personal control. The future was seen even more in social rather than in personal terms over the time period. In addition Danziger found a marked decline in the number of time-related plans, which are necessary for the co-ordination of ends and means. A time sense is critical for rationally organizing one's resources and ordering actions into a coherent scheme. The absence of this temporal framework is crucial for understanding future plans, and for the sense of futility that was found in many of the respondents. The clear change over time and the sense of flight from reality which he found were less strong in the women he studied, because the impact of official policy on the career aspirations of women is less than for men. It was fairly reasonable for them to plan the future in terms of marriage, children and a home even though more "hopeful fantasies" may be abandoned.

If one can generalize from the Danziger research it could be expected that those whose lives accommodate to the system, who have not looked beyond that which was quite clearly available and given, would develop attitudes that are less hostile than those who are on a path that because of the choices it opens, make most likely conflict and frustration. This is in line with the work of Gurr, but what is clear is that the accommodation may have already been dearly bought, through the abdication of personal control and a withdrawal from decision making and rational planning. The work of Brett on the attitudes of a sample of middle class Africans shows that even those who are in jobs which pose no threat to the established order, such as clerks, express feelings of insecurity, pessimism and dejection. His results emphasize once again the need to take cognisance of the wider society in understanding the psychological functioning of the individual. The subjects generally saw relationships within the African community as influenced by the wider system, and that the total system is responsible for the thwarting of their needs and aspirations.

What are the implications of all of this for the study of African high school students? According to Erikson they are in a period of transition during which they will have to resolve a number of conflicts. The nature of the resolution will influence their future adult functioning in a critical fashion. In fact, Erikson believes that the adolescent period is of importance equal to that of the initial developmental period. The type of resolution reached might be related to the individual's level of cognitive functioning. According to Piaget the adolescent will, if his cognitive system attains the level of formal operational functioning, be able to think of solutions to problems which are not already apparent in the real world outside himself. It might be expected therefore that the types of resolutions found to conflicts, the ability to plan, the finding out of who one is and the preparation for the future will relate to the capacity to abstract from the real world: to make the transition from the real world to an ideal one.

The study of African High School students set out to examine these issues in detail. The aim was to describe the beliefs and aspirations of a group of young people who, by virtue of their ability and education, could form the nucleus of the leadership of the African community in the years to come, and to see how these values and ambitions were influenced by home and by school.

# 9

# Content and Context

Almost one thousand students, drawn from four Soweto high schools, participated in the study. Two of the schools—Arcadia and Water-kloof—were full, five year Senior High Schools, and two—Sunnyside and Groenkloof—offered only the three year programme of the Junior High School. Students were not selected for admission to the particular type of high school on the basis of ability, and all the students who wished to continue their education at high school had to successfully pass the examination at the end of Standard 6, that is at the end of the Higher Primary School programme. The study involved students in the second, third and fourth years of high school all of whom completed a questionnaire about their backgrounds, aspirations, beliefs and expectations. A smaller subsample also completed a version of the Thematic Apperception Test (TAT) which was designed and analysed to inform about the students' expectations about particular social relationships and social situations—how these would be characterized, what would happen and what outcome could be anticipated.

The fine detailed analysis of data is a source of great interest to the researcher and to others who have done or anticipate doing research in the same general field, and not necessarily other readers. Therefore we have placed the detailed information about the sample, the tests and the results in the Appendices. Here we summarize the essence of the research findings before we embark on an interpretation and explanation of the results of the study and show how it relates to the actual activities of Soweto students in 1976.

As a whole, the sample was drawn from unskilled parents, most of whom had only a minimal amount of education. There were some children from educated middle class families but they were relatively few. The students were receiving an education far more advanced than their parents, and were therefore already mobile. They were at school at an age when most of their parents were working and when most of their age mates had abandoned education. However, they were living in conditions and circumstances not necessarily better than those of the rest of the Soweto population. Their parents were not wealthier, their families more stable nor smaller than the rest of the residents in Soweto.

We were interested in particular areas of belief and aspiration. According to the arguments in earlier chapters, the aspirations and ambitions developed at school are of critical importance in relation to the way the individual evaluates the wider society. Insofar as the system as a whole accommodates the individual's aspirations he is likely to evaluate it positively and find favour in those elements within it which are supportive. If however, the system rejects the values and the aspirations which have been encouraged or developed while at school, the individual could be expected to repudiate the outside social system, and negatively evaluate those factors and forces which frustrate him. The questionnaire and the Thematic Apperception Test (TAT) were both designed in this study to provide information about aspirations with respect to schooling and future occupation and expectations about the attainment of these goals. They were also sources of information about values, attitudes and evaluations of the society as a whole, and about various interpersonal relationships in particular.

The responses that were obtained from the students were analysed in relation to four sets of non-psychological variables that could have played a determining role in the reactions that were produced. The first set of variables concerned the student's background, those factors that he or she brings into the situation that might mediate his or her experiences. These background variables concerned the structure of the family, the educational achievements and occupations of parents and siblings, the urban-rural origin of the student. The second factor considered was gender. Most societies socialize boys and girls differently, although the clarity of the distinctions made may vary from place to place and change over time. These varying demands and expectations may well influence the way the student evaluates his or her experiences and opportunities. As discussed previously, regardless of official policy and the opportunity structure of the society, it remains reasonable for young women to plan a future in terms of marriage, children and a home, even though occupational paths may well be barred.

The third and fourth sets of factors considered in relation to the students' responses both concern the educational process. Subjects were drawn from the second, third and fourth years of the high school programme. It is possible that the number of years that the individual has spent at school could influence both his assumptions about himself and the aspirations that are developed. In addition two types of schools were examined. Each offers the students different "success ceilings". It is possible that the full five year programme, such as offered by Arcadia and Waterkloof, would produce different aspirations from those encouraged by the three year programme available at the Junior High Schools of Sunnyside and Groenkloof.

The study started with the assumption that the school would be of major influence in determining the attitudes expectations and aspirations of the students, and that its influence would be greater than that of home or acculturation. The schools open to the students, paths to future achievements which are not opened by the family. It was believed that in a strong colour-based social system variations within each colour group according to class would be depressed. The data show that the influence of the school is pervasive, that it operates most strongly on aspirations for jobs and education, on the general evaluation of the environment and also on the patterning of the responses to the pictures in the TAT. However, when we consider expectations about work and earnings, rather than aspirations, we find that while these are still significantly related to school they also seem to take account of the opportunity structure outside the educational sphere and they are modified according to the reality of the political and economic world. The schools might open to the students the vistas of educational and occupational achievement, but at the same time the students are aware of the world outside the school system, and temper their expectations accordingly.

It was anticipated that since the students came from schools of two different sorts—Senior Secondary Schools with five year programmes and Junior with three—that the different opportunity ranges presented to the pupils would be reflected in differing patterns of response for each type of school. The data do not strongly support this. Although in certain respects the two Senior Secondary Schools are similar—as in the level of occupational aspiration and the length of TAT protocol—in most other respects they are different. And although the Junior Secondary Schools present a number of similarities in response there is enough variability to allow firstly, for a fairly good prediction of particular school membership on the basis of particular attitudes and evaluations, and secondly to strongly suggest that the curriculum structure of the school is not the major factor influencing the beliefs and aspirations of the students.

What emerged is that the schools, instead of presenting dichotomous responses, according to the nature of the curriculum seem to offer constellations of attitudes which allow one to distinguish them on dimensions other than the structural. On some dimensions, especially those relating to attitudes towards the society and the nature of relationships within it, Arcadia and Groenkloof were to be found at opposite ends of the dimensions, with Waterkloof and Sunnyside somewhere in the middle range. On other dimensions relating to occupation the more extreme position was marked by Sunnyside, the other pole by Waterkloof, and Arcadia and Groenkloof were around the central area. The results of the analysis support the view that schools can be identified in terms of the types of values that are manifest so that they fall into different quadrants when the two major dimensions of attitudes and aspirations are presented graphically.

The influence of the school appears to increase the longer the individual remains within it. The commitment to education is greater the longer the person stays at school, and encourages higher educational aspirations and hopes for careers in the top professions. There is also a greater similarity between the attitudes and values of students in the higher forms to those expressed by the African professional and middle classes as described by Brett (1963) and Sherwood (1958), and to those of university students as found by Bloom (1960), Danziger (1963) and Mann (1962).

One of the most interesting groups is the third form. Attendance figures show that the third form is the major point of departure from school for those pupils who get into the high school system. It is therefore an important decision point in the careers of the African students. There was greater variability amongst the responses of the third year students than amongst the second and fourth years, and on the discriminant analyses, where we used attitudes and aspirations to predict form at school, we were less successful in predicting third forms than predicting second or fourth. There was a pattern of third form responses, but there were also patterns like the second and fourth forms. One is encouraged to speculate that these attitudes may in some way influence the nature of the final decision at this educational choice point. There is greater shift in values, attitudes and aspirations between the third and fourth form than between the second and third, and it may well be that some form of "preparedness" is already occurring in the relatively small number of students who will stay on at school.

As indicated, we expected the influence of the family to be less pronounced than the British and American literature has suggested because of the general depression of class factors in a colour based social system. In addition we thought the school system to be stronger than the family and therefore it would overwhelm it. Essentially these assumptions were supported. The influence of the family is less than that of the school, both in terms of the force of those relationships that are in evidence and in the number of variables that are family related. There were no effects due to overcrowding as such—but then the range of density for the sample was rather narrow. The occupation of the parents is of no particular influence except in a subsample of boys who were incorrectly allocated to form in the discriminant analysis. This technique sorts individuals into groups on the basis of certain variables selected as defining. A number of boys in the second form were allocated to the fourth form because their responses on the critical variables were similar to those of the fourth form boys, and a number of the fourth form boys were assigned to the second form in the analysis. We were interested to see whether there were any characteristics which distinguished these "misassigned" students in terms of their previous experience or school membership. We found the distinction in the fathers' occupations. The boys in the second form who responded like the fourth form boys had fathers who were unskilled workers and those in the fourth form whose responses were like the second form boys came from families where the father was in a more middle class job. It is almost as if the protection afforded some boys by the security of the middle class family allowed them to be more accommodating and less negative in their attitudes to a variety of elements in the society. Other family variables—size and the type of structure—were not important in relation to aspirations or attitudes, and ordinal position was of some minimal influence for the third form students. For these there was a direct relation between their aspirations and the attainments of older brothers, a relation which is reversed for the fourth form students. There are a number of possible explanations for this shift. It is possible that in the lower forms the achievements of older siblings act as a positive reference point, but that once the major decision to remain in education has been made the example of older siblings becomes redundant. Alternatively there is the possibility that older siblings, having been limited in the attainment of higher educational qualifications assist their younger sibs to achieve what they could not. There is some support for this explanation in the discussions with students during which a number mentioned that their school fees were being paid by older working siblings, who in some cases saw in the success of their younger brothers and sisters some satisfaction of their own un-attained ambitions.

Throughout the study there were differences in the responses of the girls and boys. Critical differences seemed to be the fact that occupational roles are closely sex-linked, so that it was necessary to employ a different classification for the aspirations of the boys from that utilized for the girls. Only the professional occupations were shared as aspirations and as expected eventual jobs, and this we divided into two groups—Professional I including law, medicine, and other occupations demanding prolonged training and Professional II which included teaching, nursing and social work. There was a clear tendency for the boys to aspire to occupations in the Professional I category and girls in the Professional II, but their job expectations differed from this. It was clear that the girls actually anticipated that they would work in those fields to which they aspired, while for the boys there was a considerable variation in their expectations about their future job. They did not necessarily expect that their aspirations would be achieved. Translating this into a relative deprivation score it is clear that the score for boys, reflecting a shift from the desired to the expected, is greater than that for the girls.

A number of variables can therefore be seen to influence the aspirations, and indeed the expectations and attitudes of this group of Soweto students, and those with the greatest force are the sex of the individual, the form they have reached at school and the particular school they attend. The power of some schools, in particular Arcadia, is such that the female students attending the school manifest response systems that are different from those of girls at other schools. Using the discriminant analysis technique to assign students we were able to classify correctly at levels well beyond chance our respondents according to sex (being more successful however, with girls than with boys), according to form and according to school. Our success at this reflects the cohesion of the subjects' response patterns. Girls' responses are less variable than those of boys and we were therefore able to correctly assign more girls than boys. The third form pupils show a less coherent pattern of responses than those in forms two and four. Of the schools, Arcadia students show the most coherence in their patterns of responses and the Arcadia students are most often correctly assigned to their school. These results hold for the questionnaire alone and for analyses combining the questionnaire with the TAT; in the TAT analysis alone the polar opposite of Arcadia, namely Groenkloof, is easier to predict than even Arcadia.

The relationship between the sets of structural variables and the students' responses is only part of the picture. What is of greater psychological interest is the actual interrelations of the variables of aspiration, expectations and evaluation. By examining interrelations it is possible to describe a cognitive structure which gives insight into particular ways that the individual may construe his world and locate himself within it. We utilized a technique which allowed us to plot the responses of the subjects in Euclidean space* and this enabled us to look at the clustering of responses for the questionnaire and the TAT independently and for the two combined, and to relate the clusters to particular marker variables (sex, form and school). For the questionnaire alone two main dimensions could account best for the variations that occurred. These were a dimension of political attitudes, marked at one end by a conservative set of responses and the other by a radical (or rejecting) one, and a dimension of aspirations, polarizing high and low aspirations. These dimensions were clear when the sample as a whole was analysed and when separate subgroups were analysed. On the TAT the major dimension was one reflecting interpersonal relations, anchored at one end by hostility and the other by friendly and supportive personal interactions; the second major TAT dimension related to the concept of control. This idea has been discussed previously and refers to the way the individual perceives the control of rewards, the factors which could determine the outcome of ventures and plans. This dimension was marked by the opposition of external and fatalistic control—that is control through others—with internal control, personal striving and social responsibility. The major dimension when the TAT and the questionnaire were combined again reflected the political; it was a combination of radical attitudes combined with cognitive complexity contrasted with polical conservatism and simple cognitive structures. The second dimension characterizing the combined data was one of achievement and striving as opposed to constraint and helplessness.

Within the space defined by these dimensions it is possible to describe

*See Appendixes B and C, pp. 166–193.

three clusters of responses. The first reflects a conservative set of attitudes and evaluations, which while not necessarily accepting the status quo nevertheless does not actually reject the political system, and does endorse the traditional supports of Church and tribe. The job expectations of this group are relatively high as are their aspirations. The second constellation is a radical one, rejecting the political and tribal institutions, and showing doubts about the educational system as a cure-all—whereas the conservative set tends to be optimistic in their assumptions about the power of education to solve personal and social needs. The radical group views personal and family relations positively and in their relations with the formal authorities they are resistant rather than compliant. This constellation of evaluations is associated with high cognitive complexity and with fluent responses on the TAT. The third group of responses is one of constraint and depression. The constraint is seen in the reasons the students give for their support of the tribe—there is no choice—in evaluating the political system and in the reasons for their particular aspirations and expectations. These are generally low, lower than could be realistically anticipated given the level of education that they will have attained, and the reasons given for the choice again indicate a lack of choice, the absence of options, a constraint. They endorse the status quo, generally for reasons of personal identity and support and in their TAT stories produce simple themes marked by high levels of hostility and criminality.

These three response clusters—the accommodated, the radical and the constrained—are not independent of structural variables. The girls are mainly associated with the accommodated group, and the boys with the radical, but these overall associations must be qualified. It is mainly the boys from the fourth form and from Arcadia who are associated with the radical constellation, and there are other school differences which overlay the sex differences. Waterkloof and Groenkloof schools are associated with the depressed, constrained cluster and Sunnyside with the accommodated one.

The constellation of attitudes manifest by the Arcadia fourth form students is particularly interesting. This group has high aspirations and produces pleasantly toned stories with positive, supportive interpersonal relations. They are fluent and complex in their responses and they reject the political and social system. They are aware of the nature of the issues that confront them, concerned with national progress and they understand that political issues demand political solutions. And yet, despite their awareness of the problems and the necessary actions to solve them, the students seem to feel no real competence in actually being able to achieve their aims. There is some helplessness in their responses, and although they are conscious of the notion of resistance it remains at the verbal level rather than being translated into action.

The above cluster of responses is in some contrast to that which is associated with low aspirations. The low aspirers not only tend to a general constraint, but they are also interesting in their perceptions of the social world. The stories they produce in response to the TAT contain few barriers, that is obstacles to the attainment of an end, or a feature of the situation which moves the actors to respond. Where barriers are reported there is little evidence of any strategy for dealing with them; personal relations are avoided or if reported seen as hostile, and the tenor of the responses is that of fatalistic resignation. The impression is of a situation that is barren and helpless, empty of hope and of succour.

These three constellations of attitudes and aspirations which we have defined are in some ways reminiscent of the three groups of clerical workers that Sherwood (1958) was able to distinguish in her study to which we have previously referred. Examining successful and unsuccessful clerks, as rated by their supervisors, she found that the high rated group were older and less urbanized than the others and had lower educational achievements. The group set high value on adjustment and control and accommodation to the work situation. They were earnest and placed heavy emphasis on self-development; they were highly involved with their work and had an almost exclusively positive image of the clerk. Sherwood suggests that these people seem to use a great deal of their energy in controlling and repressing their impulses in order to conform to their ego-ideal, and in terms of personality this group is the most passive, dependent and depressed, with poor self-esteem, marked anxiety, overt compliance but resentment and hostility. The low-rated group displayed generally an apathetic and uninvolved attitude to their work and stressed the formal aspects thereof. They did not see a need for accommodating attitudes and did not see work as a means of personal growth. They were the least passive and dependent and showed less anxiety than the other group. In addition they expressed hostility and were generally non-compliant.

The intermediate group Sherwood characterizes as reality-oriented and more free and potentially mature in their social relations. They saw the jobs in positive and creative terms but with a dominant emphasis on security. They showed a greater verbal recognition of the conflicts inherent in their jobs, but at the same time enjoyed the work, expressed less low self-esteem and faced up to their own ambivalences. The parallels with the constrained, the radical and the accommodated clusters of high school student responses are clear.

We thought that the perception that obstacles to success and achievement lie within the social system would encourage a number of responses directed to removing these, and not to attempts to locate the blame within the individual. In our exposition about the relation of the educational services to the wider social system, we suggested that accepting that the social structure was the major barrier to attaining those goals that school encouraged, would lead to an externally located system of perceived responsibility, and to activity directed to group rather than personal goals. That is, that the individual would perceive that the individual's achievement and mobility could not be based on his own efforts alone. His definition would be a group definition and his movement limited by the movement of the group. Although there is no direct confirmation of this, there is some support, but the mediating variable is not high aspirations. However, where the individual recognizes that obstacles to his advance are external to himself, that is are economic or legal and not directly in his control, he tends towards a system of moral judgement based on social expediency. Further, those who recognize that the barriers to their advance are socially determined reject the social system. Those who report more social-legal barriers are politically more dissatisfied on the questionnaire measures and report more confrontations with power and authority in their TAT stories. This high-dissatisfaction-externalized barrier combination relates to the centrality of moral judgement to the responses. The social good is seen as the basis for such judgements. It also relates to a greater acceptance of the end justifying the means, of social needs legitimating illegitimate behaviour.

This study used the TAT to investigate the individual's perception of his environment, particularly in relation to its characterization as supportive or hostile and in order to see where in the environment the individual saw the major obstacles to particular ends. It can generally be claimed that this method was successful in that coherent response

systems were produced and that these were sensibly related psychologically to the attitudes and aspirations that were reported on the
questionnaires. The TAT not only fills out the skeleton of attitudes and
values that the questionnaire was able to structure, it also has permitted the construction of a pattern of interrelationships between the
nature of the environment, the most likely type of action to be undertaken and the likelihood of success. It has presented particular perspectives concerning the interrelationships between people in a variety of
contexts and tied together the threads linking the individual's personal
aspirations and the values and attitudes that these engender within a
particular social context.

There is a study rather comparable to this one, undertaken in East
Africa by the Ainsworths (1962). Using very similar instruments
(questionnaire and TAT) on populations of similar ages and circumstances (their study was done prior to independence) the two studies
have produced rather similar results. Both found remarkably little
aggression in the TAT protocols, a strong emphasis on community
service and "unrealistically" (to quote Ainsworth) high hopes for
future training. The patterns of responses which the East African study
found characteristic of the more acculturated high school pupils, are
similar to the constellations that we found for the fourth formers and
for Arcadia. The association of more interpersonal interactions in the
TAT stories, better handling of aggression, greater verbal fluency,
more political awareness and dissatisfaction, more expressed frustrations is a familiar constellation in our study. The Ainsworths attributed
the identical constellation to high levels of acculturation, where we
have assumed a school effect. However, they characterized the acculturation level of an entire school and the effect they observe is,
therefore, like ours, a school effect. We cannot on the basis of our data,
compare the Soweto schools in levels of acculturation: all are urban
schools, staffed by trained teachers, serving an urban community. The
East African schools varied in closeness of contact to city life: the
differences of output may therefore indeed be due to differences
in input.

Where variations in results exist these can be ascribed to the fact that
at the time of the study both Uganda and neighbouring Kenya were
coming to the end of their colonial history. The young Africans at
school did not necessarily see their future lives in terms of continued
subordination to White rulers, and could identify easily with the

leaders of the new order and culture. The contrast between this and the position of the young African in South Africa is clear. He is not part of a colonial empire giving independence to subject peoples; he has no evidence to suggest that his subordination is about to end. And each time the changes in neighbouring African states give him hope, his immediate experience is of increasing subjection to legal restraints.

The similarities between the results of the two studies and the attribution of this to particular conditions of social mobility is strengthened by the study of LeVine (1966) which was described in a previous chapter. In explaining the differential achievements of the Ibo in Nigeria LeVine emphasizes the role of assessment of the opportunity structure of the society and the information that is received about this from the agents of socialization. The growing child perceives the chances of rising socially and the behaviours that are thought to lead to success in the system. His perception is influenced by the information that he receives from family, from representatives of institutions, from the media and from school. LeVine writes:

> If his image is that the chances of his rising socially are good and that individual competition with a standard of excellence is what leads to success, then he will manifest the achievement motive. If his image is that he has little chance of rising socially and that obedience and social compliance lead to what success is available, then he will not manifest the achievement motive. Intermediate examples will vary between these extremes, according to the amount of the perceived opportunities and the strength of the perception of achievement behaviour as instrumental in success. Thus the frequency of n-Achievement in a population will co-vary with the strength of the incentives for achievement behaviour perceived by the men as being offered by the status mobility system during the years in which they were growing up. (LeVine, 1966)

This thesis of LeVine, therefore, places emphasis on the transmission of information, and suggests that neither parental values nor child rearing techniques are involved as determining factors in the production of n-achievement. The constellation of attitudes that he has shown in his Ibo sample is very similar to that of Ainsworth's acculturated sample and our high aspiring-rebellious subjects. High expressed n-ach, low frequency of obedience and social compliance and of authoritarianism, a high value on self-improvement and national progress, and on community benefit were characteristic of the Ibo. It is worth noting that LeVine used a measure of acculturation to see whether this influenced the results, taking as his measure parent's education. His findings confirm ours that this is not a significant predictor of responses.

The three studies therefore suggest that differential mobility within a sample in the peculiar conditions of social change in Africa relates very closely to a process of socialization which presents to the child differential views about the opportunity structure of the society and of his ability to take advantage of it. This implies that there are two steps to the process, although the ordering may vary. The child must firstly be aware of his own competences, and secondly he must be aware of the method by which these competences are expressed and rewarded. Mobility could be deterred at either point. An accurate perception of the opportunity structure without believing that one possesses the abilities that are rewarded will not encourage high aspirations, and high aspirations, that is a sense of competence, will not be translated from fantasy and wishful thinking into action unless it is clear that the social system gives rewards for the sort of skills one possesses.

These studies are at odds with that of Lystad (1970) comparing stories written by urban Swazi with those of urban Black South Africans in which she suggests that the policy of separation associated with the real proximity of the Blacks to highly organized technologies increase the level of frustration of the South African youth and inhibit a rational response to his social situation. Apart from the difficulties of determining what a rational response would be, Lystad seems to stress only one mode of response where we have found several. The one she emphasizes is that of intrapunitiveness, low overt hostility to the White group, a "nostalgia for a more traditional way of life" (p. 1396) and no indication how one might utilize education, for example, in order to attain one's goals.

Two South African studies which we have previously mentioned lend support to the belief that the attitude constellations we found are a concomitant of mobility. Both these examined the values and attitudes of middle class Africans, individuals who have already achieved status and respect within the community. The study by Brett (1963) investigated the social, racial and political attitudes of African professional men, teachers, clerks, clerics, students and high school students, a small sample however, of only 150. Sherwood (1958) examined a sample of clerks and lower professional workers (teachers, nurses, social workers). Sherwood found a high motivational value placed on community service, and only secondary place given to self-oriented satisfactions.

Of the self-oriented values self-development and intrinsic job interest were of major importance. The Brett study did not find as much orientation towards community service as have the other studies but then he asked about the things the sample wanted for their children and not only for themselves, which is likely to considerably alter the responses. He did, however, find evidence of legal and political awareness, and high dissatisfaction with the status quo (including tribe and Church).

> The material suggests that the nature of their experience had led in some to submission . . . but more often to the acceptance of the validity of political action of an extreme and uncompromising kind. (p. 77)

He found, however, very low levels of expressed hostility and aggression, as did Ainsworth and Ainsworth, and this study too. A study by Shalit (1970) raises the question of whether the high levels of real violence might depress the production of fantasy hostility. He found levels of hostility on TAT responses of new recruits to the Israeli army much reduced after the Six Day War. Given the crime statistics for the Soweto area, and the enormous emphasis given to violence in the reports of life in the township which the matriculating students wrote, it may be suggested that the reality of aggression diminishes the production thereof in TAT protocols.

Brett found that the better educated middle class men manifested higher degrees of self-confidence and a greater ability to take effective action, and on the whole his sample indicated rather similar trends on the projective tests that he used as did ours on the African TAT:* environmental hostility, thwarted action, the individual unable to freely control his fate. These similarities within the samples of South African studies suggest consistencies which mark them off from studies in ex-colonial Africa.

The middle class and potential middle class are different from their fellow Africans of lower status. The high emphasis on service which has also been documented by Gillespie and Allport (1955), Danziger (1963), Bloom (1960) and Mann (1962) on student samples, was not found in the De Ridder (1961) study of bus drivers and bus company employees. He reports low levels of aggressive control, more volatile behaviour with low levels of frustration tolerance, selfish and ma-

---

*He used a version of the van Lennup four picture test, and his own adaptation of the TAT.

terialistic motivations, moral laxity and id-dominated behaviour. These are not the types of characteristics that have been found in other studies which have focussed more particularly on potential achievers and those who have attained professional or middle class status, both in South Africa and in other African states. It is quite possible that those who are unable to adjust to the demands of urban living and to the rapidity of social change are those who manifest high levels of personality disintegration whereas those who can adapt and cope are the more integrated and achieving.

There is no doubt that adjusting to changing social circumstances is stressful. Erikson's descriptions of the difficulties of the Sioux Indians (Erikson, 1950), Turnbull's of the lonely African (Turnbull, 1962), Ausubel's (1960) study of acculturation stress in Maori adolescents are all evidence of the difficulties that attend this process. Apart from these studies one by Gough (1970) on Aboriginal children shows that low social status and acculturation even where the personality does not manifest stress, do not of themselves bring about high aspirations and a sense of community service. It is not simply social change and the development of national pride that can explain the similarities in the results of LeVine, Ainsworth and others. Nor is it possible to look simply to the fact of education or schooling and assume that its effect is direct. All the studies report differential school effects. For the Ainsworths this is said to be due to the level of acculturation of the school. A study by Armer (1970) suggests that the relation is more complex. Armer examined the relationship of education to modernity and alienation among a sample of young Nigerians. He suggested that there were two possible nexuses—change could be the equivalent of loss, and therefore greater modernity would mean greater alienation; alternatively change could be selective and therefore there would be no frustration, and so no alienation. The evidence was clear that education differentially operated on sets of attitudes so that those with modernistic attitudes and high educational attainment demonstrated low levels of alienation, those with traditional attitudes and high education showed high alienation.

What it is in the "modernistic" attitudes that is critical these studies do not illuminate. It certainly is not that a dominant cultural group— the British colonial powers, White South Africa or Western technological society—exerts an attraction as a reference group, and that with this certain model to guide them the African middle and aspirant middle classes internalize their values. Research that has compared the attitudes of White and Black South African students have found fairly consistent differences between the groups. Africans and Indians were found to be more concerned with political and social issues and White students with private; non-Whites attributed negative features to the "White" civilization while the Whites attributed positive (Danziger, 1958). Even if one were to assume that the rather vaguer reference group is some continental European stance on these issues there is little supporting evidence. Gillespie and Allport show that there are differences between the newer and older nationalisms in relation to concepts of social utility; in her study of English school leavers Veness (1962) found no evidence of the altruism nor of the emphasis on education that the African studies show. There is therefore no support for the view that change is shifted from tribal or traditional values to attitudes and values in line with those of the dominant culture. Change is not a simple step from an experienced point to an observed point; it is a process of adaptation, of creation, of uncertainty and doubt.

Given the specificities of societal forces it is particularly striking that our study of Soweto and the other studies in Africa have found so many common elements.

This uniformity is even more striking in the light of a study by Nutall (1964) of the correlates of high need achievement of Negroes in the U.S.A. Men living in the northern states present quite different clusters of attitudes from those living in the southern states. In the north, clustering with high need achievement were less religiosity, greater militancy and higher educational levels, and a greater sense of being victimized than were found associated with low need achievement. In the south the cluster was of repressed hostility, denial of victimization, more religiosity and higher incomes.

In our study we found both these constellations, and suggest that it is the former that leads to middle class achievement. In this we are supported by evidence from the rest of Africa. However, the conditions for the Blacks in South Africa are more similar to the pre-desegregation South than they are to Nigeria or even to colonial Uganda.

This anomaly in the research findings needs to be explained, and it can only be accounted for if the context within which aspirations and attitudes develop are not only "taken into account", but fully integrated into the explanation. The transition from cognitive representation to action, from attitude to behaviour; from that which we

derive from our measures of aspirations, from our scales, TAT protocols, future autobiographies, informs us only in part of the relation
between the individual, the group and the society at large. As Fishbein
has so convincingly demonstrated, the translation of a belief into an
intention, and an intention into an action depends on more than
simply the assessment of an evaluative response (1975). It depends also
on one's knowing the attitude to the relevant behaviour and the social
or normative factors involved. This factor deals with the influence of
the social environment on behaviour, and without taking it into any
equation the prediction of behaviour or of behavioural intentions is
limited in its success. But equally, the normative variables may help
shape the intentions and the beliefs, and thus the social situation is
doubly implicated in the translation of the cognitive to the active. That
this perspective is essential in understanding the development of the
construction of the social world has been argued elsewhere (Geber,
1977; Geber and Webley, 1980). It is crucial here where it must be
stressed that the type of behaviours by which a particular need, value
or aspiration may be attained will be context dependent. It may well
be that in the northern states the most appropriate behaviours would
be aggressive and assertive, in the southern states they would be accommodated and compliant. To see only one set of behaviours as
adaptive in the complex reality of social pressures is to indulge in
wishful oversimplification. It might be easier for psychological research, but it would be a gross misrepresentation of reality.

We have suggested in the research findings that one set of attitudes
and intentions is more likely to lead to success than another: this
assumption has some support in the literature. We cannot however
rule out the possibility that the accommodating acceptance of the
status quo may also be a viable means of adjusting to change and
achieving success.

# 10

# The Dialectics of Development

The technique used to gather data in this study affords no before-and-after design with intervening manipulations. This limits the type of relationships that can be deduced from the data. Furthermore we have used a cross-sectional rather than a longitudinal design, with the result that the changing patterns that have been observed cannot be linked directly to changes in the life circumstances of particular individuals but only to rather broad variations in the conditions of the critical groups.

If we want to make generalizations beyond the present study it is necessary to put the results into a process-oriented perspective. What do we think can account for the interactions that we have discerned, and can we uncover processes from the data collected in one particular historical time, and in one particular social context that will enable us to account for more than the single event? It has been argued (Holmes, 1970) that often social psychological survey research has been too concerned with the immediate, and unready to integrate the fact with the theoretical system that is necessary to give it meaning. And if one argues, as has been argued here, that in order to understand the psychology of cognitions and behaviour one must be prepared to relate these to the wider social and historical context within which they occur, then the onus of turning the unique into the generalizable finding becomes even more necessary. Just as a personality theory has to be able to account for the ideographic while establishing the nomothetic, so social psychological theory has to be able to account for the specificity of experience within one context, while allowing for comparisons and theory which apply to the full range of actual or possible contexts.

Holmes has argued that frequently "the knowledge that we gather is but a record of the passing moment and so cannot readily translate itself into those generalizations that alone could allow us to predict". He continues that much of the information we collect is "transient", and not easily "subsumed" into the abstract and the timeless. Holmes offers one solution to the dilemma he poses—the use of cross-cultural research to sift "news" from "science" and to enforce the testing of laws and measures in new venues. A second solution, not offered in his paper is that which is being proposed now, namely to move from the transient data to the processes which underlie them, from the specific to the general. One should not be content simply to describe, important though it might be: it is necessary to attempt an explanation of what is observed. A criticism of the so-called ethological method raises similar anxieties. Despite the noble aim of detailed unbiased observation which guides much behavioural description, it is clear that the datum alone is of little meaning or moment. And it is equally clear that observation without direction by theory or expectation is not feasible. In a major longitudinal study of boys at schools in London at age 13 and then later as young adults, Himmelweit (1967, 1969) examined the development and stability of their attitudes, values, aspirations and self-concepts. She explains the processes of influence and change, particularly at school, by reference to a model of the school as a socializing agent. The major proposition is that the extent of the influence of the school will vary according to the particular rewards it is able to dispense. We have already discussed this aspect as the "strength" of the system. The model shows the child progressing through the school, directly influenced by parents and school, indirectly by the society which governs the goals and objectives of both. Himmelweit examines the school's influence by looking both at "inputs", the characteristics the child brings to the school, and at outputs, that is the attitudes, aspirations, skills and values developed within the system. Quite clearly the influence of the school operates within the context of the social structure as a whole. The society gives to the school sets of objectives, and the structure within which to achieve these. The objectives can be set by a variety of agents. The universities may make demands on the schools in relation to the level of achievement required prior to acceptance into the tertiary sector of education. Industry can demand certain types of skill, certain minimal levels of literacy and numeracy, or routine time keeping habits. The schools output is there to serve not only the cultural needs of the individual but also more than this the output is there to serve the general economic needs of the community. These demands vary over time, and the relationship between schools and the society as a whole is not static. The wider society exerts its influence on the student as he moves through the school system not only through the mediation of the school, but also through the mediation of other agencies which in turn feed back into the school system. The mass media, the family, the peer group directly impinge on the developing person, but also indirectly present to him the "zeitgeist".

One of the interesting aspects of the South African study is that the socializing agents and the wider society itself make competing demands on the Black high school pupil. The competitive school system encourages the adoption of achievement oriented behaviours, of skills and knowledge appropriate to a Western technological society. The wider society, implicitly in segregation and explicitly in the political ideology, insists on the recognition of separateness and inequality. This separation implies not only a variation in rights, but also that there are differences in the success of the adoption of those things that the school system is teaching. The culture of the school is assumed by the Whites to be part of their heritage, indigenous to them and alien to the Blacks.

The schools can dispense rewards in terms of skills, knowledge and the qualifications necessary for advance. The society in its turn can bar the use of these through legislative restrictions on occupations and control over the intake of schools and universities. The strength of the school system in this situation cannot be gauged simply by the success with which it eases the individual from, for example the working class to the middle class. The outputs of the system are more tenuous and less certain. Schooling may be a necessary condition for success, but in the South African context it is even more than in other societies not a sufficient condition.

This does not however, obviate all influence of the school. Although this study indicates that for most of the sample an awareness exists of the limitations imposed by the outside world, and that for many this constrains the extent of their adoption of the values of education, it is equally apparent that the school still exerts an influence. This can be seen in the fact that the pupils place high value on those skills and conditions that are consequent upon the resources that the schools bestow. Advancement and achievement, status and prestige, technological and social progress, job satisfaction are all spontaneously produced values of the African high school student. The longer the pupils remain in the school the more the experience of school gains value. The *process* of education and of learning gains strength as opposed to the outcomes of the process. The educational process achieves a functional autonomy, becoming rewarding in itself and not simply as an instrument for the acquisition of other ends. Both these sets of evidence indicate that the schools' values are recognized, and to varying degrees accepted. The school, by virtue of the rewards it can dispense develops in its pupils those behaviours and values that it encompasses.

What the model as it stands cannot illuminate is the observed difference between the schools in the range and power of impact. The idea of differences in strength through differences in the rewards dispensed may well account for the secondary-modern/grammar school variations observed by Himmelweit. This study has produced few differences based solely on variations in the formal structure and curriculum of the school. The most tempting condition for explaining the results observed in this study is the coherence of the value system within the school to which the child is exposed. Certainly the results indicate that at the extremes of submission and radical rejection, represented by Groenkloof and Arcadia, are consistent systems of attitude and value which may simplify the learning process for the pupils. However, such an explanation would be circular: simply because we observe coherence in the responses of the pupils attending the same school we cannot assume that this is because there is a consistent value system at the school. Coherence cannot be both a dependent and independent variable. Unfortunately we have no measures of the variations between schools other than those reflected in the responses of the pupils.

Unlike English schools the schools in this study are not selective. They do not take in, according to curriculum, children of restricted ability ranges or social class composition. All of the schools are "élitist" in the sense that the African high school pupil is a voluntary scholar and a statistical minority, especially after form one. This means, more perhaps even than was found in the Himmelweit study, that we have to look to what happens within the school for an explanation of differences between individuals at different schools. We cannot rely on "input" variables for the explanation.

A paper by Hemming (1966) quoted by Sealy and Himmelweit (1966) summarized four types of educational model which might be of help in understanding the results of this study. There is firstly the "potentiality-opportunity model", which sees education as a process of matching the child's potential with social opportunities. The child is static, the school a mediator, an institutional "matchmaker". It is interesting to note that this model is reflected in the Bantu Education Act, which structures African education. The act does see the school as preparing the young African for his predetermined position in society, and amongst other things recommends the teaching of gardening and carpentry as suitable skills. The second model is a stimulus-response model. The child is again passive, and is acted upon by the school. Variations in the "input" of the school would be of no moment, and the "output" should vary only according to effectiveness of the school in inducing appropriate responses. Although tempting in its simplicity and in its immediate referability to an established psychological process the model fits the facts neither of the Himmelweit nor of this study.

In the third model the child is seen as more active. He is seen as a system of needs and potential which is developed as a personality structure through the agency of home, school and peer group. The influence system is wide and relatively undefined, the points of contact undifferentiated. Although this is possibly the most widespread model (see for example Andersson, 1969) its lack of specificity diminishes its value. The fourth model is a transactional one, as opposed to the inter-active bias of model three. Through his interactions with society the child develops confidence in dealing with it: the school experiences will provide a sense of acceptance, "a set of values and a positive view of himself" (Sealy and Himmelweit, 1966, p. 107) which will feedback into the way the child handles and responds to reality.

This fourth model is the one which can indicate the points at which the observed differences in the schools of this study are located. Beyond the detail of the Arcadia responses lies a sense of confidence, competence and worth which is not reflected in the responses of the other schools. Seeing people as supportive, not avoiding the real obstacles that society presents, presenting a sense of readiness to accept challenge Arcadia pupils give a different interpretation of the social world from pupils at other schools. It would need more specifically directed research than is available from this study to test the validity of this "self-image" mediated assumption. However the study by Himmelweit cited above and one by Coopersmith (1967) suggest that high self-esteem is related to reports of good supportive family relationships which lend the belief some support. The transactional nature of the fourth model implies that the consequences of low self-confidence or of low acceptability within the school would be widespread. It is not simply that a learned response or attitude is absent, but rather that all interactions are influenced by this. Reality is not only differently experienced but is actually different. It becomes extremely important therefore to begin to discover what Sealy and Himmelweit (1966) call "points of vulnerability" in the interactional system, points which can be critical in the development of esteem and confidence.

For our purposes the main "point of vulnerability" is the fact that the world outside the school is not only likely to be frustrating to the African child, but is also likely to reduce his sense of his own worth. It might be that the first step in the progress of an oppressed group is the development of pride in those features which distinguish it from others and have been the focus for its devaluation, the "politicization of ethnicity" (Kilson, 1970). The majority of the pupils in this study did not yet manifest this pride in their national culture. However, what this particular identification of a "point of vulnerability" does suggest is that any system that can compensate for, or counteract the impact of the wider society must in itself be extraordinarily strong.

The stress on the nature of the system external to the individual as a source of disruption does not preclude vulnerability actually being located within the individual. The fourth model, after all, is a trans-actional one, and this demands that all the elements in the system be taken into account, those within the individual and those in the environment. We have previously interpreted the notion of fit to apply to the relationships between various types of social experiences—the family and the school, the school and level of acculturation, the school and the wider society. It is equally proper to look for fit within the cognitive and personal spheres of functioning of the individual and the school.

The importance of the role of language in the social development and intellectual functioning of the individual has been described by Bernstein (1971). He sees language as a way of developing a social identity, as the basis for communicating one's uniqueness, for developing sophisticated and articulated concepts and behaviour in interpersonal interaction, for developing subtleties of meaning and intent. Restricted, predictable language usage limits these developments. This has consequences for the child in interpersonal relationships, in receiving communications at school, in being able to communicate adequately the subtleness and complexity of his own thinking. What is implicated in the development of linguistic codes is a particular type of socialization process as well as demands on the child to express his experience explicitly in a verbally differentiated way.

Bernstein and Henderson (1969) have examined patterns of mother-child interaction in the training of specific skills in order to discover some of the sources of variability in the development of linguistic codes. They suggest that mothers use particular control techniques in inter-action with their children and place emphasis on verbal interaction differentially according to social class. Geber (1977) has suggested that the differential responses may well be mediated not simply by class but more particularly by stress, which might (but need not) be class related. However, whatever actually mediates the interaction and its influence on cognitive functioning, it seems that this control process may be implicated in the responses of African children.

Two aspects of socialization which are important in test-related be-haviour of children in Kenya are suggested by Harkness and Super (1977). Both are to do with verbal productivity. The first is that, in comparison with American mothers, the Kenyan mothers (Kipsigis) offer very little practice in the kinds of talking that are required by psychological tests in their verbal interactions with their children. The second refers to a profound change in the relationship between the child and important adult figures which occurs during the second and third years of life. This change produces a social distance between the child and the adult. Harkness and Super found that the majority of the Kipsigi mothers assumed that children learn language from other children, and the most mentioned language teaching technique was giving commands; only $40\%$ of the mothers reported that they taught their children the names of things. In their analysis of actual speech, Harkness and Super report that imperatives were the most common form of utterance, and these, of course, demand a response in action, not in language. In fact, the emphasis in language is on comprehension, not production, and the total amount of speech from the adults to the children was remarkably small in comparison with American samples. In addition, the verbal interaction between the Kipsigi mothers and children became more directive and more negative as the children grew older, and were pushed from being the favoured youngest child by the birth of a new baby. These trends point to an important fact in the socialization of the behaviour of the Kipsigi child, namely a silence in the presence of older or higher status people. This, the authors maintain, is one of the reasons why researchers in Africa have often found it difficult to test the African child.

We are not assuming that the students in our sample were like the

Kipsigi child. However, there are some pieces of evidence which suggest that the language learning in the home, which may or may not facilitate the child's adjustment to school, might not be too different from that which Harkness and Super describe. Firstly, there is the prolonged absence of the parents from the home during the day and the reliance on children to look after the pre-schoolers. Second there is frequent reference to the despotic behaviour of parents and their rule by decree. Finally there is the research by Albino and Thompson (1956) which indicates that at least amongst the Zulu there is to be found sudden weaning and the distancing of the child from adults, similar to that reported for the Kipsigis.

It is possible to take this argument further. Cognitive activity, especially of the sort encouraged by the schools, depends on the ability to formalize thinking, to work with impersonally transmitted information. Goody (1977) has suggested that one of the consequences of literacy is the externalization of knowledge, rendering it timeless. This process of "distancing" is used by Sigel and Cocking (1977) in their description of the interactive base of representational thinking. They make use of three concepts—distancing, discrepancy and dialectics. Distancing behaviours can arise from social, physical or verbal events, and have the characteristic of activating a separation between the individual and the immediate present, thereby encouraging representational thought. The kinds of distancing behaviours employed will vary according to social and cultural characteristics, situational factors and the idiosyncratic characteristics of the participants in the interaction. The important thing about distancing behaviours is that they create discrepancy and this mismatch propels the organism to change. This is not simply another tension reduction model but "rather an action model in which certainty or a reduction of ambiguity is a key construct" (p. 216). The outcome of the solution of the mismatch is a new organization of behaviour, not only in quantity but also in quality. The resolutions can involve at least three strategies—assessing alternatives, anticipating the future or reconstructing the past. Each of these discrepancies Sigel and Cocking conceptualize within a system of dialectics. Three laws of dialectics are utilized. The first is that of unity and the struggle of opposites, which states that forces or categories that are mutually exclusive presuppose each other. The second is the transformation of quantity to quality, for instance the change from one level of cognitive stage structure to another, or to take a more frivolous example, the transformation from simply losing hair to being bald. The third law is the negation of the negation, where the old is replaced by the new, and that in turn by another new. In other words development is seen as never ending, one is dealing with a system which is ongoing. The model emphasizes the interaction between the individual and the external world which influences both the creation of cognitive conflicts through the provision of discrepant information, and the particular strategies available for conflict resolution. It also allows for factors inside the individual to influence his responses to the external events.

This model of Sigel and Cocking allows one to suggest the following: the outside world, both directly through the teaching strategies of others (which might encourage distancing) or in a manner mediated by cultural artifacts—writing, films—varies in the extent to which it encourages the individual to externalize and reflect upon events. To the extent that cognitions can be externalized so can they be evaluated. The process of separation of self from the products of thought also allows one to operate directly upon those thoughts. Popper (1976) refers to the distinction between statements in themselves and subjective thought processes and implies that it is only the former that can stand in logical relation to each other, and therefore be dealt with in contradiction to those of others. Thought processes, unexternalized, cannot be contradicted by another, or by one's own thought processes at another time. If this holds, then it would imply that factors which encourage the externalization of thought would be implicated in the process of cognitive growth.

The parallel with Bernstein, with Sigel and Cocking and with Goody is clear. Cognitive development and the processes of externalizing thought and making it independent of time and place are closely related. Experiences which work only on the implicit without making it explicit—tradition, restricted language code, ritual—do not necessarily encourage development. It may well be that to understand the differential influence of particular socializing agencies one has to be alert to those factors internal to the individual which might facilitate receptivity (intelligence, the nature of schema, level of maturity) and also the availability in the outside world of appropriate strategies for encouraging the externalization of thought.

One problem must be considered. The fact that thought can be made objective, that is made the subject of thought itself, does not say anything about the particular contents of thought. This point is discussed at length by Geber and Webley (1980). The gist of the argument is this: the individual has available to him an abundance of problems, issues, inputs. Each of these potentially can become not only thought, but also a "statement". There is nothing in the concept of distancing, or of development, which a priori predicates the phenomenon to which attention will be paid. It cannot be assumed that just because the potential for objective thought or logical analysis exists in the individual, that each and every issue will be dealt with in this way. Wason (1977), in a critique of Piaget's notion that formal operational thinking transcends content, has shown that thought is significantly influenced by content. Whether a problem is presented "abstractly" or in the form of concrete content determines the ease of solution. Therefore, although the environment through particular distancing behaviours facilitates the creation and solution of discrepancy, one is still left with the problem of accounting for the particular issue selected.

What might happen is not simply that particular socializing experiences promote critical thinking, but that they also legitimize the content of that thought. They may make it proper to call into question something which has previously been taken for granted. The second part of the Sigel and Cocking model must also be taken into consideration, namely the nature of the discrepancy created and the nature of the resolutions possible. It may well be that in order to understand the processes implicit in their model one has to adopt a specifically social psychological approach, and emphasize the nature of the salient issues in each context. One school may legitimate personal concerns, and through the processes of questioning inherent in distancing strategies, create discrepancy in schema related to this; another may legitimate questions about the society. Alternatively, the differences could be explained in terms of the resolutions proffered. The discrepancies could be of a general nature but one solution could be found in the reconstructing of the past (affirmation of the tribal tradition) the other in anticipating the future (nationalism and radicalism). The model allows for fluency and complexity to be associated with particular attitude constellation. Affirmation of the traditional, or unquestioned compliance discourages distancing. No discrepancies will be discovered, and simple cognitive structures will be retained.

The data of this study have indicated clearly that the linguistic skill of the subjects (as measured by fluency) and also their levels of cognitive differentiation and complexity are closely associated with the nature of the attitudinal and evaluative structures that are to be found. Those who are fluent and complex tend to reflect more questioning and radical responses than those who are cognitively less differentiated. This is interesting, because the testing was carried out in a language which was not that of initial socialization, which would normally be one of the Bantu languages. It may therefore be that the elaborateness of the particular code learned, or the development of the linguistic tools necessary for translating thoughts into statements, transcends the specificity of a particular experience.

The relationship between complexity, distancing and cognitive development is interesting in the light of the study's finding concerning aspects of moral judgement. The projective test responses showed a clustering of social comment, of the idea of legitimacy and of moral evaluations. Quite fortuitously the cards extracted from the sample spontaneous references to ideas of right and wrong, justice and retribution and legitimacy and the social good. These responses could be seen to conform to the two stages of morality which Piaget (1932) defined, and two patterns emerged. The pupils at Sunnyside presented what is broadly a picture of heteronomous morality. Moral authority is divine or supernatural. Wrong is absolute and unrelated to intentions. Authority is powerful and demands submission. The pupils at Arcadia, with their impression of competence and confidence present a picture of autonomous morality. So do fourth form students at Waterkloof. Morality is located in the social good. Wrong is not absolute—social benefit can legitimize "wrong" behaviour. Morality resides, not in the divine or in authority but in the social group. Authority can be challenged, and moral systems like all else are seen to be subject to scrutiny.

Since there is nothing in the input to the schools that can explain this divergence of moral evaluative systems, it must be due to the experiences of the student at the school. The developing individual restructures his experience and adjusts his assumptions in line with his experience through interaction with the environment. For this to occur the individual must be open to experiences and prepared to meet those which challenge his current cognitive structures. Sealy and Himmelweit (1966) cite two points of vulnerability that may mitigate against this "lack of confidence to explore the world" and "lack of external direction . . . leading to inappropriate exploration". If the school, or parents, or peers cannot help to build up self-confidence against the current of denigration by the wider society then there will be restricted exploration. Without guidance the areas of exploration may be inappropriate.

The moral evaluations that are made, and the conditions that encourage their development may relate to the way the individual perceives the power relations in the social system, and to the causal concepts that he employs. If actions are determined by non-personal forces, if the individual cannot control his own acts, if the outcomes of actions are controlled by others or by the supernatural then it is surely beyond the power of any person to alter the social order, and the moral order, of the world. Both would be inviolate.

The TAT responses of the students contain a preponderance of unresolved or unsuccessful story endings. The less able the individual is to maintain control of events the more likely it is that disaster will occur. Fate, chance, the elements, other people—none of these are necessarily benign. The only area where the individual was perceived as exercising any control was in the limited one of work. The individual is not the centre of power controlling his own destiny. Most often he is seen as helpless, isolated and controlled. It is not surprising, that given their causal view and the characteristics they attribute to the individual that most students were passive and perceived themselves to be impotent. They may not like their world but they do not see themselves as able to change it.

The origin of this causal system is not clearly established, though it is possible to speculate about it. The power of the central authority is so great that the causal system may well reflect an accurate assessment of reality. The individual is subjected to control over so many areas of his life and behaviour that a sense of powerlessness is likely to permeate all of it. In addition the cosmology of the tribal tradition, which Jahoda (1970) has shown continues to operate in West Africa in discrete areas of cognitive functioning, stresses the magical and the animistic. Scientific simplicity does not foster a concept of chance or of personal efficacy without the intervention of some supernatural aid. It is worth stressing again that this sense of incapacity does not permeate all the sample equally. Arcadia pupils make more attempts to control the environment than the others, but although they are no more successful, they appear less overwhelmed by it. They are also the least accommodated and the most rebellious.

There is one finding that arose out of a subsidiary analysis of the data which is interesting. Taking in the first instance job aspirations, and in the second political dissatisfaction, regression analyses were performed to establish for the sample of boys how much of the variance in these measures could be accounted for by particular dimensions. It was found that the best predictors of job aspirations were job expectation, and fluency as measured on the TAT, and for political dissatisfaction the best predictors were cognitive complexity and the evaluative and attitudinal variables. Aspirations do not predict dissatisfactions, we do not seem to have an example of the operation of the frustration-aggression thesis to account for political discontent. We do have a network of values and social judgements that is coherent, and related to the individual's cognitive style.

There may be more than simply a cognitive basis for the variations that were perceived, and more than an intellectual basis for the influence of the school on the sense of competence of the student. Competence implies more than the intellectual—it involves in a very real sense the idea of ego strength. It is clear that the schools differed in ways other than the content of the moral systems and assumptions about causality. The flatness of the emotional tone of the Sunnyside stories and the gloom of the Groenkloof, contrast with the greater gentleness of the Arcadia protocols. The avoided emotional commitment of the junior high schools related to the avoidance of representation of actual interactions between the characters of the stories. They present people as isolated or unrelated to each other; the absence of obstacles in many of the stories indicates an avoidance of social situations which may threaten or overwhelm them. The general impression is of people defending against uncertainty and anxiety. It might be that intellectual achievement provides the fodder for an increased sense of personal worth and competence, rather as learning a new skill may. For example, Clifford and Clifford (1967) examined the self-concepts of a group of adolescent boys before and after an Outward Bound School course. These courses are intended to build physical stamina and extend the individual to the limits of his strength and endurance. The ideal self-image of the subjects showed no change from before the training to after, but the real self was viewed much more positively. What is more, the changes in self-image were general, rather than specific. In a similar way, a sense of intellectual worth may effect a change in the way one views oneself in other spheres as well. It is also possible that particular distancing procedures encourages one to examine in a more dispassionate manner one's relations to the world outside. Whether the effects are long lasting, this study cannot say. It is quite possible that when the students leave their schools, and are thrust entirely into the strong system outside it, that the benefits and advantages that particular school experiences bestow may dissipate. It is likely that once out of school and faced with the immediate need to cope with the facts of the South African scene new interpretations will have to be made, and new self-concepts will develop.

One of the consequences of the educational process is that value systems are encouraged that are not easily accommodated outside the educational system itself. The value of achievement, of concern for the process of learning, for the enjoyment of the job itself, care for others, all of these are stimulated in the school. Ideals of progress, development and growth, of self-realization are not unusual in the responses of school pupils. While it is perhaps true that in all societies values taught at school are not necessarily directly relevant to the life that is led outside it, it is not all societies which present such firm, race dominated obstacles to the translation of these school values to adult working life. It is possible that the reaction to this frustration will be rejection and aggression, and the whole system of values will be discarded.

It is quite possible that many of the students, out in the world as adults, will find that the benefits in terms of ego-strength that the school gave are corroded by the problems facing them in the world outside it. The symptoms of the lack of ego-integrity—strong latent aggression and insufficient control, high anxiety—that are noted by de Ridder (1961) may have more to do with adult experiences than with those of childhood. Indeed, as Orpen has shown (1976), Black clerks regard extrinsic or context factors as more important in their job than equivalent age and educated White clerks do, and this is not surprising in view of the relative poverty and insecurity of the Black as opposed to the White worker. The importance of actually feeding and sheltering oneself and one's family may well wreak havoc with the ideals and values that are developed in the relatively more sheltered environment of the school. Once development and functioning are conceptualized in terms of the model that Sigel and Cocking suggest, the importance of the continuous nature of experience is emphasized, and changes in both the endogenous and the exogenous systems have to be taken into account. This leads to some interesting speculations in relation to the girls in the sample.

It was not surprising to find strong sex differences in the responses of this sample. On TAT measures (Murstein, 1963), in field dependence (Witkin *et al.*, 1954), in conformity (Crutchfield, 1955) the psychological literature has reported greater conservatism and conformity for girls than boys, a trend towards what has been called the "mediocrity of women" (Heim, 1970). There was no reason to expect the African girls to be excepted from this trend. However, the model of development that we have presented demands that we take account of events over a longer time scale than is often found, and that we consider the socialization of the present generation to be determined not only by current concerns, but also in response to the past. It is as socializers of the next generation that these young girls will have a great influence on the nature of the African population in towns, and it is in this role, as well as in others, that they may make a major impact on society.

In the lower classes at high school there are as many girls as boys. They are not a first generation of educated women (although in some cases this may be so). As the general level of educational expectation rises, as the demand for education becomes more widespread so more girls are going to absorb the ethos of family life and child rearing common in the world opened to them by learning. Not only the expectations and aspirations, but also the behaviours necessary for success are going to be made available to the next generations of young Africans. How these are accommodated, how far the social system will bend to meet the needs and aspirations of these young people may be a critical feature of the social structure.

Where there have been no examples of success, where the barriers facing the individual are insurmountable, it is likely that there will be no hope, and no disappointment. This is not the experience in South Africa. There are successful Africans to serve as an example to the younger generation in South Africa. More important they have before them the example of independent Africa.

Whether the behaviours we have observed are viewed primarily driven from within (as in the fluency dimension) or from outside, or whether, as we suggest, it is more accurately viewed as a transactional process between the individual and his social world, there are certain general broad implications for society that stem from it.

Most people, it appears, accommodate to the reality of their social world. They may not like what they have, but they adapt and mould their hopes and expectations and moderate their values and attitudes in line with its demands. Whether this is achieved at great cost to the individual is a matter of speculation: it may well be that for some the cost is withdrawal, or ego disintegration.

There are others, however, for whom accommodation is not an easy solution. How they adjust to this we do not know. Whether they rebel, and attempt to change society, or in time adapt to the demands of society will depend on more than an understanding of their own needs and capacities.

# 11

# Evaluations and Events

On June 16, 1976 students from a number of Soweto schools began marching to Sunnyside school and the large stadium at Orlando, a part of Soweto. They were there to protest against the use of Afrikaans as the medium of instruction for some subjects at school. The march was organized and instigated by students at four secondary schools, and prominent amongst these was Arcadia. Although these schools were not yet receiving instruction in Afrikaans they believed that this would soon start. Approximately 15 000 students carrying placards critical of Afrikaans converged on Sunnyside, which had already been boycotting classes for some time. The students were halted by a group of police and after some teargas cannisters had been thrown to disperse the crowd, the police began firing. The exact numbers killed and injured that day is not clear, but in the following few days a running battle between police and students developed throughout Soweto. By June 24, the official statistics reported 140 dead, over 1000 injured and 908 arrested. By the end of June the trouble appeared to be on the decline and at the beginning of July it was announced that headmasters could choose their own medium of instruction (*World* July 2, 1976).

Relative calm prevailed over the township for the first few weeks of July. The police maintained a large presence there, and the calm allowed the schools to reopen on July 22. Attendance was low. Soon afterwards many Black schools throughout South Africa were burnt down. By August 3 Soweto and the surrounding townships were again in uproar, and the unrest spread to the Cape Province where both African and Coloured schools were closed and more people were killed and wounded by the police. On two occasions during the protests the students attempted to organize strike action by the Black workers in the townships. Both were partially successful, with the second strike called to begin on September 13 resulting in a reported half a million Black workers staying away from work.

Protests continued in Soweto and other areas. The boycott of schools remained in force through much of 1977. There were continuing raids by the police on schools as well as the reported arrests of both student and parents in the African areas. 1977 continued with student walk-outs, examination boycotts and arson. Even during the middle of 1978 the attendance at schools in Soweto was sporadic, and there were press reports which claimed that Bantu Education was collapsing.

There are three questions that can be raised about the events in 1976 that have relevance for social psychology; detailed documentation of the rebellion and of the political consequences is not necessary. The first is concerned with the continuity of evaluations and beliefs over time, not by the same individuals, but by people who successively occupy certain social positions. The second has to do with establishing the conditions which can shift discontent to protest and action. The third has to do with the issue of the role of the institution on the development of beliefs of its members in successive generations, and the process by which this occurs.

The statements made by the student protestors, and indeed by a number of parents and teachers interviewed about the student movement, show that much that was a cause for concern in the previous decade remained as potent discontents at the time of the Soweto march. The students disliked Bantu Education, and considered it inferior and a symbol of their position in the wider society. The schools and the school system remained the most immediate and daily reminder to the students of their social and political deprivations. Education remains the main means of social progress. Taking that path reinforces dependence. When the disliked system aligns itself to the disliked language—Afrikaans—the situation becomes explosive.

It was clear from the original study of Soweto students that the language spoken was a highly symbolic issue, and preferred language was one of the measures that distinguished the politically dissatisfied from the conservative students. The radicals preferred to speak English when with their friends, the conservatives their own vernacular. Neither group selected Afrikaans as the language they liked to speak. In all their responses the Afrikaans language was clearly associated with the Afrikaners, with Apartheid and with domination. Many studies of attitudes, as we discussed in Chapter 10, show that Africans differentiate between the English and the Afrikaans-speaking Whites, showing their greatest approbrium to the latter. Although historically the English-speaking South Africans have not indicated a willingness to radically alter the role of the African, and separation and subservience were to be found in both the old British colonies and in the original Union Constitution, nevertheless, the Afrikaner is seen to be the cause and the perpetrator of Black political discrimination. Where competition for jobs existed it was more likely to be between the Afrikaners and the Blacks or Coloureds. The petty officials who implement central government, provincial or even local policies, are more likely to be Afrikaans than English speaking, and certainly the police force is Afrikaans speaking. A study by Melville Edelstein, who was tragically killed in the Soweto rioting, showed that a sample of matriculation students in Soweto would prefer their children to be educated in English than in Afrikaans, and would prefer the vernacular to Afrikaans. He also found, on various measures of social distance that the Afrikaner was the least preferred in every category (Edelstein, 1972). The African student is not well disposed to either the Afrikaans language nor to those who speak it.

Although the issue of language as a medium of instruction was highlighted as a principle reason for the uprising, and was certainly a precipitating factor, it was not the only issue which affected the students. However, it did serve as a focal point for protest, and was sufficiently strong and clear to arouse students to protest, and can clearly be seen to have been a contentious matter over a period of time.

It is worth noting that the regulations, under which the language ruling was made, had been in existence for some time. Before the implementation of the Bantu Education Act in 1955, either English or Afrikaans was used as a medium of instruction in school after Standard 2, and by the end of the Higher Primary School all instruction was being given in that language, and most often this was English. In 1955 the Government insisted on mother-tongue education up to Standard 6. Thereafter, in Secondary School, religious instruction, home language, and, in some instances music and physical instruction, were to be taught in the mother tongue. All the remaining courses were to be divided equally within each school between English and Afrikaans. This was known as the "50-50 system", and led to a student entering Secondary School faced with instruction in three languages. Headmasters were however, allowed to apply to the Department of Bantu Education for exemption from this policy.

By requiring their home languages to be used in the early education of Africans, tribal and cultural differences between groups could be emphasized. This was in line with the government policy of establishing tribally based homelands and discouraging the development of a united Black movement. Since mother-tongue education was planned to continue up to Standard 6, by which stage most students have left school, few would learn in any other language. The recurring fear that the Afrikaans language would be replaced by English and/or fall into disuse, led to both languages being placed on an equal footing in secondary schools.

When the "50-50 system" was introduced, exemptions were granted almost automatically. One of the reasons for this was (and still is) that comparatively few African teachers are proficient in Afrikaans. The "50-50 system" proved to be extremely unpopular and a number of representations were made to the government to have it changed.

Considering South Africa as a whole (i.e. including the areas under Homeland government control) by 1975 only 32% of African Secondary School pupils were being taught under the "50-50 system". 68% were taught in English and only 81 pupils (0·025%) were taught in Afrikaans. The position is decidedly different if one excludes the schools under the jurisdiction of the Homeland governments and considers only those under the control of the Department of Bantu Education. In 1975, 76% of these were taught in the "50-50 system" and the remaining 24% were taught in English (Annual Report Department of Bantu Education, 1975).

In August 1974 a circular sent to all schools in the Soweto area from the Department of Bantu Education informed the schools that the "50-50 system" was to be enforced for all classes from Standard 5 to Standard 10 as from 1975. Nine Soweto schools applied for exemption. When they received no reply by the beginning of the academic year they began to teach only in English. Eventually in May 1975 the nine schools received refusals from the authorities. Despite representations to relax or abandon the "50-50 system", it remained. In May 1976 students at Sunnyside school began boycotting classes with the complaint that they could not understand the courses that were given in Afrikaans. The boycott was joined by a number of schools in May, and by June 4 six schools in Soweto were affected by boycotting classes.

Critical though the language issue undoubtedly was in focussing student discontent there is a second educational factor that is of some importance. We have seen throughout the studies that education is a major concern of the students in high school, it is seen as closely allied to their future career plans, and is perceived as both important for the development of the individual as well as for the progress of the community as a whole. In 1975/1976 Standard 6 was removed from the educational system. This, it will be recalled, was an extra year at the end of the Primary School course which operated only in African schools, and marked a major transition point. Passing the examination at the end of that year with a good grade determined whether or not the student would be admitted to high school. The actual removal of this class could be seen as either beneficial or not, depending on the general view about the intentions of the authorities, but whatever the attitude taken there was one major result—increased overcrowding. At this point, not only was the regular Standard 6 graduate eligible for entry to Secondary School, but also those now completing Standard 5. The number of secondary school pupils increased by 31·5% between 1975 and 1976 (*Hansard*, April 1976).

Commenting on the expected overcrowding that would result when Standard 6 was removed, an editorial in the Bantu Education Department's journal stated:

> Finding methods of allowing the tide to flow through the schools without the collapse of the whole system is of more importance to all of us. Now is the time to consider ways and means of finding a temporary solution to the problem *even if our methods should be unacceptable in normal circumstances*. The factual position is that even the most ardent optimist would admit that the erection of 4,000 additional classrooms in order to accommodate the tide simply cannot be realised. (*Bantu Education Journal*, August 1975)

One way of handling this tide was to continue to teach students who were nominally High School students at the primary schools, and using the Primary School staff. However, now added to this was the use of Afrikaans by these teachers who previously had actually taught in the home language. The overcrowding and the feeling that they were now being additionally handicapped, could explain why, in the very first boycotts, it was the students from Standards 5 and 6 who were involved. Even before these fairly tumultuous changes were made, it was evident that in the early years at high school, education was a highly prized process, and seen, as reflected in the measures of educational optimism, to be the critical solution to a variety of problems.

Two elements that were frequently mentioned by the students who participated in this study recur in the statements made a decade later.

One had to do with the relationship between parents and children, the other with students' anger at the beerhalls that are built.

The Soweto revolt was a students' revolt. Comments indicated that not only did the students reject the authority of their parents, but that they blamed their parents' passivity and submissiveness for their own present predicament. Their position stemmed from their parents' behaviour.

> It is our parents who have let things go on far too long without doing anything. They have failed. (Soweto student. *World*, 1976)

Interviews with parents indicated that they did not entirely reject this view, and that the students, having started on a course of action were not lacking parental support. The students organized strikes of workers, and tried to broaden their protest to involve the considerable labour force on which industry is dependent. There were strikes, the parents did follow the children, but the reality of the economic and political situation proved stronger than the immediate influence of the students. However, the leadership of the children was not unexpected, and was reflected in the assumptions voiced in the essays and protocols of the students of the 1960s. Parents did not know about their children, they did not speak to them, the discipline was authoritarian, and indeed the study showed that their influence on the aspirations and beliefs of the students was minimal. But the peer group is a powerful socializer, both in the streets and in the schools. This rejection of the older generation is a strong theme in the responses of Soweto students.

In their criticism of their parents the students claimed that the older generation had been seduced by alcohol, that they had been satisfied with beer and failed to see the wider issues. Beerhalls featured prominently in the essays of the students, and beerhalls, drunkenness and deprivation were associated in the TAT responses. After a long struggle Africans had been allowed to buy and drink alcohol legally. The government built a large number of beerhalls which sold vast amounts of beer to the inhabitants of the townships. Suspicion about the motives behind this was voiced by the students in the original study. It is reflected a generation later in a statement by Barney Makhatle, a member of the Soweto Students Representative Council formed in July 1976, and in the fact that beerhalls were the main target for the attacks of the students, some 67 of these being burned as early as the end of June (*SAJRR*, 1977). Makhatle said:

There are more beerhalls than schools and you find these beerhalls are situated right at the terminus of the buses, stations and offices where you pay rents. So when your father comes home from work he either goes to the beerhall or pays rent . . .

These beerhalls is what is breaking down and lowering the dignity of Black people. It is taking money from their parents and their fathers are coming home drunk. Beerhalls messes up all the Black people in Soweto. The beerhalls are made by the government of White people.

So we find similarity of attitude across time and behaviour on the part of schools that is congruent with the attitudes previously evoked. But action only occurred in 1976. Why? We have discussed some of the educational changes that acted as precipitating factors, but these did not operate in isolation. Events outside the school system must be understood if we are to begin to adequately explain how general discontent can be transformed into political action.

The first general change in the period leading to 1976 was economic. There was a slowing down of the economy in 1974 and 1975, an increase in the consumer price index from 5·2% in 1970 to 13·5% in 1975. In addition, the real gross domestic product slowed from an increase of 4·9% in 1970 to 2·1% in 1975. Both these indicate a remarkable downturn in the economy which had grown 76% in the ten year period to 1970. Taking into account the rapidly increasing population (especially the African population) it is clear that an expanding economy is required to offer employment to new job seekers. With an increase of 5% in the real gross domestic product, the increase in the per head gross domestic product is only 1·7%, declining to 0·7% in 1975, and negative by 1976 (Nedbank, 1977). One result of all this was an increase in Black unemployment, which, in the absence of accurate figures, some have estimated to have reached almost two million. In addition to this and despite considerable improvement in the wages of many Black workers, the Blacks who constitute 71·2% of the population received only 21·1% of the total wages and salaries in the country. Whites, 16·7% of the population, accounted for 68·2% of the 1973 wages and salaries total. In 1976 therefore, the African population was faced with a high inflation rate which eroded most of the wage gains made earlier and also with rising unemployment. The already limited job market open to the Black high school graduate was further constrained, making their prospects far from enviable.

The constant and considerable concern of the student for the poverty and the deprivation of the African communities featured in every single source of data collection. It permeated the reports about township life, it marked the essays about childhood and adolescence, it was prominent in the TAT responses. Whether the subjective experience of deprivation is magnified after a period of relative improvement in conditions cannot clearly be affirmed. Gurr's analysis of relative deprivation which we have described in an earlier chapter would lend some support to this idea. Hopes raised and then disappointed may well be worse than no hopes at all.

In his analysis of the relation of belief to behaviour Fishbein (1975) introduces two concepts that are relevant in this context. His theory deals not so much with the direct prediction of behaviour from beliefs, but with the prediction of behavioural intentions from which one can predict behaviour. According to his theory there are two major factors that will determine behavioural intentions—the individual or attitudinal factor and the social or normative factor. These attitudes and norms relate not necessarily to the object of an attitude but to the behaviour itself:

> ... a person's attitude towards a specific behaviour is proposed to be a function of the perceived consequences of performing that behaviour and of the person's evaluation of those consequences. (Fishbein and Ajzen, 1975, p. 301)

There is however a second component involved in predicting behavioural intention, and this is the subjective norm, that is:

> ... the person's perception that most people who are important to him think he should or should not perform the behaviour in question. (Fishbein and Ajzen, 1975, p. 302)

The theory therefore integrates both individual belief and the social norm, and proposes that the intention to perform an act will relate to the individual's own beliefs about the consequences of his actions, and also the perceived or actual beliefs about the expectations of relevant others. In the TAT protocols that we analysed the outcome of the plot was a critical variable. It related to the type of action undertaken to overcome the perceived barriers and distinguished between the various groups in the sample. Stories that dealt with conflict with authority, with apartheid or with the position of Africans in society tended to have unfavourable outcomes; those that dealt with striving at the personal level, in terms of achievement, stressing hard work and individual effort, showed favourable outcomes. It was as if the stories reflected the belief that it was only in the areas that relate to their own immediate careers that there is any possibility of a successful conclusion to the course of action selected. The prevalence of this belief makes it understandable that political action aimed at altering the basic conditions under which the individual lives was rare. Why the change?

Two factors in particular seem to be involved in the change that occurred between the original study and the events of 1976. First, there were major political changes in the countries which border on South Africa. The old British Protectorates became independent. The Tswana, Swazi and the Basuto could be free and independent in Botswana, Swaziland and Lesotho, govern themselves and participate in world councils. But not if they lived in South Africa. Even more important however was the collapse of the Portuguese colonial empire in Mozambique and Angola.

From 1970 the South African Government had engaged in a policy of courting those African countries which they considered moderate. This was put to the test when it became clear that the decolonization of Portugal would result in an obviously hostile government in the neighbouring territory of Mozambique. From the statements of the leader of the only sizeable liberation movement in Mozambique, it appeared that he would allow the country, when independent, to be used as a base for attacks on South Africa. Many people expected vast changes to occur in South Africa with the independence of Mozambique. This was not to be. Prime Minister Vorster maintained that a Black government in Mozambique held no fear for South Africa, and subsequently the interlocking economies of the two countries did lead to continued co-operation.

A large number of Black Mozambiquans, approximately 100 000 per year, work on the South African mines. This labour is sorely needed by the mining industry which is unable to recruit enough local Black miners, and the benefits for an independent Mozambique are clear. The Portuguese had required the Black miners' salaries to be paid directly into the government coffers in gold, and in turn paid the miners in local currency on their return. Migrant labour in the mines of South Africa offers employment and gold reserves for any Mozambique Government. Besides the mining and migrant labour exchange, mutual benefits derive from South Africa sending goods through Mozambique ports, and maintaining the hydro-electric power station at Cabora

Bassa which supplies electricity to South Africa and Mozambique and was built with finance from South Africa. South Africa sent experts to assist in the running of the port of Maputo and a special rescue team following a mining disaster. The result was that Mozambique's independence did little to change South Africa. It did serve to establish that in the 1970s Blacks could be handed control of a country successfully, in a short space of time.

The Nationalist Government argued that it would adopt the same attitude towards Angolan independence that it had to Mozambique. But the position in Angola was much more complex, with three active liberation movements, the MPLA, FNLA and UNITA.

UNITA, active in the south of the country, stated that they wanted peace with South Africa. The two other movements stated that they would assist in the liberation of South Africa (Legum, 1975). The MPLA was the largest movement and was far more active than the others in the later period of the war against the Portuguese. UNITA and FNLA, however, put in claims for having some role in the independent government. The Portuguese managed to establish a transitional government including all the liberation movements in March 1975 which enabled them to withdraw from Angola. The transitional government soon collapsed and the three movements became embroiled in a civil war. The MPLA received aid from Russia, Cuba and other Eastern European states, while the FNLA and UNITA received aid from the U.S.A. and some pro-western African states, amongst others. In the early stages of the war, South Africa provided military aid to UNITA, then in July 1975 a small number of South African troops took up defensive positions around a dam inside the Angolan border. South Africa became increasingly involved in training UNITA troops and finally in October that year sent a column of troops into Angola in support of UNITA. These combined forces advanced far into the country. In November 1975 ships arrived in Luanda harbour and Cuban troops began to come ashore to bolster the MPLA. In November and December 1975 the South African forces are understood to have suffered heavy casualties and finally South Africa decided to withdraw in February 1976 (Johnson, 1977).

The impact on the public of South Africa of the withdrawal of the supposedly strongest power in southern Africa in the face of a guerrilla army was considerable. International criticism of South Africa increased, the share market fell and most important for the economy, foreign investors began to suspect the security of South African investments. The reports of the public response illustrated the differences in reaction between Black and White. While Whites expressed concern, Blacks are reported to have welcomed the news broadcasts of South African casualties (Callinicos and Rogers, 1977). To Blacks the withdrawal indicated for the first time that Whites were not invincible. It became clear that military action and guerrilla warfare could effect a change. Barriers could be attacked and had been seen to be capable of successfully being surmounted. A basic belief had been shown to be fallacious.

The second change that occurred between the original study and the events of 1976 was also presaged in the responses of the Soweto students in the 1960s. This was the growth of Black Consciousness—seen in some form in the emphasis on the need for nationalist not tribal affiliations, for community advance, and in the opinion that the Church was a White man's thing. However, in our study the sense of group belonging was expressed only by the more advanced students, by the boys and mainly by the students in Arcadia. A series of events led to these views being more publicly articulated.

Until the segregation of the universities in 1959 there were two main student movements—NUSAS which was active in the English-speaking universities, those which accepted African, Coloured and Asian students together with White, while the Afrikaans-speaking universities which were segregated had their own body, the ASB. In 1969 the student leaders from the then existing Black universities met and formed the South African Student Organization (SASO), a totally Black federation* of students. This attempted to establish branches at all Black universities and institutions of higher learning, thus breaking from NUSAS. Its 1970 constitution gives a clear idea of the position adopted by SASO.

> We the Black Students of institutions of higher learning in South Africa believing:
> (1) that Black students in South Africa have unique problems and aspirations pertaining to them;
> (2) that it is necessary for Black students to consolidate their ranks if the aspirations are to be realised;
> (3) that there is a crying need in South Africa for Black students to re-assert their pride and group identity; . . . (SASO Constitution, 1970)

*SASO defined Black to include Coloured and Indian students.

The emphasis SASO placed on Black pride and the need to overcome the inferiority developed through continual subjugation, can be appreciated from the following resolution:

> SASO is a Black student organisation working for the liberation of Blacks first from psychological oppression by themselves through inferiority complex and secondly from the physical oppression accruing out of living in a white racist society.

Other Black Consciousness movements* arose after the first leaders of SASO saw a need to form a broader based movement. The most important of these for understanding the events of Soweto are those concerned with school students. By 1972 a number of Black Consciousness groups for school pupils had been formed. The South African Student Movement (SASM) was founded by Soweto High School students with the main aim of co-ordinating activities of High School students (*Black Review*, 1972). The Government's concern with Black Consciousness was clear. They continually harassed, banned and arrested many of the office-bearers of Black Consciousness groups. At the time of the 1976 protests a number of officials of SASO and another organization were on trial for alleged subversion. Finally in October 1977 the Government banned 18 Black Consciousness organizations including SASO, SASM and the Soweto Students Representative Council.

The exact role of the Black Consciousness movement on the school students in Soweto is difficult to gauge. The first president of the Soweto Students Representative Council, now living in exile, in an interview, suggested that the organization of the uprising was due to the Black Consciousness movement and its various bodies, and was not, as had been claimed, the work of the exiled old political movements, the African Nationalist Congress and the Pan-African Congress. The psychological impact of the movement needs to be stressed in its role as reference group. If the group was active and vocal it would make clear its view about the need for concerted action and would feed in positively to the equation drawn by Fishbein to account for the behavioural intentions. It may be that this operates as a legitimating process, or it could be that it rewards in the numerous ways that groups can reward members—approval, status, acceptance. Alternatively it

---

*The multiracial University Christian Movement had a well-developed Black theology group. At its 1968 conference a group of Black students formed a group which in part led to the formation of SASO (*Black Review*, 1972).

could make salient new ways of viewing old issues. Lobban (1975) has found that African students identified with American Blacks, Independent Africans and urban Africans and that these groups exemplified the ideal image—free, civilized and *Black*. They were not lacking in self-esteem due, Lobban argues, to the readily available external locus of responsibility for their shortcomings, the White Government. The self-esteem and the positive evaluation of Blackness, as well as the militancy were found in the original sample, but mainly in one particular group. Its extension to a larger group may well be due to the existence of a group articulating and making salient this particular set of beliefs. Black Consciousness as a psychological reality was always there. Positive evaluation of this, a shift in the psychological meaning of the experience, may well have been determined by the formal expression of the sentiments by a political body.

Thus, the confluence of elements. The concern for education and fear and dislike of proposed changes. A worsening economic situation and the chance of leaving school, with the sacrifices that schooling demands and then not finding a job. A new sense of group cohesion and a feeling that no one else will change the situation. An opponent now seen to be vincible and a growing pride in one's own characteristics. Some elements old, some new; together they combined to change the students of the 1960s to the activists of the 1970s, to shift beliefs about action to action itself.

# Appendix A

# The Study: The Sample and the Tests

Data for the study were derived from the responses of a sample of 992 boys and girls drawn from four high schools in Soweto. All testing took place at school in the classroom, and all students in the class participated in the study. A smaller number of the total classes was used for the second part of the study, which utilized an African Thematic Apperception Test (de Ridder, 1961).

It was clear from the outset that the study would be heavily dependent on gaining the support and interest both of the teaching staff and of the students themselves, and further that any comments and objections raised had to be taken seriously and accommodated. The major requirement was anonymity. Not only was it necessary that no single student be identifiable, but it was also clear that in the stages of the study no student would be willing to be tested out of the group situation. All testing in the first (questionnaire) and second (projective test) stages of the research took place in the classroom even though by the second testing period the students were no longer anxious about the project. By the time the third stage (interviews, discussion and essay groups) occurred it was possible to use a variety of settings, both in Soweto and at the researcher's home. The issue of anonymity however, remained prominent, and in the tests the subjects were allowed to use pseudonyms, provided that the same name was used in all test conditions. In addition, it was clear that some matters were sensitive, in that the information could have been used to the detriment of the subjects, or so they felt. Therefore, in all demographic questions, those who were "at risk" (not really entitled to be in town, or unable to buy books, or having lodgers in their homes) were permitted not to reply.

## The sample

In the lower forms there are as many girls in the class as there are boys, although after the third year of the programme the number of girls drops dramatically, and they constitute only one-sixth of the sample in the fourth year. The students are slightly older than their White counterparts, and the boys on the whole present an older age profile than the girls. Over half the girls were 17 and 18 years old (57%) and only 16·2% were older than this. In the case of the boys 48% were 17 and 18, and 32% were older than this. The students were quite clearly an urban born and bred group. Over 60% were born in the Johannesburg metropolitan area itself, and only 13% were born in the country. The tribal origins of the sample show that Johannesburg has drawn its Black population over the years from many areas, though mainly from the north and east of the Transvaal. Sotho, Pede, Tswana, Ndebele and Zulu were all represented in the sample.

The educational and occupational background of the parents of the students can be seen in Tables 7, 8, 9 and 10. It is clear that fewer mothers than fathers completed their schooling, but also that fewer are totally without any formal education. The modal level of mother's education is at the Higher Primary level, that of the father's is at two years of High School. The fathers tend to have jobs mainly in unskilled occupations and the mothers are employed in domestic service, taking in washing, or in unskilled factory work. The fairly high number of non-responses can be accounted for in part by the structure of the family.

Less than half the sample lives in a simple nuclear family, and as many as 35·9% in families that do not fit the father-mother-offspring pattern, living with siblings or with other relatives, or in single parent households. The families of origin of the sample are large, averaging 4·3 children per family, and 38% of the students come from families in which there are more than six children. We attempted to get indices of residential density for the sample, but this was one of the questions which raised great apprehension, and over one-third of the sample failed to answer. However, working on the ratio of rooms to inhabitants from the information provided, it was clear that 16·1% were living in overcrowded conditions, assessed as 10 or more people in a four-roomed house, one room of which would be the kitchen.

The sample as a whole is drawn from the working class, and lives in conditions and within a family structure that does not differ from the rest of the Soweto population.

## TABLE 7
### Distribution of sample by father's occupation

| | No response | Unemployed | Unskilled | Semi-skilled | Skilled | Clerical | Upper middle class | | | Total |
| | | | | | | | Skilled Clerical | Professional I | Professional II | |
|---|---|---|---|---|---|---|---|---|---|---|
| Boys | 24·3% (138) | 2·5% (14) | 24·3% (138) | 16·0% (91) | 6·3% (36) | 18·8% (107) | 2·3% (13) | 5·0% (28) | 0·5% (3) | 100% (568) |
| Girls | 28·4% (120) | 2·8% (12) | 18·6% (79) | 21·2% (90) | 4·7% (20) | 17·2% (73) | 1·9% (8) | 4·3% (18) | 0·9% (4) | 100% (424) |
| Total | 26·0% (258) | 2·6% (26) | 21·9% (217) | 18·3% (181) | 5·7% (56) | 18·1% (180) | 2·1% (21) | 4·6% (46) | 0·7% (7) | 100% (992) |

## TABLE 8
### Distribution of sample by father's education

| | No response | No schooling | Infant school | Higher primary | Two years high school | Junior certificate |
|---|---|---|---|---|---|---|
| Boys | 16·7% (95) | 16·7% (95) | 5·1% (29) | 22·8% (129) | 24·0% (136) | 7·7% (44) |
| Girls | 19·1% (81) | 9·7% (41) | 4·5% (19) | 21·5% (91) | 28·0% (119) | 9·4% (40) |
| Total | 17·8% (176) | 13·7% (136) | 4·8% (48) | 22·2% (220) | 25·7% (255) | 8·5% (84) |

| | Standard 9 | Matriculation | College | University | Total |
|---|---|---|---|---|---|
| Boys | 0·7% (4) | 2·6% (15) | 2·5% (14) | 1·2% (7) | 100% (568) |
| Girls | 1·2% (5) | 4·5% (19) | 0·5% (2) | 1·6% (7) | 100% (424) |
| Total | 0·9% (9) | 3·4% (34) | 1·6% (16) | 1·4% (14) | 100% (992) |

TABLE 9

Distribution of sample by mother's occupation

| | No response | Unemployed | Housewife | Unskilled | Semi-skilled | Clerical | Professional I | Total |
|---|---|---|---|---|---|---|---|---|
| Boys | 24·6% (140) | 19·0% (108) | 14·6% (83) | 29·6% (168) | 6·0% (34) | 2·1% (12) | 4·1% (23) | 100% (568) |
| Girls | 10·3% (44) | 21·2% (90) | 15·6% (66) | 34·0% (144) | 8·0% (34) | 3·8% (16) | 7·1% (30) | 100% (424) |
| Total | 18·5% (184) | 20·0% (198) | 15·0% (149) | 31·5% (312) | 6·9% (68) | 2·8% (28) | 5·3% (53) | 100% (992) |

## TABLE 10
### Distribution of sample by mother's education

|  | No response | No schooling | Infant school | Higher primary | Two years high school | Junior certificate |
|---|---|---|---|---|---|---|
| Boys | 13·2% (75) | 15·1% (86) | 10·0% (57) | 31·3% (178) | 19·2% (109) | 7·4% (42) |
| Girls | 11·3% (48) | 6·4% (27) | 6·4% (27) | 28·1% (119) | 32·1% (136) | 10·6% (45) |
| Total | 12·4% (123) | 11·4% (113) | 8·5% (84) | 29·9% (297) | 24·7% (245) | 8·8% (87) |

|  | Standard 9 | Matriculation | College | University | Total |
|---|---|---|---|---|---|
| Boys | 0·2% (1) | 0·4% (2) | 3·2% (18) | — | 100% (568) |
| Girls | 0·9% (4) | 0·7% (3) | 2·8% (12) | 0·7% (3) | 100% (424) |
| Total | 0·5% (5) | 0·5% (5) | 3·0% (30) | 0·3% (3) | 100% (992) |

## The tests and measures

The data to be reported here are based on two main methods of getting information. The first, a questionnaire was given to the full sample of 992 subjects. It consisted of 65 questions designed to extract information about the respondents' background and attitudes. Background variables included age, sex, form, place of origin, education and occupation of mothers, fathers and siblings, position in the family, household structure, finances, spoken language(s), spare time activities and membership of organizations, clubs and societies. Composite scores were obtained regarding tribal affiliation; the attitudes towards the church, orientation to urban life; political attitudes; educational involvement, aspirations and expectations; occupational aspirations and expectations; motivational reasons for occupational and educational choices; reference groups and nationalism.

These measures are all self-explanatory. There are however, some measures which need clarification. Two of these relate to education— educational optimism and educational pessimism. These do not say anything about the value of education *per se* but rather express an opinion about the utility of education as a means of social change. Educational optimism therefore implies that through education the individual and/or the group can improve their lot. Educational pessimism implies the opposite view. The term cognitive complexity which is sometimes used in the literature to refer to the cognitive structure of the individual as assessed by a variety of repertory grid techniques is employed in this study, but is assessed by the structure and organization of the replies to a variety of open-ended questions.

A number of the questions in the questionnaire were open-ended. Political attitudes in particular could not be approached directly. Three coders coded the responses and all measures yielded an inter-coder reliability of no less than $r = 0.9$.

The second method used was the African Thematic Apperception Test (de Ridder, 1961); this is not the only test devised specifically for use with an African population. Sherwood (1957) produced a test for use with a Swazi population "assimilating Western culture"; Baran (1971) one for Zulus on the urban-rural continuum, also concerned with the process of acculturation. In all instances the particular test was devised so as to have a technique of "penetrating foreign cultures in an unbiased fashion" (Baran, 1975, p. 10). There is no evidence that the TAT is less biased than any other measure, and certainly any test that attempts to be culture-fair needs to take care that the categories then used to classify the content do not nullify the virtuous object of not importing the assumptions of one culture into another.

The projective tests were not intended to establish ideographic portraits of each subject, nor to build up a picture of *the* personality of *the* African in towns or in transition. It was a means of understanding the way that the social environment is structured, to see the sets of expectations that are built up about the probability of certain events occurring, of the outcomes of these events, of the means regarded as most likely to be effective in determining outcome. The test was used as an avenue to the reality that has been constructed about the world the student lives in.

Because the intention was more social-cognitive than concern with unconscious processes the actual cards selected for use were chosen to represent particular aspects of social living. The cards used by de Ridder are a subset of a larger group tested on the African working population of Johannesburg and Durban. Out of the range available two matched sets of seven cards each were constructed. These cards were selected by psychology graduates (White and Black) on the basis of their manifest content for the representation of one of seven themes; the individual alone, the family, the township (general), achievement, heterosexual interaction, group interaction and multiracial.

In a criticism of the de Ridder cards Baran (1975) selects the fact that certain cards are designed so as to "almost guarantee" that certain stories will be produced. This may be criticized (although any test which assumes that the manifest content of the card is irrelevant in stimulating and directing the response can be accused at least of naivety) but if one is attempting to direct evaluations towards the social world of the subjects and to the sort of issues which are likely to be important to them and to the central concerns of the study, it appears to be sensible. There is no purpose in presenting test material which is likely to give information about matters which are outside the interest of the hypotheses.

The tests were administered to the subjects at school in their classrooms. Group administration made certain demands on the test presentation. First, it necessitated written responses. This was not thought to be a problem, since the subjects were all high school pupils, literate and able. Secondly, because there were no projector facilities available in the classrooms, each subject had to be given an individual set of cards. Finally, to discourage co-operative work since subjects sat two or three to a desk, two equivalent sets of seven cards were provided, so that neighbours were not describing identical cards.

There are a number of points arising from this particular method of administration that are worth comment. Firstly, although group administration of the TAT is not uncommon there are differences in the lengths of protocols in this as opposed to individual testing. What is affected does seem to be only length, not content (Lindzey and Silverman, 1957). The amount of time that is spent on each card seems to be the factor that the experimenter loses control of. In their group administration Lindzey and Heinemann (1955) used five minutes as the maximum exposure period for each card; in this test situation it was decided to eliminate as far as possible all speed-related variables to maximize the difference between this task and a "test". This reduced the control over length.

Secondly, in addition to limiting the amount of control over length this particular method of administration also reduced the number of cards responded to. The school allowed a generous period of time for the completion of the test—but some of the subjects were slow, a few were unenthusiastic and anxious to escape from the classroom to the playground (which is where they were sent once they had finished so as not to disturb those still writing). However, across the sample as a whole an average of 5·2 cards were completed and these cards were equally distributed across the sample by sex, form and school so that the results are not biased by the lack of total control. No card particularly favoured and none was specifically avoided: this is important since the instructions particularly permitted the subjects to deal with the cards in any order they wished. There have been some studies of order effects (Lowe, 1951; Mason, 1952; Dollin, 1960) but the results did not seem to justify a rigid adherence to a particular order of presentation, particularly where two sets of cards had to be used.

In the original set Murray (1943) provided sets of cards for each sex so that the sex and age of the hero would be related to that of the subject. Although there is evidence of sex differences in responses to the test (Lindzey and Goldberg, 1953; Veroff et al., 1953; Moss and Kagan, 196i) there does not seem to be clear indication that these are due to the nature of the stimulus, nor the sex of the hero. There is some suggestion (Murstein, 1963) that girls find it equally easy to respond to cards featuring boys or girls, boys do not respond as well to cards featuring girls. The same cards were therefore used for all subjects, and on those where a single figure was featured a male figure was represented. The particular scheme adopted for analysis of the TAT protocols does not need to make any assumptions about the identification of the respondent with the "hero" and therefore the similarity between the subject and the people depicted on the cards, in age and sex, is unimportant.

It is possible to approach the TAT story-telling as a cognitive task (see Ladkowitz, 1959; Kenny, 1961). The stimulus is perceived, categorized and then the categories are related to schema, which Kenny sees as imaginative thought sequences. Such schema are sets of expectancies about environmental regularities, which reflect the individual's world, both social and material. Such an approach has obvious links with theories of cognition, with a constructivist view of the nature of reality. As such it is possible to link it with the work of Bartlett (1932) with Bruner (1954) and with the general theory of Piaget (see Geber, 1977). Its links with the dynamic personality theories which were the mainstay of the testers are more tenuous.

The coding frame devised for this study stresses both categories relating to form and categories relating to content. In research subsequently confirmed by others (e.g. Smith, 1970) Lindzey and Silverman (1959) showed that verbal productivity significantly correlated with many of the dimensions of TAT analysis, for instance with theme $(r = 0.54)$, achievement $(r = 0.34)$, number of figures $(r = 0.53)$. It would be possible to partial this variable out of the analysis, but if one is concerned with the way in which the individual construes his world, verbal features or ability may be an important contributing variable, a factor which mediates between the responses of the individual and his world. A study by Tamhankar (1968) found that the length of protocol showed a significant positive relation with n-ach in boys of high and average ability. Since structural variables may influence the nature of the relation between the individual and his world, particularly in a developing population, it was deemed necessary to give weight to the structural or form dimensions of the protocols and not ignore them. The detail of the categories used can be seen in Appendix D.

Before we examine the responses of the students to see the effects on their aspirations and beliefs of the four sets of independent variables we have mentioned, it is worth looking at the relationships that the TAT produced across the sample as a whole. It helps elucidate the general view of the individual and his world that has already emerged from the essays we have presented, and it also helps establish the influence of the stimulus material itself on the variations that we actually perceived. Analysis showed that three dimensions relating to content were highly influential in relation to the others, and also the verbal fluency of the subjects emerged as important.

The first content dimension that emerged was that of theme. The focus of the TAT card seems to suggest a logic of its own which influences many of the dimensions of the response. It relates to the complexity of the presentation and to the concreteness or abstractness with which the subject is handled ($p < 0.001$). The most concrete themes are those which deal with crime, followed by those which describe interpersonal behaviour and work. The stories that deal with the political structure of South Africa are high on all abstract categories, while stories dealing with financial deprivation and personal effort are high on the simple abstract and abstract categories.

The theme is related to aggression, both to the type of aggression described and to the reason given for its occurrence ($p < 0.001$). Robbery occurs most often in crime stories, but also in themes dealing with poverty and economic deprivation. Interpersonal themes, whether between same or opposite sex characters are high on fighting with some assault and rape, whereas the family, like individual effort and economic deprivation is seen to be related to hypothetical or potential violence. The reasons given for aggression are similarly theme linked. Drunkenness, which appears quite often does so in a variety of themes, but interpersonal themes give rise to aggression as emotional release following frustration or conflict. Within the family retaliation as a cause of aggression is fairly frequent.

Three other dimensions of content are related to theme—the barriers stressed in the story, the means the actors use and the nature of the outcome of the action. Crime stories are highest on unfavourable outcomes. Symbolic conflict stories, those that deal with Apartheid or the position of Africans in South Africa, also show a strong trend towards unfavourable outcomes.

The stories that are highest on favourable outcomes are those that deal with striving and achievement. These stress individual effort and hard work as major means of action, and the barriers that these themes encourage are those that result from individual deprivation. Stories that deal with economic deprivation tend to end with what we have called a statement of precept. This is not an avoided ending, but one which, while not resolving any conflict states the moral or principle on which such resolution should be based. Examples of this are stories that end, after describing a situation, with a statement such as "Hard work does not harm" or "if they marry they should not divorce".

The outcome of the story too, serves as a focus for particular dimensions. The perceived source of responsibility for a particular outcome and the nature of the outcome are significantly related. If the self is responsible the outcomes tend to be more favourable than unfavourable. Responsibility attributed to others is associated with unfavourable outcomes, and shared responsibility produces fewer favourable than unfavourable results. Non-personal and impersonal sources of responsibility are associated with a high proportion of unfavourable outcomes.

The relationship between responsibility for outcome and success in surmounting barriers shows similar trends. Where the self is responsible the highest number of successful attempts occur, but where others are responsible we find the highest percentage of failure. Impersonal and non-personal forces produce a high proportion of avoidance responses, that is there are no attempts to overcome the barriers.

Story outcome relates not only to the source of responsibility but also to the type of action. Criminal, political action or avoidance/withdrawal tend to lead to unfavourable outcomes. Individual effort leads to the highest number of favourable outcomes. This dimension of type of barrier is the third critical dimension of content in the protocols.

Type of action relates to the nature of the barriers perceived. Barriers located within the individual's limitations or in economic deprivation encourage individual effort as the means of action, those located in rivalry between groups encourage criminal activity or persuasion. With these relationships it is not surprising that the success of the outcome is related to the nature of the perceived barrier. Those located within the family are most frequently overcome, those due to social isolation or to interpersonal conflict less successfully. Where the barrier is located in the social system—either in economic deprivation or in the power structure, the conflicts are seldom resolved and the stories likely to end in a statement of precept. Individual effort, co-operative action and prayer are more likely to lead to success in overcoming obstacles than are criminal or political action. These either do not succeed at all or encourage objection but no action.

The success of a venture is frequently regarded as sufficient grounds for the legitimization of normally unaccepted actions or conduct; a case of the ends justifying the means. This is particularly true if the action is directed against the environment or a social institution. Action, however successful and against whatever target that is instigated by alcohol or drunkenness is seldom legitimized.

These patterns of interaction between the thematic variables suggest a world where *it is possible for the individual to be relatively successful if he is dealing only with his own shortcomings. Where the problems are external to himself the success of any venture is doubtful.*

Across the sample as a whole the TAT cards stimulate a view of a world which is relatively hostile and within which the individual has little chance of succeeding except against his own shortcomings. While a certain amount of the responses appears to reflect general cultural norms, two other sources are of interest. Firstly, particular ways of viewing the world can derive from the different schools, by differing amounts of education and by being socialized as either a girl or a boy. These variables are the focus of attention of this study and would be expected to influence responses to the cards especially in the light of the force these variables played in the questionnaire data.

The second source of responses can be considered those that reflect particular individual experience. It is possible that experiences in the township could be so particular as to render any influence of the school, form attended or sex, insignificant. Alternatively, the experiences of township life could be so similar as to render little individual difference, and no particular influence of the variables of sex, school or form.

# Appendix B

# Family and Gender Effects on Responses

On examining the responses of the sample to the questions regarding occupational choice, it was quite clear that overall aspirations exceed expectations. Within these general findings the patterns for boys and girls were sufficiently different to warrant separate consideration.

For both boys and girls two professional occupational groups were distinguished—Professional I which involve long periods of study and are ranked highest on any status measure (medicine, law, science) and Professional II (social work, nursing, teaching) which are still of high status, but require less preparation. The remaining aspirations and expectations in relation to occupation were so different that separate categories for the two sexes were described. The category for girls after Professional II contained creative occupations—acting, singing—followed by the next group of skilled and semi-skilled jobs (dressmaking, typing, hairdressing and shop work). The final category contained all unskilled work, which for this sample meant domestic work and unskilled factory work.

For boys the category which followed the two professional groups included clerical and white collar jobs. After this was a category of entrepreneurial and independent occupations, such as store-keeping, or taxi driving. The next was a group of unskilled but non-manual jobs, and finally the unskilled category included street-sweeping, road building, factory work, construction and domestic work. No mention was made of skilled work that is based on a formal apprenticeship system—since apprenticeships were not open to Blacks.

TABLE 11

Percentage distribution of occupational aspirations and expectations of African high school girls (N = 427)

|  | Professional I | Professional II | Creative | Semi-skilled | Unskilled | No response |
|---|---|---|---|---|---|---|
| Aspired to | 26·74 | 65·5 | 0·7 | 5·6 | 0·96 | 0·5 |
| Expected | 14·15 | 67·0 | 0·4 | 9·85 | 4·7 | 3·9 |

## TABLE 12

Percentage distribution of occupational aspirations and expectations of African high school boys (N = 567)

| | Professional I | Professional II | Clerical and white collar | Entrepreneurial | Skilled non-manual | Unskilled manual | No response |
|---|---|---|---|---|---|---|---|
| Aspired to | 48·67 | 15·78 | 7·93 | 4·76 | 5·29 | 0·9 | 16·66 |
| Expected | 30·89 | 18·0 | 26·62 | 3·88 | 9·41 | 1·2 | 10·0 |

The girls tend to have high aspirations, with 92·4% aspiring to professional work, and 81·5% expecting jobs in these categories. Only 64·45% of the boys aspire to professional occupations while only 48·89% expect to achieve that position. The difference between the sexes is that the boys aspire to and expect to obtain more Professional I occupations (doctors, lawyers, etc.) than Professional II (teachers, social work, nursing) while for the girls the position is the reverse. This is not surprising as Professional II category includes most of the helping professions, occupations commonly occupied by women. A large proportion (26·62%) of the boys expect to occupy white-collar positions, although they do not aspire to them.

It should be noted that the proportion of boys who were unsure of their choices and therefore unable to respond to the question, was far greater than that of the girls. Thus the boys are both more varied and less certain of their future career pattern than are the girls.

Gurr's relative deprivation (RD) measure* was adopted to examine the discrepancy between aspirations and expectation and indicated that a greater degree of relative deprivation was experienced by the boys (0·25) than by the girls (0·05). There is greater congruence between aspirations and expectations for girls as opposed to boys. Other personal variables such as age and place of birth (rural or urban) were found not to correlate with job expectations and aspirations but as was expected in a society stratified on a basis of sex, this variable plays an important role in structuring job expectations and job aspirations. More important however is the fact that the boys show a larger discrepancy than girls as measured by our relative deprivation index. If it can be assumed that this measure relates to political discontent then the boys should show more discontent. This will be discussed later.

The potent impact of sex-role differentiation on the samples' job aspirations and expectations is not matched by the impact of family. The occupation level of the father was found to be significantly related to job aspirations but not expectations. Although most pupils aspire to professional occupations, this was particularly apparent for students whose fathers occupied skilled jobs. The influence of this trend is reflected in the relative deprivation index where the largest amount of

---

*Formula adopted: Aspired level—Expected level./Aspired level. For boys a score of 6 was assigned to Professional I category and 1 to manual with other occupations arranged between these two. A similar system was adopted for girls.

RD is found in children whose parents occupy occupations intermediate on the scale (see Table 13).

TABLE 13
Relative deprivation score by father's occupational level

|  | Middle class | Clerical and skilled | Semi-skilled and unskilled manual |
|---|---|---|---|
| Boys | 0·14 | 0·23 | 0·16 |
| Girls | 0·025 | 0·07 | 0·023 |

No correlation was observed between either job aspiration or job expectation and ordinal position, family size and type of family structure. Since, in general, the family variables including parents' education and occupation exert no influence on job *expectation*, it can be argued that expectations about the occupational future are constrained by factors extraneous to the family.

Examining the jobs aspired to by the sample the occupation of the father was a significant influence ($p < 0·01$). Although most of the students aspire to professional jobs this is particularly marked for those whose fathers are in the skilled clerical and the skilled manual categories. Fathers in lower grade professional jobs (teaching and social work) have children who tend to aspire to entrepreneurial occupations. This trend was particularly pronounced for the boys. Father's education however correlated only with the job aspirations of boys and then only in Forms 2 and 3. No such relationship was found for girls. However, the correlations found suggest that the father has some role in patterning the child's desires in the wider society.

Both boys and girls relate their educational plans to the jobs to which they aspire. Since there are sex differences in the latter, it is reasonable to find differences in the former. Over 60% of the girls who would like to go to University aspire to jobs in the Professional I category. Girls who want to go into nursing or social work seldom anticipate education beyond Form 3, or beyond Matriculation. Depressed job expectations relate to educational aspirations that are limited to high school.

There is an interesting relationship between job expectation and educational pessimism. This latter variable reflects the individual's belief in the potency of educational success as a means of attaining goals. Educational optimism refers to the belief that through education a means can be found to resolve personal and social problems. Pessimism reflects the opposite viewpoint. Girls were generally more optimistic in their attitudes to education than boys, and the greater the job expectation the greater the level of educational pessimism. Even though education is seen as a necessary condition for personal advance, it is not seen as a sufficient one.

The way that the social system is perceived also indicates sex differences, and these are one of the major distinctions in the study. By and large, with some variation according to education to which we will later refer, girls are less critical of the environment than are the boys.

It had been predicted that the nature of the aspiration, given the character of South African society, would relate to attitudes towards both traditional and present day institutions. As has been discussed earlier the tribe has a peculiar role both as the vestige of tradition and as an element in the segregation policy of the Government. The tribe could therefore be viewed and evaluated on a number of different bases.

The results showed that for boys evaluation of the tribe was significantly related to occupational aspiration ($p < 0.01$), and linked high aspirations with negative evaluation. This relationship is not found for the girls. Firstly they endorsed tribal membership far more than the boys, and what variance is found is not significantly related to aspiration.

Tribal affiliation which is a measure of tribal involvement follows a similar pattern with a significant negative relationship at the 5% level for boys and none for girls. For boys the higher the occupation aspired to, the lower the level of involvement with the tribe.

The reasons the pupils give to support their particular evaluation of the tribe relate meaningfully to aspirations. The tribe is evaluated (usually negatively) in terms of community progress and advance by both boys and girls aspiring to jobs at the Professional I level. Boys aspiring to clerical and semi-skilled jobs tend to give reasons of constraint, of inevitability in explaining their evaluation of the tribe. These relationships occur only in respect of job aspiration. For neither boys nor girls is there any significant relationship between the tribal measures and job expectation.

The measure which we have called cognitive complexity is not an attitude measure nor an evaluation nor a value. It is an indication of the articulateness and complexity with which these are expressed. It is a structural rather than a content variable, and its relationship to occupational aspirations and expectations is interesting. It must be stressed that in the absence of any I.Q. measure we do not know the relationship between complexity and intelligence.

Boys are significantly more complex than girls in their responses on the questionnaire ($p < 0.001$), but those girls who are high on complexity are significantly more likely to aspire to Professional I jobs than those who are less complex. For boys the relationship is significant at the $0.01$ level, and a similar picture emerges. There is an increase in the percentage of boys aspiring to Professional I jobs as the complexity rating increases.

The evaluation of the existing politico-legal system in South Africa shows similar relationships to the aspirations of the school children as does the measure of tribal evaluation. At a level of significance of $p < 0.01$ political dissatisfaction and job aspiration relate. The higher the level of job aspired to the greater is the dissatisfaction with the existing structure. This trend is particularly significant for the boys. For the girls it is discernible but does not reach acceptable levels of significance.

Unlike tribal attitudes political dissatisfaction also correlates significantly with job expectation, although at a lower level ($p < 0.05$). For girls this relationship is not evident.

Although only 58.2% of the pupils indicated any political dissatisfaction in turn it correlates positively, as would be expected, with rejection of the tribe and concern for the community. This recurring association between tribal rejection and concern for the community appears to reflect a movement of the reference group to the urban situation and a rise in political discontent.

In general it appears that those boys who have high aspirations have broken with traditional life and appear to show more political discontent. In that aspirations can be considered to reflect a value system, it is clearly in this group that a clash between the values upheld and aspired to and society at large is apparent.

The additional finding that pupils who express political dissatisfaction tend to reject links with the church suggests a general politicization has taken place where the two major conservative forces in the life of a young Black have been rejected. Thus we have a group of Black pupils who have not only broken with the past but also with the constraining force of the church. It is this group who show political discontent and it

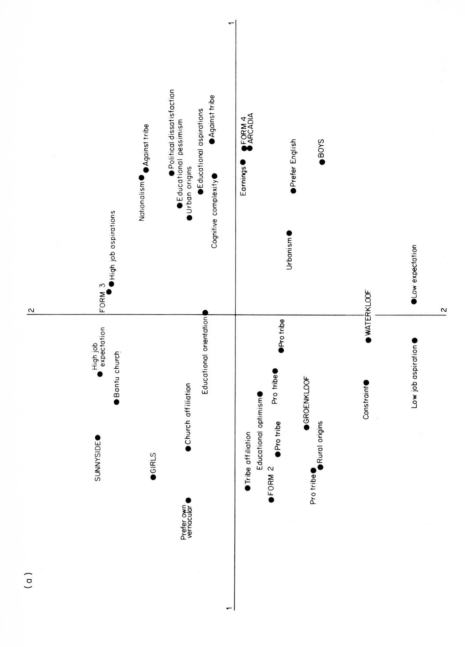

(a)

(b)

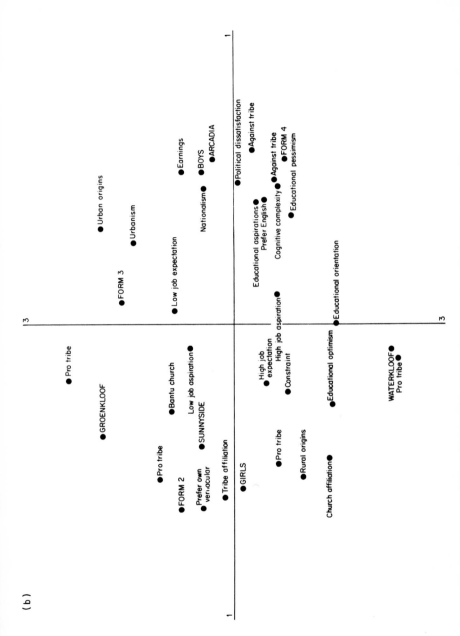

Fig. 4. Small space analysis. (a) Dimensions 1 and 2 for questionnaire. (b) Dimensions 1 to 3 for questionnaire.

has high job and educational aspirations. The finding that political dissatisfaction correlates with cognitive complexity furthermore suggests that this group is articulate. So we appear to have on the basis of the correlational analysis a group of individuals, more likely to be male, who show a decided form of antagonism to the society at large.

In order to be able to see simultaneously how these various dimensions interact and how they distinguish between the sexes, we used the 41 variables (these are listed in Appendix E) of the questionnaire and analysed them by means of a Small Space Analysis (SSA).* This projects the plots of the variables in Euclidean space, showing their relationship by means of the distance between them which is projected on to two, three or more dimensional space. 3-dimensional space produced a good projection,† and this is shown in Fig. 4(a) and (b).

In this figure (4a and b), the sexes are polarized on dimension 1 which is associated on its rightmost point (Boys) with a preference for English, urbanism, cognitive complexity, opposition to the tribe, political dissatisfaction and aspirations with regard to education. Movement to the opposite end of this dimension reflects a move to a

---

*The data was subjected to the Guttman Lingoes Small Space Analysis 1 (Guttman Lingoes, 1973. This non-metric computer programme is especially suited to the analysis of correlation matrices. The programme proceeds by plotting in Euclidean space the factors in the correlation matrix with the distance between each variable reflecting their order in the original correlation matrix. As distance can be represented along any number of dimensions the data can be considered in 2, 3 or more dimensions. Associated with each projection is a measure of stress (co-efficient of alienation) which indicates the extent to which the data is misrepresented in the projection. Obviously as more dimensions are added so less distortion of the data will occur. For interpretative purposes the data is considered in two dimensions at any one time regardless of how many dimensions have been projected. Therefore if the 4-dimensional solution is used two dimensions will be displayed on the first diagram and the remaining 2 on the next. In addition the dimensions are ordered in the extent they account for the variance of the data. Dimension 1 accounts for most variance followed by dimension 2 and so on. Therefore if dimensions 1 and 2 are used from a 4-dimensional solution their projection will account for considerably more variance than the projection of the remaining two dimensions.

The interpretation of the SSA proceeds by viewing the clustering of the variables around the points representing the typical performance of a member from one of the subdivisions of the population.

†The 2-dimensional solution produced a rather poor fit (coefficient of alienation = 0·29). Consequently the 3-dimensional solution was used (coefficient of alienation = 0·21). There was a close resemblance between the projections on dimensions 1 and 2 on the 3 and 4-dimensional solutions which lends further support to the 3-dimensional picture and any interpretation placed upon it. The stress on the 4-dimensional solution was low (coefficient of alienation = 0·16).

pro-tribal, pro-church and pro-vernacular position. Thus the girls reflect a conservative attitude in comparison to the boys, or more accurately a position which favours conservative institutions. This result parallels the findings on the preliminary analysis which indicated a similar difference between the girls and boys.

Dimension 2 (Fig. 4a, vertical axis) reflects a move from low to high aspirations and expectations. Girls occupy a position on this axis closer to the high aspirations/expectations position than boys. Dimension 3 fails to distinguish between the sexes.

In order to examine which variables were primarily responsible for the sex differences a Discriminant Analysis* was performed with 10 selected variables: educational aspirations, job aspirations and expectations, cognitive complexity, political dissatisfaction, church affiliation, tribe affiliation, educational orientation, educational optimism and educational pessimism. The results of this analysis are displayed in Table 14.

TABLE 14
Discriminant analysis for sex with 10 predictor variables*

| Actual group | % Predicted | |
| --- | --- | --- |
| | Boys | Girls |
| Boys | 66·9 | 33·1 |
| Girls | 26·9 | 73·1 |
| $X^2 = 114\cdot589$; $p < 0\cdot001$ | | |

*Variables used in the analysis were: tribal affiliation, church affiliation, job aspirations and expectations; political dissatisfaction; cognitive complexity; educational aspirations, optimism, pessimism and orientation.

According to the discriminant analysis girls appear slightly more coherent than boys on these 10 variables. The stepwise method was selected for performing the analysis.† This ranks the variables which

---

*The Discriminant Analysis technique is designed to apply to a new sample. In this instance we do not have a new sample but we have used the technique to confirm the interpretation placed on the data.

†The particular method selected was the Wilks method which ranks and in certain instances excludes variables on the basis of their contribution to the overall F ratio for the test of differences among the group centroids. (Nie et al., 1975).

All missing data was excluded from this analysis.

The same technique was used in all the remaining Discriminant Analyses.

(.a)

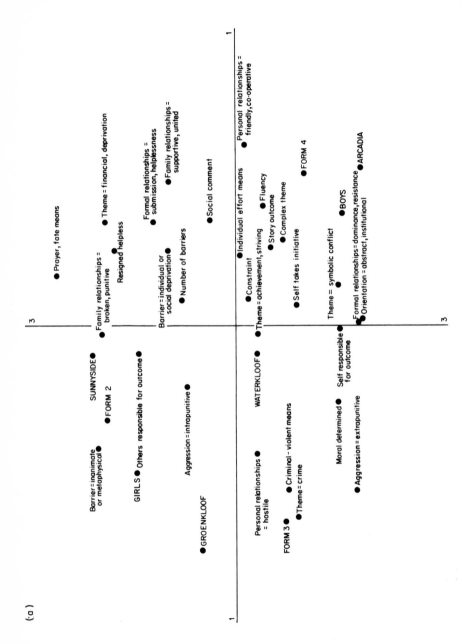

3

Prayer, fate means

Family relationships =
broken, punitive

Theme = financial, deprivation

Resigned helpless

Formal relationships =
submission, helplessness

Family relationships =
supportive, united

Barrier = individual or
social deprivation

Number of barriers

Social comment

Barrier = inanimate
or metaphysical

SUNNYSIDE

FORM 2

GIRLS Others responsible for outcome

Aggression = intrapunitive

Individual effort means

Constraint

Fluency

Theme = achievement, striving

Story outcome

Complex theme

Self takes initiative

FORM 4

GROENKLOOF

Theme = symbolic conflict

Personal relationships =
friendly, co-operative

WATERKLOOF

BOYS

Personal relationships
= hostile

Self responsible
for outcome

Formal relationships = dominance, resistance

ARCADIA

FORM 3

Criminal - violent means

Orientation = abstract, institutional

Theme = crime

Moral determined

Aggression = extrapunitive

3

1

1

(b)

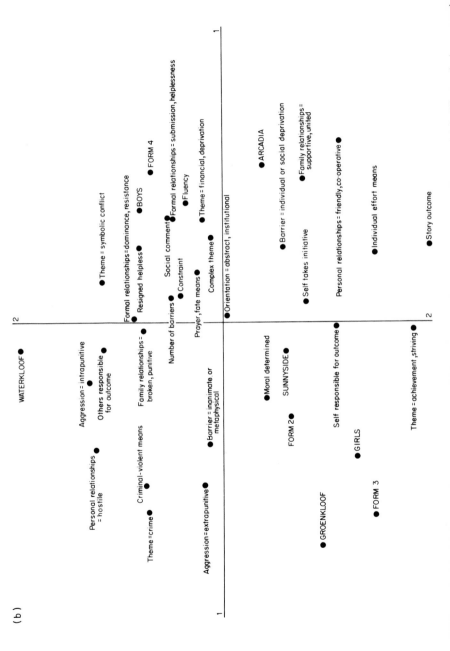

Fig. 5. Small space analysis. (a) Dimensions 1 and 3 for Thematic Apperception Test. (b) Dimensions 1 and 2 for Thematic Apperception Test.

(a)

4

Need/achievements ●

Theme = striving ● ● Theme = financial
SUNNYSIDE ●

● Pro tribe
Educational
optimism ●

Barrier = social deprivation ●

● Anti tribe
Urban ●
Earnings ●
High job aspirations ●

FORM 2 ●

Prefer vernacular ● ● Tribal affiliation
Barrier = physical,
inanimate ●
Church affiliation ●

Job motivation = altruism ●
Educational
orientation ●
High job expectations ●

Family relations = supportive ●

Educational pessimism
● Political dissatisfaction
● Complex
● FORM 4
ARCADIA ●
● BOYS

Prefer English ●

Educational
aspirations ●

Formal relationships = submission ●

Positive emotional tone ●
● Personal relationships = hostile

● GIRLS

GROENKLOOF ●

Family relationships
= broken ●

Pro tribe ●

Negative emotional tone ●

FORM 3 ●
WATERKLOOF ●
Constraint ●
Pro tribe ●

Low job aspirations ●

Low job expectations ●
● Personal relationships
= friendly
Formal relationships ●
= resistant

Aggression ●

Barrier = isolation ●
Anti tribe ●

Job motivation
= personal ●

Nationalism ●

● Anti tribe

4

1

(b)

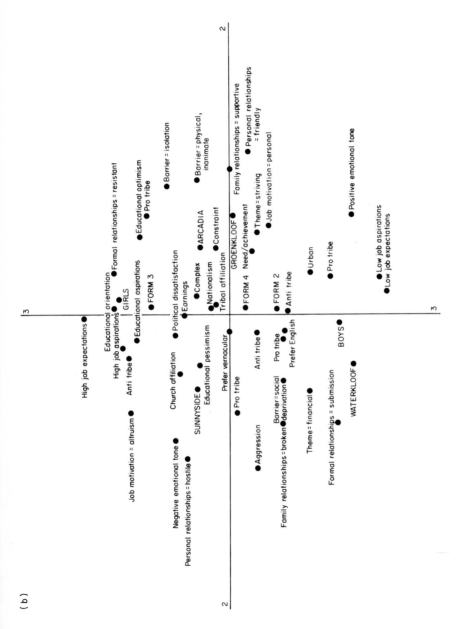

Fig. 6. Small space analysis. (a) Dimensions 1 and 4 for combined data. (b) Dimensions 2 and 3 for combined data.

fail to make a significant contribution to the analysis. The variables contributing most to the distinction between the sexes were job aspiration and expectation, cognitive complexity and educational aspirations. None of the 10 variables were excluded from the analysis.

The dimensions on the TAT which showed sex differences confirm the findings from the questionnaire. The boys produced longer, more complex and more abstract stories focussing more often on politics and deprivation than did the girls, and the girls produced fewer barriers. However, as can be seen from Fig. 5(a) and (b), the patterning on this test is less clear than for the questionnaire. What does emerge is that the differences between the sexes involve the greater hostility and aggression of the girls, coupled with a view that events of the world are out of their control, in contrast with the boys, and stress on bad personal and family relationships. The boys are more associated with friendly and supportive relationships, but also with a recognition of deprivation. The boys see control as deriving from within the individual in relation to personal action, far more than the girls. When the data from both techniques are combined, the sex differences remain, and are most clearly seen on dimension 1 of Fig. 6. Here we find the boys located on the pole of dimension 1 that is associated with political dissatisfaction, cognitive complexity, opposition to the tribe, resistance to domination, abstract themes and supportive family relations. Girls appear at the opposite end of the dimension, along with membership of the church, a pro-tribe attitude, preference for speaking one of the Bantu languages and simple themes. The sexes are polarized on this dimension even when it is paired with each of the other dimensions that appear in the solution to this particular SSA, and this emphasizes the potency of sex-role differentiation on attitude development. The sexes are again polarized on dimension 3, as seen in Fig. 6(b), which had appeared when the questionnaire alone, was analysed. This dimension reflects a move from low to high aspirations and expectations with girls associated with the latter and boys with the former. Again this points to the strength of occupational role differentiation in relation to responses on a sample of students.

The data show that the aspirations, expectations and evaluations of the world that students present, are minimally influenced by experiences that they bring with them to high school. Very little variation in the responses was found to be associated with factors from the family circumstances of the students, either in terms of the physical conditions under which they live, or in terms of those dimensions that are associated with social class. However the impact of sex-role differentiation is considerable. Firstly, it directly influences the occupational ambitions and expectations of the students, and the educational programme that they hope to follow. Secondly, whether mediated by these occupational plans or not, the boys and girls evaluate their society differently. It now remains to be seen how the educational system interacts with these gender related responses.

# Appendix C

# Aspirations, Evaluations and the Educational System

This study drew its respondents from three forms (or years) at four high schools in the Soweto area. The high schools were of two types: Junior Secondary Schools (Sunnyside and Groenkloof) which offer a three-year programme, and Senior Secondary Schools (Waterkloof and Arcadia) which offer a full five-year course. These structural features of the study allow the testing of the role of the school over time in developing aspirations and beliefs about the world and the individual's role within it. The role of the type of school can also be tested by contrasting the responses of students at schools which offer the example and the opportunity for successful completition of the full high school programme and those at schools which only offer the shorter course.

The data on aspirations indicate that these not only increase with increased schooling but also that there is more consistency within the sample as one goes up the school: the students in the higher forms show less variability than do those in the lower. The positive relationship between aspirations and form is more apparent for the boys than for the girls, with more boys in the fourth form aspiring to high professional careers than those in the lower forms and fewer hoping for lower grade professional jobs. Clerical and other white collar work decreases in attractiveness with more schooling, and so does work in the independent entrepreneurial category. The same trend is found for girls, though it is not significant: in the fourth form more girls aspire to high professional occupations and there is a consequent diminution in the numbers aspiring to the other types of jobs. The form differences for the boys can be seen reflected in the scores on a measure of relative deprivation, which indicates the discrepancy between aspirations and expectations (see Table 15). The boys raise their aspiration levels as they proceed through school but not necessarily their expectations, and as a result the discrepancy score increases from Form 2 to Form 4. Girls however show a reasonably constant discrepancy score between these measures. If relative deprivation is a measure of discontent then it would be expected that boys in the higher forms would show more dissatisfaction than those in the lower. The result may be anticipated

TABLE 15
Relative deprivation score for boys by form

| Form | Score |
|------|-------|
| 2 | 0·145 |
| 3 | 0·23 |
| 4 | 0·44 |

slightly by the finding that when asked for the reason for their choice of job those aspiring to professional careers gave answers which implicated altruistic concern for others, while those with lesser aspirations offered job-related reasons. This was true for both the boys ($p < 0.001$) and for girls ($p < 0.01$). However, the reasons for job expectation showed much less relation to the individual's value system, and the only significant result was that those boys who anticipate finding themselves eventually in manual occupations relate this to constraints within the environment—the cost of further education, the limited possibilities in the job market. Most students in fact had a fairly negative view about the job prospects within South Africa. When asked where they thought it would be easiest to find a good job, all, with the exception of those aspiring to social work, thought that the opportunities outside South Africa were better than within.

There were significant form differences in the variables that examined evaluations of the society. These can be seen in Fig. 4(a) and (b) in Appendix B. What the results show is that on dimension 1, which is a conservative to politically critical dimension, Form 2 is located at the conservative end and Form 4 at the politically critical, with the third form in the middle. This implies that cognitive complexity, educational aspirations, opposition to the tribe and increasing political dissatisfaction develop as the student moves through the school system. That these attitude differences are important can be seen in the results of a discriminant analysis, in which students were allocated to forms on the basis of ten selected variables. The results can be seen in Table 16. While approximately 65% of the second and fourth year students were correctly assigned, only 28·5% of the third form were correctly identified. A large percentage of them were predicted to be of the lower form.

TABLE 16
Discriminant Analysis for forms with 10 predictor variables*

| Actual group | % Predicted | | |
| --- | --- | --- | --- |
| | Form 2 | Form 3 | Form 4 |
| Form 2 | 65·8 | 18·8 | 15·3 |
| Form 3 | 42·3 | 28·5 | 29·2 |
| Form 4 | 17·4 | 18·2 | 64·5 |

*Variables used in the analysis were: tribal affiliation; church affiliation; job aspirations and expectations; political dissatisfaction; cognitive complexity; educational aspirations; optimism; pessimism and orientation.

This intermediate form does not present as distinctive and coherent a cluster of responses as the others. The most powerful variables discriminating between the forms were cognitive complexity, political dissatisfaction, tribal affiliation, educational aspirations and job expectations.

The form differences that have been noted can be considered independently of any variations in responses that might be found in relation to the type of school attended. In both the Junior Secondary Schools the second form is associated with the conservative end of the dimension and the third form shows movement towards the more critical pole, and a similar trend is found at the Senior Secondary Schools. (These analyses are not displayed here.)

As with the questionnaire, the TAT responses obtained from the sample indicate that the length of time spent at school influences the responses of the students to the critical stimuli. Table 17 shows those TAT variables on which students in the three forms responded differently. The relation between these responses and the variations produced on the questionnaire substantiates the general trends described. The fourth form students produce the longest, most abstract and most complex stories, and the greatest number of stories which refer to interpersonal and symbol conflict. Their writings tend to include most barriers, and these are mainly political or relate to deprivation and isolation. To overcome these barriers they utilize mainly political action or individual effort. They are the group least constrained by the stimulus demands of the cards, and produce the largest amount of verbal aggression. Form 2 stories were in the main simple and concrete, stressing interpersonal barriers, and the main means that they employed in the plots were co-operation and avoidance. Students from the third form included the least number of barriers, had the most favourable outcome to their plots which stressed isolation as the chief barrier, and violence as the main means of overcoming obstacles.

TABLE 17
Differences in responses of pupils from different forms on TAT cards

| | TAT dimension | $p<$ | Differences observed |
|---|---|---|---|
| 1. | Theme | 0·01 | Form 2 more achievement/deprivation |
| | | | Form 4 more interpersonal/symbol conflict |
| 2. | Thematic complexity | 0·001 | More abstract and more complex with higher forms |
| 3. | Story length | 0·001 | Form 4 longer stories |
| 4. | Number of barriers | 0·001 | Form 3 least barriers |
| | | | Form 4 most barriers |
| 5. | Type of barriers | 0·001 | Form 2 interpersonal |
| | | | Form 3 isolation |
| | | | Form 4 political, isolation, deprivation |
| 6. | Story outcome | 0·001 | Form 3 most favourable |
| 7. | Means employed | 0·02 | Form 2 cooperation; avoidance |
| | | | Form 3 violence |
| | | | Form 4 political action; individual effort |
| 8. | Card constraint | 0·001 | Form 4 least constrained |
| 9. | Type of aggression | 0·02 | Form 4 greatest verbal aggression |
| 10. | Family relations (nature of) | 0·02 | More supportive and united with higher forms |

The relationship of the forms' responses to the two types of techniques used to collect information can be seen in Fig. 6(a) and (b). The fourth form occupies an extreme position on dimension 1, which is the dimension associated with opposition to the tribe, abstract themes, cognitive complexity and a preference for English as the language of communication. In Fig. 6(b) the marker for fourth form students is located near the origin of the two dimensions which reflect low to high aspirations and expectations and negative to positive interpersonal relations. Form 2 students are more conservative, linked with church and tribe, and a preference for speaking in one of the Bantu languages. The third form is associated with constraint, negative emotional tone, broken family themes and isolation as a barrier—altogether a gloomy and unhappy constellation. They are also associated with higher job aspirations and expectations than the other forms.

A discriminant analysis using five variables emphasizes the lack of homogeneity in the third form. As Table 18 shows, some 60% of form 4 and 56% of form 2 students can be correctly allocated to their group on the basis of these variables, but only 38% of the third form can be so located. The results suggest that the students in the third form are in a transitional position, and not members of a group with a coherent posture.

TABLE 18
Discriminant analysis between forms with five predictor variables*

| Actual form | Predicted form % | | |
|:---:|:---:|:---:|:---:|
| | 2 | 3 | 4 |
| 2 | 56·3 | 22·9 | 20·8 |
| 3 | 32·5 | 38·1 | 29·4 |
| 4 | 22·4 | 17·6 | 60·0 |
| $X^2 = 37·63; p < 0·001$ | | | |

*Variables used in the analysis were: political dissatisfaction, cognitive complexity, complex theme, number of barriers and constraint.

The two Junior Secondary Schools show varied differences between forms 2 and 3. At Sunnyside there is a movement from the form 2 position of being cognitively simple, pro-tribe and church and using simple themes, to a third form position that is anti-tribe, cognitively complex and more politically discontent. Cognition and awareness clearly develop with progression through the school. Groenkloof, on the other hand, shows no such simple relationship. Students in the second form are associated with variables reflecting a concern for and awareness of deprivation, with the production of some complex themes, while at the third form level the association is with a pro-tribe and church position, simple themes and card constraint. Only students from forms three and four participated from Arcadia, and the SSA reflects the increase in political awareness and cognitive complexity with increased schooling. Waterkloof, which was the only school to supply students from all three years clearly supports the general pattern, namely that increased schooling leads to a more radical and critical position, as well as to cognitive advance. There is a clear progression from the conservative pole occupied by form 2 to the political discontent, rejection of the tribe and cognitively complex position occupied by form 4. (These analyses are not displayed here.)

Not only is the time spent at school of importance in the development of aspirations and attitudes, but the particular school at which time is spent has an impact on the nature of the responses. The school effects are however, not simply based on the Junior/Senior Secondary School distinction. The proportion of Arcadia pupils aspiring to professional careers is significantly greater than for the other three schools ($p < 0.02$). This difference holds even when the group is split by sex, and is also observable in relation to job expectation.

Waterkloof, Sunnyside and Groenkloof do not differ from each other significantly on job aspirations and expectations despite differences in curriculum. The variations in the schools' responses can be seen in the projection of the SSA that is presented in Fig. 4(a) and (b) indicate that on the questionnaire Arcadia is clearly positioned on dimension 1 surrounded by the variables associated with the anti-tribe, politically discontented constellation. The other three schools are towards the conservative end of the dimension. The position of the schools on this dimension remains no matter with which of the remaining three dimensions of the four dimension solution it is paired, confirming the strength of this in accounting for the largest amount of the variance in the school differences. Arcadia students are more radical, more cognitively complex and have higher educational aspirations than the other three schools, even if they share a similar school structure. On dimension 2, which is marked by low and high aspirations, Arcadia occupies an intermediate position and the other Senior Secondary School, Waterkloof, appears to be primarily associated with the low end. Sunnyside lies furthest in the direction of high job aspirations and expectations. Looking at the SSA projection it is clear that each of the four schools is associated with a different attitude cluster, and utilizing 10 variables it is possible to predict school membership on the basis of the variations in the attitudes held. The results are displayed in Table 19. The school with the largest number of pupils correctly predicted was Arcadia, with nearly 50% correct placement; Waterkloof does not show a clear and distinctive pattern, again indicating that the structural similarity is not sufficient to ensure attitudinal similarity. The two Junior Secondary Schools are about equally easy to predict.

The variables most powerful at predicting school membership, and by implication the major difference between pupils at the different schools, were cognitive complexity, political dissatisfaction, church and tribal affiliation and educational aspirations. As may have been expected these were the variables which discriminated the groups along dimension 1 of the Small Space Analysis.

A comparison between the Junior Secondary Schools (Sunnyside and Groenkloof) and Senior Secondary Schools (Waterkloof and Arcadia) by means of a discriminant analysis resulted in 58·7% of all pupils being correctly classified ($X^2$ 22·5; $p < 0.001$). The most powerful discriminating variables were the same as those found in the discriminant analysis for all schools. This suggests that the most significant differences between the two types of schools reflect the variables associated with dimension 1 of the Small Space Analysis, i.e. those associated with the politically conservative-politically radical dimension.

TABLE 19
Discriminant analysis for school with 10 predictor variables*

| Actual school | % Predicted | | | |
|---|---|---|---|---|
| | Waterkloof | Arcadia | Sunnyside | Groenkloof |
| Waterkloof | 26·5% | 25·1% | 22·3% | 26·1% |
| Arcadia | 15·0% | 49·6% | 20·3% | 15·0% |
| Sunnyside | 19·2% | 19·2% | 38·5% | 23·1% |
| Groenkloof | 17·1% | 20·7% | 27·0% | 35·1% |
| | $X^2 = 41.96$; $p < 0.001$ | | | |

*Variables used in the analysis were: tribal affiliation; church affiliation; job aspirations and expectations; political dissatisfaction; cognitive complexity; educational aspirations; optimism; pessimism and orientation.

The SSA suggested that the pupils from Arcadia may constitute a distinctive group; this was confirmed when a discriminant analysis was performed. 67·7% of all pupils were correctly assigned to either Arcadia or the three remaining schools combined according to their positions on the 10 predictor variables ($X^2$ 92·18; $p < 0.001$). The most powerful variables were the same as the two previous discriminant analyses with the addition of job expectations.

When the differences between schools are examined for each sex separately the differences which appeared in the combined analysis continue to be in evidence. The boys present a pattern of school associated attitudes and aspirations the same as that for the total sample, and an SSA for girls again clearly isolates Arcadia. Despite the fact that girls are more conservative than boys, Arcadia girls are more radical, or politically critical, than the girls at the other schools. Sunnyside girls have higher job aspirations and expectations, and the projections for Waterkloof and Groenkloof, although different types of school, are similar. (These analyses are not displayed here.)

It is possible that the school picture is confounded by the fact that not all schools contributed pupils in the higher form, and that Arcadia's peculiar prominence is due to the absence of form 2 students, whom we have seen to be the most conservative. An analysis was therefore performed to test this by using only form 3 students. Since all four schools contributed subjects from this group it is possible to test for school differences with years of education held constant. This analysis verifies the close association of Arcadia with measures of political dissatisfaction and radical attitudes. The other three schools are clustered around the political dimension in an unordered fashion. Dimension 2, again one associated with job aspirations and expectations finds Sunnyside at the high aspiration end and Waterkloof towards the low (not displayed here). Further, although the pattern of responses, as we have previously seen, is not as clear for third form students as it is for the other two forms, a discriminant analysis nevertheless still significantly distinguishes between the four schools with 39% correct allocation. As Table 20 indicates, Arcadia and Groenkloof students are the easiest to assign. There is one interesting result in the analysis of the third form responses which re-

TABLE 20

Discriminant Analysis for schools with 10 predictor variables.* Form 3 pupils only

| Actual group | % Predicted | | | |
|---|---|---|---|---|
| | Waterkloof | Arcadia | Sunnyside | Groenkloof |
| Waterkloof | 35·7 | 23·2 | 19·6 | 21·4 |
| Arcadia | 24·6 | 40·6 | 11·6 | 23·2 |
| Sunnyside | 17·6 | 20·3 | 37·8 | 24·3 |
| Groenkloof | 10·0 | 18·0 | 26·0 | 46·0 |

*Variables used in the analysis were: tribal affiliation; church affiliation; job aspirations and expectations; political dissatisfaction; cognitive complexity; educational aspirations; optimism; pessimism and orientation.

lates to the type of school attended, and is probably the strongest case for an argument relating to curriculum variations. A discriminant analysis dichotomizing third form students into Junior and Senior Secondary Schools resulted in 60% of the students being correctly assigned, and this suggests that the nature of the models available at the school may well be involved in decisions about the future, such that those students who work within the longer time perspective that the Senior Secondary Schools offer may in some instances be more alike than they are like students in the same year of study at the Junior schools. Finally it is worth noting that if Arcadia is opposed to the other three schools combined at the third year level, 63·6% of the students can be correctly assigned to their group on the basis of the most powerful variables, which were tribal and church affiliation, cognitive complexity and educational aspirations, optimism and orientation. At this level however, political dissatisfaction is not as potent a discriminator as it is for the total sample, although it does add significantly to the difference between Arcadia and the other three schools.

The schools differed on a number of variables measured by the projective test. Again Arcadia shows a distinct pattern which is different from that of the other schools. The variations are shown in Table 21. The pupils from Arcadia produce stories which include significantly more political barriers, more resistance to power, more verbal aggression as well as reflecting the most gentle emotional tone and the largest number of favourable outcomes. What is also of interest is that their

TABLE 21

Differences in responses of pupils from the different schools on TAT cards

| | TAT dimension | $p <$ | Differences observed |
|---|---|---|---|
| 1. | Theme | 0·02 | Waterkloof the most crime and conflict Groenkloof the most deprivation and achievement |
| 2. | Thematic complexity | 0·001 | Sunnyside and Waterkloof more concrete |
| 3. | Story length | 0·001 | Waterkloof then Arcadia longest stories |
| 4. | Number of barriers | 0·001 | Sunnyside lets barriers |
| 5. | Type of barriers | 0·001 | Arcadia most political/isolation Groenkloof most deprivation |
| 6. | Surmounting of barriers | 0·001 | Sunnyside no attempt Waterkloof success |
| 7. | Story outcome | 0·001 | Sunnyside most unfavourable Arcadia most favourable |
| 8. | Emotional tone | 0·001 | Sunnyside most moralistic Arcadia most gentle |
| 9. | Card constraint | 0·001 | Sunnyside most constrained |
| 10. | Type of aggression | 0·05 | Arcadia more verbal aggression |
| 11. | Family relations (nature of) | 0·01 | Arcadia more supportive |
| 12. | Interpersonal relations (nature of) | 0·001 | Arcadia most positive |
| 13. | Power relations (nature of) | 0·05 | Arcadia most resistance Sunnyside most submissive |

stories suggest the most positive interpersonal relations and the most family support. When the results are subjected to an SSA analysis (see Fig. 5) there is evidence that the schools are associated with clear and distinct attitude and aspiration clusters and that the position of the schools is not dependent on the nature of their structure. Arcadia is a polar opposite of Groenkloof on the first dimension, which is defined at one end by positive interpersonal relations and at its other extreme by hostile relations. The other two dimensions in the solution associate Arcadia with complex and fluent stories, and a stress on internal control, striving and conflict with authority.

The patterning for Sunnyside links that school with broken family relationships and a moral tone to the stories, and it is also associated with the main character taking the initiative—as indeed is Arcadia. Waterkloof occupies an extreme position around variables of poor relationships, aggression and external control of outcomes. Arcadia presents the most clear constellation of responses, but each of the other schools has something distinct in the responses of the students. The clarity of the Arcadia associations is further illustrated by the fact that when various discriminant analyses were performed on the data the most significant, and in percentage terms the most successful, was that which simply dichotomized the sample between Arcadia and the rest. In this case 66% of the students were correctly assigned.

When the data from the questionnaire and the TAT are combined the school distinctions continue to show. Arcadia is clearly associated with the variables of political dissatisfaction, cognitive complexity, abstract handling of themes, opposition to the tribe, a preference for English, and resistance to domination. Its opposite is Groenkloof, with simple themes, tribal and church affiliation, and a preference for the vernacular. Sunnyside is associated with achievement, striving, and a position of support for the tribe, while Waterkloof is linked to constraint, isolation and negative emotional tone. Sunnyside reflects negative and Arcadia positive interpersonal relations, and Waterkloof is tied to low aspirations and expectations, submissiveness and helplessness and de-privation. It is a school which reflects a decidedly pessimistic and negative position.

Using the five predictor variables to see if the students could be allocated to school appropriately by means of a discriminant analysis it appeared that again the most homogeneous school was Arcadia, and we were able to allocate 50% of its students to the right school. The results can be seen on Table 22. When however we oppose Arcadia to all the other schools we still get a highly significant result $X^2 = 41 \cdot 6$; $p < 0 \cdot 001$) and the correct assignment of $68 \cdot 4\%$ of the students. Since on the dimension that seems to be the most persistent on the SSA (dimension 1) Arcadia and Groenkloof were opposed, we were interested to find that comparing these two schools alone $70 \cdot 3\%$ correct assignment occurred. The variables from the questionnaire of poli-

TABLE 22

Discriminant Analysis for schools with five predictor variables*

| Actual group | Predicted group % | | | |
|---|---|---|---|---|
| | Waterkloof | Arcadia | Sunnyside | Groenkloof |
| Waterkloof | 45·7 | 18·5 | 12·3 | 23·5 |
| Arcadia | 21·4 | 50·0 | 9·2 | 19·4 |
| Sunnyside | 19·8 | 24·7 | 35·8 | 19·8 |
| Groenkloof | 21·3 | 17·0 | 21·3 | 40·4 |

$$X^2 = 56 \cdot 94; p < 0 \cdot 001$$

*Variables used in the analysis were: political dissatisfaction, cognitive complexity, complex theme, number of barriers and constraint.

tical dissatisfaction and cognitive complexity, and from the TAT of complex theme, number of barriers and constraint can therefore account for a great deal of the between-school variance. When the same variables are used to make discriminations between the type of school, opposing the Senior and the Junior Secondary Schools, $61 \cdot 6\%$ of the cases are correctly classified. There is less likelihood of misclassifying the Junior Secondary students as Senior than the other way around. This can be accounted for by the fact that Waterkloof is more like the Junior Secondary Schools on many of the measures than it is like its fellow Senior School of Arcadia.

The process of education influences the aspirations and the evaluations of the Soweto student in two main ways. Firstly, the length of time the student spends within the educational system relates to the nature of his and her view of what should be the role eventually played in the outside world. It also effects the way that outside world is perceived. That this may be part of the impact of education in terms of the opportunities it makes possible is supported by the fact that the major differences are between the second and the fourth forms, which are associated with in the first instance simply being at school, and in the second case having made a conscious decision to remain and join the small group of high school graduates, or even eventually, of University students. The third form students are not as clearly defined: some will continue and therefore would be similar to the fourth formers, others will be undecided, and therefore might resemble the second form, and yet a third group may well know that they are soon to leave school, and find a place in society, and this could well mark their evaluations. Thus schooling in terms of progression through the system must be seen in relation to the role of that system in preparing the student for work outside.

Potent though this progression is its strength is somewhat curtailed both by the impact of sex-role differentiation, and also by the nature of the school in which the student is being educated. The school effect is important, and although in some instances the observed variations could well be explained in terms of the course available, in many others this is an inadequate assumption. Each school seems to present a profile, some clearer than others. These profiles are consistent across the many analyses to which the responses were subjected. The differences are coherent, and important.

# Appendix D

# Distributions of TAT Responses

## Percentage distributions of TAT responses on form categories

### (a) Story length (words)

| 0–30 | 31–60 | 61–90 | 91–120 | 121–150 | 151–180 | 181–210 | 211–240 | 240+ |
|------|-------|-------|--------|---------|---------|---------|---------|------|
| 3·0% | 9·9% | 16·3% | 25% | 23·2% | 12·2% | 5·5% | 2·2% | 2·7% |

### (b) Fluency

| Low | Poor | Average | Good | High |
|-----|------|---------|------|------|
| 5·9% | 24·3% | 36·9% | 23·5% | 9·4% |

### (c) Level of complexity of theme

| Concrete | | | Abstract | | |
|----------|--------|------|----------|--------|------|
| Low | Medium | High | Low | Medium | High |
| 28·6 | 22·0 | 25·6 | 11·0 | 8·0 | 4·8 |
| Total | 76·2% | | Total | 23·8% | |

## Percentage distributions of TAT responses on content categories

### (a) Themes as per cent of all cards described

| Crime | Inter-personal | Family | Financial/deprivation | Striving/achieving | Politico-legal | Work | Other |
|-------|----------------|--------|-----------------------|--------------------|----------------|------|-------|
| 16·3 | 19·5 | 10·6 | 13·7 | 10·4 | 7·0 | 3·9 | 18·6 |

(b) Percentage distribution of sample on story outcome

| Unfavour- able | Fatalistic | Avoided | Neutral | Statement of preception | Favourable | No story |
|---|---|---|---|---|---|---|
| 23·2 | 5·0 | 8·7 | 11·6 | 14·4 | 14·3 | 22·8 |

(c) Main type of action as percentage of all stories

| Crimi- nal- violent | Politi- cal action | Argu- ment/ persua- sion | Co-op | Indi- vidual effort | Prayer | Provi- dence/ chance | With- drawal avoid- ance | No action |
|---|---|---|---|---|---|---|---|---|
| 21·1 | 4·2 | 6·4 | 6·4 | 12·0 | 1·5 | 6·7 | 3·8 | 37·9 |

(d) Percentage distribution of sample across number of barriers

| None | One | Two | Three or more |
|---|---|---|---|
| 39·5 | 55·4 | 4·0 | 1·1 |

(e) Percentage distribution of sample on type of barrier

| None | Individual limitation and deprivation | Isolation/ alienation | Interpersonal barriers | Physical/ inanimate | Socio-economic (legal) |
|---|---|---|---|---|---|
| 39·3 | 23·8 | 6·8 | 11·9 | 12·8 | 5·3 |

(f) Percentage distribution of sample across relationship dimensions: Family relationships

| Avoided | Negative | Neutral | Positive |
|---|---|---|---|
| 72·1 | 10 | 4 | 13·9 |

(g) Interpersonal relationships

| Avoided | Negative | Neutral | Positive |
|---|---|---|---|
| 59·8 | 12·0 | 6·7 | 21·5 |

(h) Formal relationships

| Avoided | Submissive | Neutral | Non-submissive |
|---------|-----------|---------|----------------|
| 84·1    | 8·3       | 2·0     | 5·6            |

(i) Percentage distribution of sample across emotional tone

| Pleasant | Moralistic | Neutral | Unpleasant |
|----------|-----------|---------|------------|
| 15·2     | 30·9      | 33·0    | 21·9       |

(j) Percentage distribution of sample across type of aggression

| No aggression | Verbal | Robbery | Fighting | Assault | Rape | Murder | Hypo-thetical |
|---------------|--------|---------|----------|---------|------|--------|---------------|
| 66·7          | 2·6    | 9·9     | 4·2      | 2·7     | 0·6  | 4·6    | 8·7           |

(k) Need achievement: Percentage distribution by subject

| None | Very low | Low  | Moderate | High |
|------|----------|------|----------|------|
| 40·1 | 36·7     | 18·9 | 2·8      | 1·5  |

(l) Card constraint

| High | Moderate | Low  | Very low |
|------|----------|------|----------|
| 13·5 | 22·0     | 33·4 | 31·1     |

# Appendix E

# Variables used in SSA analyses

## Questionnaire: Variables in Small Space Analysis

1   Tribe affiliation
2   Urbanism
3   Church affiliation
4   Earnings
5   Political dissatisfaction
6   Nationalism
7   Cognitive complexity
8   Educational aspirations
9   Educational orientation
10  Educational pessimism
11  Educational optimism
12  Waterloof
13  Arcadia
14  Sunnyside
15  Groenkloof
16  Boys
17  Girls
18  Form 2
19  Form 3
20  Form 4
21  Rural origins
22  Urban origins
23  Prefer own vernacular

24  Prefer English
25  Bantu church
26  Constraint
27  High job aspirations
28  Low job aspirations
29  High job expectations
30  Low job expectations
31  Pro tribe (membership—inevitable + legislative demands
32  Pro tribe (membership—ethnocentric)
33  Pro tribe (membership—individual support)
34  Pro tribe (membership—identity)
35  Against tribe (membership—factions, divisions, inequalities)
36  Against tribe (membership—nationalism, oppression by government or tribe, progress)

## Thematic Apperception Test: Variables in Small Space Analysis

| | | | |
|---|---|---|---|
| 1 | Fluency | 21 | Theme=symbolic conflict |
| 2 | Complex theme | 22 | Orientation=abstract, institutional |
| 3 | Story outcome | 23 | Social comment |
| 4 | Number of barriers | 24 | Family relationships= broken, punitive |
| 5 | Constraint | | |
| 6 | Criminal-violent means | 25 | Family relationships= supportive, united |
| 7 | Individual effort means | | |
| 8 | Prayer, fate, means | 26 | Personal relationships= hostile |
| 9 | Barrier=individual or social deprivation | | |
| | | 27 | Personal relationships= friendly, co-operative |
| 10 | Barrier=inanimate, or metaphysical | | |
| | | 28 | Formal relationships= submission, helplessness |
| 11 | Self responsible for outcomes | | |
| | | 29 | Formal relationships= dominance, resistance |
| 12 | Others responsible for outcome | | |
| | | 30 | Waterkloof |
| 13 | Self takes initiative | 31 | Arcadia |
| 14 | Moral, determined (emotional tone) | 32 | Sunnyside |
| | | 33 | Groenkloof |
| 15 | Resigned, helpless (emotional tone) | 34 | Boys |
| | | 35 | Girls |
| 16 | Aggression=intrapunitive | 36 | Form 2 |
| 17 | Aggression=extrapunitive | 37 | Form 3 |
| 18 | Theme=crime | 38 | Form 4 |
| 19 | Theme=financial, deprivation | | |
| 20 | Theme=achievement, striving | | |

# Variables Used in Small Space Analysis:
## Combined Data

| | | | |
|---|---|---|---|
| 1 | Tribal affiliation | 32 | Rural origins |
| 2 | Urban | 33 | Prefer vernacular |
| 3 | Church affiliation | 34 | Prefer English |
| 4 | High job aspirations | 35 | Pro tribe (inevitable) |
| 5 | Low job aspirations | 36 | Pro tribe (ethnocentric) |
| 6 | High job expectations | 37 | Pro tribe (individual support) |
| 7 | Low job expectations | | |
| 8 | Political dissatisfaction | 38 | Pro tribe (identity) |
| 9 | Nationalism | 39 | Anti tribe (faction fights) |
| 10 | Complex | 40 | Anti tribe (nationalism) |
| 11 | Need achievements | 41 | Anti tribal opposition (progress) |
| 12 | Earnings | | |
| 13 | Educational aspirations | 42 | Job motivation = personal |
| 14 | Educational orientation | 43 | Job motivation = altruism |
| 15 | Educational pessimism | 44 | Theme = financial |
| 16 | Educational optimism | 45 | Theme = striving |
| 17 | Simple themes | 46 | Barrier = isolation |
| 18 | Abstract complex themes | 47 | Barrier = social deprivation |
| 19 | Negative emotional tone | 48 | Barrier = physical inanimate |
| 20 | Positive emotional tone | 49 | Family relationships = broken |
| 21 | Constraint | | |
| 22 | Aggression | 50 | Family relationships = supportive |
| 23 | Waterkloof | | |
| 24 | Arcadia | 51 | Personal relationships = hostile |
| 25 | Sunnyside | | |
| 26 | Groenkloof | 52 | Personal relationships = friendly |
| 27 | Boys | | |
| 28 | Girls | 53 | Formal relationships = submission |
| 29 | Form 2 | | |
| 30 | Form 3 | 54 | Formal relationships = resistant |
| 31 | Form 4 | | |

# References

Ainsworth, L. H. and Ainsworth, M. D. (1962). Acculturation in East Africa: 1. Political awareness and attitudes to authority 2. Frustration and aggression 3. Attitudes to parents, teachers and education. *J. Soc. Psychol.* **57,** 2.

Albino, R. and Thompson, V. J. (1956). The effect of sudden weaning on Zulu children. *Br. J. Med. Psychol.* **29,** 177–210.

Allport, F. (1955). "Theories of Perception and the Concept of Structure." Wiley, New York.

Allport, G. W. and Pettigrew, T. F. (1957). Cultural influences on the perception of movement: the trapezoidal illusion among Zulus. *J. Abnorm. Soc. Psychol.* **55,** 104–113.

Andersson, B. E. (1969). "Studies in Adolescent Behaviour." Almqvist and Wiksell, Stockholm.

Armer, J. M. (1970). Formal education and psychological malaise in an African society. *Sociol. Ed.* **43,** 143–158.

Aronson, E. and Mills, J. (1959). The effect of severity of initiations on liking for a group. *J. Abnorm. Soc. Psychol.* **59,** 177–181.

Ashford, N. (1977). Is the Afrikaner's choice between change and national suicide? *The Times,* London, 23 May.

Ausubel, D. P. (1960). Acculturative stress in modern Maori adolescence. *Child Dev.* **31,** 617–631.

*Bantu Education Journal* Editorial, August, 1975.

Baran, S. (1971). Development and validation of a TAT-type projective test for use among Bantu-speaking people. *B.I.P.R.* Johannesburg.

Baran, S. (1975). Zulu acculturation in South Africa. *In* "Contemporary South Africa." (Morse, S. J. and Orpen, C., Eds) Juta and Co., Cape Town.

Bartlett, F. C. (1932). "Remembering: A Study in Experimental and Social Psychology." Cambridge University Press.

Battle, E. S. and Rotter, J. B. (1963). Children's feelings of personal control as related to social class and ethnic group. *J. Pers.* **31,** 482–490.

Bennett, W. S. and Gist, N. P. (1964). Class and family influences on student aspirations. *Social Forces* **43,** 167–173.

Bernstein, B. (1971). "Class, Codes and Control." Vol. 1. Paladin, London.

Bernstein, B. and Henderson, D. (1969). Social class differences in the relevance of language to socialisation. *Sociology* **3,** 1.

Biesheuwel, S. (1955). The measurement of African attitudes towards European ethical concepts, customs, laws and administration of justice. *J. Nat. Inst. Personnel Res.* **6,** 5–17.

Biesheuwel, S. (1957). Moral judgements of Africans and Europeans. *S. A. J. Science* **53,** 309–314.

Bloom, L. (1960). Self concepts and social status in South Africa: a preliminary cross-cultural analysis. *J. Soc. Psychol.* **51,** 103–112.

Botha, E. (1964). Some value differences among adults and children in South Africa. *J. Soc. Psychol.* **65,** 241–248.

Boyle, R. P. (1966). The effect of the high school on students' aspirations. *Amer. J. Sociol.* **71,** 6, 628–639.

Brett, E. A. (1963). "African Attitudes: A Study of the Social, Racial and Political Attitudes of some Middle Class Africans." South African Institute of Race Relations, Johannesburg.

Bruner, J. (1951). Personality dynamics and perceiving. *In* "Perception: An Approach to Personality." (Blake, R. R. and Ramsay, G. U., Eds) Ronald Press, New York.

Bureminal, L. G. (1961). Differences in educational and occupational aspirations of farm, small town and city boys. *Rural Sociol.* **26,** 107–121.

Callincos, A. and Rogers, J. (1977). "Southern Africa after Soweto." Pluto Press, London.

Caro, F. G. and Philbard, C. T. (1965). Aspirations and expectations: a re-examination of the basis for social class differences in the occupational orientations of Hall High School students. *Social and Soc. Res.* **49,** 465–475.

Clifford, E. and Clifford, M. (1967). Self concepts before and after survival training. *Br. J. Soc. Clin. Psychol.* **16,** 241–248.

Coleman, J. S. (1961). "The Adolescent Society." Free Press, New York.

Coleman, J. S. (1966). "Equality of Educational Opportunity." U.S. Dept of Health Education and Welfare, Washington.

Coopersmith, S. (1967). "The Antecedents of Self-esteem." Freeman and Co., Reading.

Crandall, V. C., Katovsky, W. and Crandall, V. J. (1965). Children's beliefs in their control of reinforcement in intellectual-academic achievement situations. *Child Dev.* **36,** 91–109.

Crutchfield, R. S. (1955). Conformity and characters. *Amer. Psychol.* **10,** 191–198.

Danziger, K. (1958). Value differences among South African students. *J. Abnorm. Soc. Psychol.* **57,** 339–346.

Danziger, K. (1963). The psychological future of an oppressed group. *Soc. Forces* **42,** 31–40.

Danziger, K. (1971). "Socialisation." Penguin, Harmondsworth.

de Preez, P. (1968). Social change and field dependence in South Africa. *J. Soc. Psychol.* **76,** 265–266.

de Ridder, J. C. (1961). "The Personality of the Urban African in South Africa." Routledge and Kegan Paul, London.

Dollard, J., Doob, L., Miller, N., Mowrer, O. and Sears, R. (1939). "Frustration and Aggression." Yale University Press.

Dollin, A. P. (1960). The effect of order of presentation on perception of TAT. Unpublished Ph.D. thesis. University of Connecticut.

Douglas, J. W. B. (1966). "The Home and the School." Penguin, Harmondsworth.

Douglas, J. W. B., Ross, J. M. and Shipson, H. R. (1968). "All Our Future." Panther, St Albans.

Edelstein, M. L. (1972). "What do young Africans think?" SAIRR, Johannesburg.

Elliot, J. and Elliot, D. H. (1970). Review of studies of birth order and achievement. *Proc. Ann. Convention* A.P.A.

Erikson, E. H. (1950). "Childhood and Society." Pelican, Harmondsworth.

Ezekiel, R. S. (1968). The personal future and Peace Corps competence. *J. Pers. soc. Psychol. Monogr. Suppl.* **8,** 1–26.

Feld, S. and Smith, C. P. (1958). An evaluation of the method of content analysis. *In* "Motives in Fantasy, Action and Society." (Atkinson, J. W., Ed.) van Nostrand Press, Wokingham.

Festinger, L. (1957). "A Theory of Cognitive Dissonance." Stanford University Press.
Fishbein, M. and Ajzen, J. (1975). "Beliefs, Attitudes, Intentions and Behaviour." Addison Wesley, London.
Garza, J. M. (1969). Race, the achievement syndrome and perception of opportunity. *Phylon* **30**, 4, 338–354.
Geber, B. A. (1971). The liberal dilemma in South Africa. *Patterns of Prejudice* **7**, 11–14.
Geber, B. A. (1972). Occupational Aspirations and Expectations of South African High School Children. Unpublished Ph.D. thesis, University of London.
Geber, B. A. (1976). Education in Soweto. *Patterns of Prejudice* **10**, 25–29.
Geber, B. A. (Ed.) (1977). "Piaget and Knowing: Studies in Genetic Epistemology." Routledge and Kegan Paul, London.
Geber, B. A. and Webley, P. (1980). Experience and society. *In* "Towards a Theory of Psychological Development." (Modgil, S. and Modgil, C., Eds) N.F.E.R., Windsor.
Gillespie, J. M. and Allport, G. (1955). "Youth's Outlook on the Future." Doubleday, New York.
Goody, J. (1977). Literacy, criticism and the growth of knowledge. *In* "Culture and its Creator." (Ben David and Clark, Eds) University of Chicago Press.
Gough, I. R. (1970). Aspirations of aboriginal children. *Austral. Psychol.* **5**, 3, 267–269.
Gregor, A. J. and McPherson, D. A. (1966). Racial preference and ego identity among White and Bantu children in the Republic of South Africa. *Gen. Psychol. Monogr.* **73**, 217–253.
Gurin, P., Gurin, G., Lao, R. and Beattie, H. (1969). Internal–external control in the motivational dynamics of Negro youth. *J. Soc. Issues* **25**, 29–53.
Gurr, T. R. (1970). "Why Men Rebel." Princeton University Press.
Haney, C., Banks, C. and Zimbardo, P. (1973). Interpersonal dynamics in a simulated prison. *Internat. J. Crim. Penol.* **1**, 69–97.
Harkness, S. and Super, C. M. (1977). Why African children are so hard to test. *Annals N.Y. Acad. Sci.* **285**, 326–331.
Heim, A. (1970). "Intelligence and Personality." Penguin, Harmondsworth.
Hellmann, E. (1948). "Rooiyard: a Sociological Study of an Urban Slumyard." Oxford University Press.
Hemming, J. (1966). Paper presented to annual Conference of Social Psychology. *In* "The School as an Agent of Socialisation." (Sealy, A. P. and Himmelweit, H., Eds).
Himmelweit, H. and Swift, B. (1969). A model for the understanding of the school as a socialising agent. *In* "Trends and Issues in Developmental Psychology." (Mussen, P., Ed.) Holt Rinehart and Winston, Eastbourne.
Himmelweit, H. and Wright, J. C. (1967). The school system, social class and attainment after school. Paper read at Annual Conference of B.P.S., Swansea.
Hodgkins, D. J. and Parr, A. (1965). Educational and occupational aspirations among rural and urban male adolescents in Alberta. *Alberta J. Ed. Res.* **11**, 255–262.
Holmes, R. (1970). The transient and the subsumed. *Compar. Ed. Rev.* **14**, 60–64.
Horrell, M. (1970). "Bantu Education to 1968." South African Institute of Race Relations, Johannesburg.
Horrell, M. (1970). "The Education of the Coloured Community in South Africa 1652–1970." South African Institute of Race Relations, Johannesburg.
Hudson, W. (1962). The study of the problem of pictorial perception among un-acculturated groups. *Internat. J. Psychol.* **2**, 90–107.
Hunter, M. (1946). "Reaction to Conquest." Oxford University Press.
Inhelder, B. and Piaget, J. (1958). "The Growth of Logical Thinking from Childhood to Adolescence." Basic Books, New York.

Jackson, B. and Marsden, D. (1962). "Education and the Working Class." Routledge and Kegan Paul, London.

Jahoda, G. (1969). "The Psychology of Superstition." Penguin, Harmondsworth.

Jahoda, G. (1970). Supernatural beliefs and changing cognitive structures among Ghanaian university students. *J. Cross-Cultural Psychol*. **1**, 115–130.

Johnson, R. W. (1977). "How Long Will South Africa Survive?" Macmillan, London.

Kenny, D. T. (1961). A theoretical and research reappraisal of stimulus factors in the T.A.T. *In* "Contemporary Issues in Thematic Apperceptive Methods." (Kagan, J. and Lesser, G., Eds) Charles C. Thomas, Springfield.

Kilson, M. (1972). The Negro and cultural pluralism. *In* "Education for Cultural Pluralism." (Eppel, E. M., Ed.) W.J.C., London.

Kuvlevsky, W. P. and Ohlendorf, G. (1968). A rural–urban comparison of the occupational status orientations of Negro boys. *Rural Sociol*. **33**, 2, 141–152.

Laskowitz, D. (1959). The effect of varied degrees of pictorial ambiguity on fantasy evocation. Unpublished Ph.D. thesis. New York University.

Lazarus, J., Kessel, F. and Botha, E. (1969). Cultural differences in n-ach externality between White and Coloured South Africa adolescents. *J. Soc. Psychol*. **77**, 133–134.

Legum, C. (1975). "Southern Africa: the Secret Diplomacy of Detente. South Africa at the Cross Roads." Rex Collings, London.

Legum, C. (Ed.) (1977). "African Contemporary Record, 1975–1976." Rex Collings, London.

Leiss, C. (1965). "Apartheid and the United Nations." Carnegie Endowment for International Peace, New York.

LeVine, R. A. (1966). "Dreams and Deeds: Achievement Motivation in Nigeria." University of Chicago Press.

Lindzey, G. and Goldberg, M. (1953). Motivational differences between male and female as measured by the T.A.T. *J. Pers*. **22**, 101–117.

Lindzey, G. and Heinemann, S. H. (1955). T.A.T. individual and group administration. *J. Pers*. **24**, 34–55.

Lindzey, G. and Silverman, M. (1957). Thematic apperception test: techniques of group administration, sex differences and the role of verbal productivity. *J. Pers*. **27**, 311–323.

Lingoes, J. C. (1973). "The Guttman Lingoes Non-Metric Programme Theory." Mathesis Press, Ann Arbor.

Lobban, G. (1975). Self attitudes of urban Africans. *In* "Contemporary South Africa: Social Psychological Perspectives." (Morse, S. D. and Orpen, C., Eds) Juta and Co., Cape Town.

Lowe, W. F. (1951). Effect of controlling the immediate environment on responses to the T.A.T. Unpublished M.A. thesis. University of Louisville.

Lystad, M. H. (1970). Adolescent social attitudes in South Africa and Swaziland. *Amer. Anthrop*. **72**, 1389–1397.

Maccoby, E. E. (Ed.) (1966). "The Development of Sex Differences." Stanford University Press.

MacCrone, I. D. (1937). "Race Attitudes in South Africa." Oxford University Press.

McGuire, W. J. (1967). Some impending re-orientation in social psychology. *J. Exp. Soc. Psychol*. **3**, 124–139.

Mann, J. W. (1962). Race linked values in South Africa. *J. Soc. Psychol*. **58**, 31–41.

Marris, P. (1967). Individual achievement and family ties: some international comparisons. *J. Marriage Family* **29**, 4, 763–771.

Mason, B. B. (1952). An experimental investigation of the effect of repetition and variation in administration upon the T.A.T. Unpublished M.A. thesis. University of Louisville.

de Mause, L. (1974). "The History of Childhood." Condor Books.

Mayer, P. (1961). "Tribesmen or Townsmen: Urbanisation in a Divided Society." Oxford University Press.

Melamet, A. M. (1977). "South Africa—its Racial Problems and Jewish Reaction." W.J.C., London.

Momberg, A. P. and Page, H. W. (1977). Self-esteem of Coloured and White scholars and students in South Africa. *J. Soc. Psychol.* **102**, 179–182.

Moore, W. E. (1969). Social structure and behaviour. *In* "The Handbook of Social Psychology." Vol. IV (Lindzey, G. and Aronson, E., Eds) Addison Wesley, London.

Morris, D. (1973). "The Washing of the Spears." Cardinal Edition, Sphere Books, London.

Moss, H. and Kagan, J. (1961). Stability of achievement—and recognition-seeking behaviour from early childhood through adulthood. *J. Abnorm. Soc. Psychol.* **64**, 504–513.

Mphahlele, E. (1958). The African intellectual. *In* "Africa in Transition." (Smith, P., Ed.) Reinhardt, London.

Murray, H. A. (1943). "Thematic Apperception Test Manual." Harvard University Press.

Murstein, B. I. (1963). "Theory and Research in Projective Techniques." Wiley, New York.

Nakasa, N. (1964). It's difficult to decide my identity. Reprinted in *Classic Magazine* **2**, 1, 1966.

Nedbank Group, The (1977). "South Africa: an Appraisal." The Netherlands Bank of South Africa.

Nie, N., Hadlai Hull, C., Jenkins, J., Steinbrewner, K. and Bent, D. (1975). "Statistical Package for the Social Sciences." 2nd edn. McGraw Hill, New York.

Nuttall, R. L. (1964). Some correlates of high need for achievement among urban northern Negroes. *J. Abnorm. Soc. Psychol.* **68**, 6, 593–600.

Olivier, N. J. J. (1954). "Apartheid—a Slogan or a Solution." SABRA, Stellenbosch.

Orpen, C. (1976). The expectancy beliefs, instrumentality beliefs and job reward valences of Black and White workers in South Africa. *Br. J. Soc. Clin. Psychol.* **15**, 365–368.

Pauw, B. A. (1963). "The Second Generation." Oxford University Press.

Perry, A. (1974). "African Secondary School Leavers: Employment Experiences and Attitudes to Employment." South African Institute of Race Relations, Johannesburg.

Piaget, J. (1932). "The Moral Judgment of the Child." Routledge and Kegan Paul, London.

Popper, K. (1976). "Unended Quest: an Intellectual Autobiography." Fontana, London.

Randall, P. (Ed.) (1972). "Power, Privilege and Poverty." Report of the Sprocas Economics Commission, Johannesburg.

Reader, D. H. (1959). "Black Man's Portion." Oxford University Press.

Reader, D. H. (1969). Summary of N.I.P.R. Afro-European Research. *Psychologica Africana* **10**, 1–18.

Rehlberg, R. A. and Westby, D. L. (1967). Parental encouragement, occupation, education and family size: artefactual or independent determinants of adolescent educational expectations. *Soc. Forces* **45**, 362–373.

Rehlberg, R. A., Shafter, W. E. and Sinclair, J. (1970). Toward a temporal sequence of adolescent achievement variables. *Amer. Soc. Rev.* **35**, 1, 34–48.

Rosen, B. C. (1961). Family structure and achievement motivation. *Amer. Sociol. Rev.* **26**, 574–585.

Rotter, J. B. (1966). Generalised expectancies for internal versus external control of reinforcement. *Psychol. Monogr.* **80**, 1.

Sampson, A. (1973). "The New Anatomy of Britain." Stein and Day, New York.

Sealy, P. and Himmelweit, H. (1966). "The School as an Agent in Socialisation." Report for the U.S. Social Science Research Council's Committee on Socialisation.

Sewell, W. H. and Shaw, V. P. (1968). Parents' education and children's educational aspirations and achievements. *Am. Soc. Rev.* **33**, 191–209.

Shalit, B. (1970). Environmental hostility and hostility in fantasy. *J. Pers. Soc. Psychol.* **15**, 2, 171–174.

Sherwood, E. T. (1957). On the designing of T.A.T. pictures with special reference to a SCI for African people assimilating Western culture. *J. Soc. Psychol.* **47**, 285–316.

Sherwood, R. (1958). The Bantu clerk: a study of role expectations. *J. Soc. Psychol.* **47**, 285–316.

Sigel, I. E. and Cocking, R. R. (1977). Cognition and communication: a dialectical paradigm for development. *In* "Interaction, Conversation and the Development of Language." (Lewis, M. and Rosenblum, L. A., Eds) Wiley Interscience, London.

Simons, H. J. (1958). The status of African women. *In* "Africa in Transition." (Smith, P., Ed.) Reinhardt, London.

Smith, J. M. (1970). A note on achievement motivation and verbal fluency. *J. Proj. Tech. Pers. Assess.* **34**, 2, 121–124.

Swanson, M. W. (1970). Reflections on the urban history of South Africa: some problems and possibilities, with special reference to Durban. *In* "Focus on Cities." (Walls, H., Ed.) Durban.

Swanson, M. W. (1976). The Durban system: roots of urban apartheid in Natal. *African Studies* **35**, 3–4.

Tajfel, H. (1972). Experiments in a vacuum. *In* "The Context of Social Psychology: A Critical Investigation." (Israel, J. and Tajfel, H., Eds) Academic Press, London.

Tamhankar, V. S. (1968). Analysis of protocols of Indian subjects on T.A.T. n-ach test. *Jap. Psych. Rev.* **10**, 2, 63–69.

Turnbull, C. (1962). "The Lonely African." Simon and Shuster, New York.

Van den Berghe, P. L. (1962). Race attitudes in Durban, South Africa. *J. Soc. Psychol.* **57**, 55–72.

Van den Berghe, P. (1965). "South Africa: A Study in Conflict." University of California Press.

Veness, T. (1962). "School Leavers." Methuen, London.

Veroff, J., Wilcox, S. and Atkinson, J. W. (1953). The achievement motive in high school and college age women. *J. Abnorm. Soc. Psychol.* **48**, 108–119.

Wason, P. (1977). The theory of formal operations—a critique. *In* "Piaget and Knowing: Studies in Genetic Epistemology." (Geber, B., Ed.) Routledge and Kegan Paul, London.

Welsh, D. (1969). The growth of towns. *In* "Oxford History of South Africa." Vol. 2 (Wilson, M. and Thompson, L., Eds) Oxford University Press.

Welsh, D. (1971). "The Roots of Segregation. Native Policy in Colonial Natal (1845–1910)." Cape Town.

Whisson, M. G. (1972). Organisations available for change. *In* "Towards Social Change." (Randall, O., Ed.) Sprocas Publication, Johannesburg.

Wiener, M. and Murray, W. (1963). Another look at the culturally deprived and their levels of aspiration. *J. Educ. Sociol.* **36**, 7, 319–321.

Witkin, H. A., Lewis, H. B., Hartmann, M., Machover, K., Meissner, P. B. and Warner, S. (1954). "Personality Through Perception." Harper, New York.

Wober, M. (1975). "Psychology in Africa." International African Institute, London.

Zajonc, R. B. and Markus, G. B. (1975). Birth order and intelligence. *Psychol. Today* **82**, 74–88.

# Subject Index

# European Monographs in Social Psychology

*Series Editor:* HENRI TAJFEL

E. A. CARSWELL and R. ROMMETVEIT
Social Contexts of Messages, 1971

J. ISRAEL and H. TAJFEL
The Context of Social Psychology: A Critical Assessment, 1972

J. R. EISER and W. STROEBE
Categorization and Social Judgement, 1972

M. VON CRANACH and I. VINE
Social Communication and Movement, 1973

CLAUDINE HERZLICH
Health and Illness: A Social Psychological Analysis, 1973

J. M. NUTTIN, JR. (and Annie Beckers)
The Illusion of Attitude Change: Towards a Response Contagion Theory of Persuasion, 1975

H. GILES and P. F. POWESLAND
Speech Style and Social Evaluation, 1975

J CHADWICK-JONES
Social Exchange Theory: Its Structure and Influence in Social Psychology, 1976

M. BILLIG
Social Psychology and Intergroup Relations, 1976

S. MOSCOVICI
Social Influence and Social Change, 1976

R. SANDELL
Linguistic Style and Persuasion, 1977

H. GILES
Language, Ethnicity and Intergroup Relations, 1977

A. HEEN WOLD
Decoding Oral Language, 1978

H. TAJFEL

Differentiation between Social Groups: Studies in the Social Psychology of Intergroup
   Relations, 1978

M. BILLIG

Fascists: A Social Psychological View of the National Front, 1978

C. P. WILSON

Jokes: Form, Content, Use and Function, 1979

J. P. FORGAS

Social Episodes: The Study of Interaction Routines, 1979

R. A. HINDE

Towards Understanding Relationships, 1979

A-N. PERRET-CLERMONT

Social Interaction and Cognitive Development in Children, 1980

*In preparation*

S. H. NG

The Social Psychology of Power, 1980

P. SCHÖNBACH

Education and Intergroup Attitudes